Children's Literature and the Politics of Equality

~

Pat Pinsent

Teachers College
Columbia University
New York and London

LANGUAGE AND LITERACY SERIES
Dorothy S. Strickland and Celia Genishi, Series Editors

Advisory Board: Richard Allington, Donna Alvermann,
Kathryn Au, Edward Chittendon, Bernice Cullinan,
Colette Daiute, Anne Haas Dyson, Carole Edelsky,
Janet Emig, Shirley Brice Heath, Connie Juel, Susan Lytle

Published in the United States of America by Teachers College Press
1234 Amsterdam Avenue, New York, NY 10027

Published in Great Britain by David Fulton Publishers 1997

Cataloging-in-Publication Data available through the Library of Congress

ISBN: 0-8077-3680-5

Manufactured in Great Britain

01 00 99 98 97   5 4 3 2 1

Contents

Acknowledgements

I would like to express my gratitude to several people from the Roehampton Institute, London: to Professor Ann Thompson, Head of the English Department, for encouraging me to apply for study leave to write this book, and to any colleagues whose work-load may have been increased by my semester's absence; to the Librarians associated with the Children's Literature Collection at Roehampton, Felicity Lander, Sue Mansfield and Julie Mills; to Isobel Walker, an MA student, for sharing her thoughts and her books about disability; to generations of graduate and undergraduate students with whom, over the years, I have discussed the themes and children's books presented here; and especially to Kim Reynolds, friend and colleague, Director of the Children's Literature Research Centre, for her continued inspiration and for commenting on parts of this book. I also want to thank Jim Docking, General Editor of the Roehampton Teaching Studies Series, for his very positive response to it, and for his helpful and encouraging suggestions.

Introduction

Figure 1 'Crusoe and the young Savage', from a nineteenth century edition of Defoe's *Robinson Crusoe*.

I beckoned [the poor savage] again to come to me, and gave him all the signs of encouragement that I could think of; and he came nearer and nearer, kneeling down every ten or twelve steps in token of acknowledgment for saving his life. I smiled at him, and looked pleasantly, and beckoned to him to come still nearer. At length he came close to me, and then he kneeled down again, kissed the ground, and laid his head upon the ground, and taking me by the foot, set my foot upon his head. This, it seems, was in token of swearing to be my slave for ever.

(D. Defoe, *Robinson Crusoe*, first published 1719; quoted from an edition published by W. & R. Chambers, Edinburgh, n.d., p. 187)

1

The copy of *Robinson Crusoe* from which the above quotation is drawn was presented by the London School Board as an attendance prize to a Standard Two scholar in 1896. Opposite the verbal description is a picture, sub-titled 'Crusoe and the young Savage' (Figure 1), graphically illustrating a scantily clad Friday subordinating himself to the somewhat overdressed narrator. This incident is central not only to this originally adult text, but also to much of the subsequent history of children's literature. For generations, images such as this, portraying the black man gratefully accepting servitude to the white man, who has brought education and Christianity to the uncivilized, probably cannibal, barbarians, went without question. But in the latter half of the twentieth century, words and pictures which depict most of the human race as inferior to a small minority of people of Western European origin, have not been allowed to go without challenge. In particular, all forms of writing to which impressionable young people may be exposed are now subjected to close scrutiny.

As well as the realization that many human beings have been denigrated on racial grounds, there is also today an increasing awareness that it is unacceptable to depict females as always taking subordinate roles or to regard them as incapable of the kind of heroic actions performed by males. Nor is it acceptable to make women and girls 'invisible' by language which overuses 'man' and 'he' and overlooks the fact that these words are no longer as inclusive as they once were. Other issues – such as disability, age, class, religion, and sexual orientation – are all now regarded as sensitive, to the extent that some arbiters have felt that the process has gone too far, and have ridiculed any attempt to make the language inclusive, caricaturing it as 'political correctness'; such critics have sometimes invented absurdities such as 'person-hole' for 'man-hole', to make their criticism stick. However, as a recent publication suggests:

> Pc is a convenient bogeyman for those who fear the diversification of our community will dislodge them from their position as typical and therefore able to speak on behalf of everyone. (*Working Group against Racism*, 1996, p. 41)

It is my intention to explore some of the many questions which arise as a result of increasing awareness in our society about equality issues. Can the attempt to make books for children consistent with contemporary views about equality go too far? In any case, are children really as much influenced by books and other material as some educationalists would claim? What can or should we do about the 'classics' of the past? And are today's children's writers so much better at avoiding giving offence to minorities? How much are children affected by the kind of prejudices and preconceptions that we all grow up with but don't always succeed in acknowledging in later life?

Matters such as these will be considered in relation to a large range of texts featuring subjects such as gender, race, disability, old age and other social issues. I begin by looking at some of the many 'guidelines' which appeared during the 1970s and early 1980s, and which on the one hand helped a number of 'liberal' thinkers to recognize their own latent prejudices, but on the other hand antagonized some readers who were perturbed to discover that books of which they had fond childhood memories were now seen as racist or sexist. I re-examine some of the key texts in the attempt to determine whether the compilers of such guidelines and the writers of books which exposed prejudice went too far, a question to which my tentative answer is that perhaps they did in some cases but if so, this was a very excusable mistake to make in the context of the pioneering work they were doing.

The analysis of children's literature which follows is based on a range of relevant educational and literary theory and an examination of the factors relating to a writer's assumptions about the nature of society. This material is integral to my understanding of the ways in which texts are experienced by young readers.

Of necessity, the main bulk of this study is concerned with books published in the UK and the USA. There is a wealth of children's literature written in other languages and all too seldom translated into English, and it is very illuminating to examine the different slant both on equality issues and on the presentation of 'taboo' subjects displayed by other cultures. Accessibility is, however, a major factor, and for a similar reason, most of the books I discuss have been written in the last 30 years. However, before going on to analyse the treatment in these books of issues such as gender, race, language, culture, and the position in society of the disabled and the elderly, I have subjected to examination a range of both the 'classics' recommended to young people, *and* the books and magazines which a recent survey of children's reading[1] shows that they choose for themselves. I have also looked briefly at the way in which children are portrayed in non-fictional literature, from reading schemes to encyclopaedias.

My most important conclusion, which underpins everything I say about selection and use of books, is that it is vitally important for children to be alerted to the ways in which literature may convey prejudice. It is impossible to remove children from any possible contamination by books which do not display a proper appreciation of the dignity of every human being. Even if it were possible, this would be to create a secondary world of literature which was sanitized by not containing the tensions which exist in the real world. I believe it is vital for teachers, librarians and parents to be able to recognize what is unsatisfactory in books written today as well as in the past; I am also convinced that they should be helping the young people within their care to recognize these aspects, so that they are better placed to avoid being influenced by negative stereotypes and prejudiced language. We need good books on all these subjects, not ones which are written simply to put forward a political point of view; rather a book needs to arise from the fact that its subject-matter is integral to the thinking of the author. We also need to make proper use of the material which exists, bad as well as good, to educate children about prejudice, so that they may develop a respect for everybody in society. Paradoxically, the use of books which display prejudice may well be among the most effective instruments to combat it.

---

1. *Young People's Reading at the End of the Century* (1996) (ed. K. Reynolds), obtainable from the National Centre for Research into Children's Literature, Roehampton Institute London, Downshire House, Roehampton Lane, SW15 4HT, referred to in subsequent chapters as the Roehampton Survey. This investigation has been in two parts, a pilot study of 321 children, carried out in 1993, published as *Contemporary Juvenile Reading Habits* (1994), and a more extensive questionnaire addressed to a demographically representative of pupils throughout England and Wales in 1995. Details are to be found in Figure 2.

Survey details (years)			
Age	**Girls**	**Boys**	**Totals**
4	18	13	31
5	59	78	137
6	150	122	272
7(1)	94	111	205
Key Stage 1 children			645
7(2)	83	80	163
8	174	166	340
9	298	257	555
10	395	350	745
11(1)	192	203	395
Key Stage 2 children			2198
11(2)	372	434	806
12	741	784	1525
13	633	666	1299
14	518	516	1034
15	416	443	859
16	217	251	468
Key Stage 3 and 4 children		5991	
Overall totals	4360	4474	8834

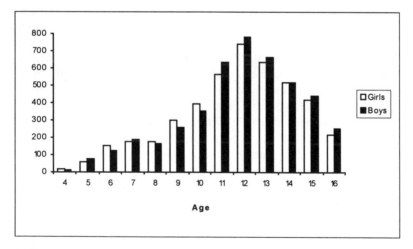

Figure 2 Numbers of young people questioned in the survey of reading carried out by the Children's Literature Research Centre, Roehampton Institute London.

4

CHAPTER 1

Prejudice in Children's Books

There is no such thing as an unbiased book (Gillian Klein, 1985, p. 1)

It was not until the 1970s that many people began to be powerfully aware of the extent to which those members of Western society who were not able-bodied middle-class white males were disadvantaged. In 1971 the Institute of Race Relations published *Books for Children: The Homelands of Immigrants in Britain*, edited by Janet Hill, who voiced her disquiet that so many of these books were poor in quality and 'blatantly biased', and her concern about African children growing up in England meeting 'patronizing, insensitive, and outmoded tales of the noble white man and the natives' (p. 7). The Children's Rights Workshop also gave some attention to sexism, race and class in children's books, but probably the most influential document of the period, in England and Wales, was the Bullock Report, *A Language for Life* (1975), which devoted a chapter to 'Children from Families of Overseas Origin'; a slightly unfortunate message was conveyed by this being located in the section of the Report concerned with 'Reading and Language Difficulties'.

During this period, it was gradually becoming apparent that women, black people and the disabled had too little autonomy in their lives, especially in the area of employment. As a consequence, legislation was enacted to enforce the rights of minorities and in Britain, the Equal Opportunities Commission (1974) and the Commission for Racial Equality (1976) were set up. On both sides of the Atlantic, people's consciousness began to be raised about the way in which reading matter provided for children was not always in line with the changes in society. There has always been argument about whether literature should simply reflect the social situation or seek to improve it; children's authors in particular have frequently sought to teach their readers the values which society wants to encourage, even to the extent of seeking to indoctrinate them. Many writers have assumed that literature *does* influence children, so it was quite natural that in this period more attention began to be given to the suitability or otherwise of much of what young people were being given to read.

It is not surprising that as soon as concerned groups started to present guidelines about particular areas of possible prejudice, especially gender and race, controversy erupted. Books which are loved in childhood naturally generate strong emotions, and frequently the reader has a special sense of possession about them. The immediate reaction of many otherwise logical readers to criticisms of writers such as Bannerman and Blyton was, 'They never did me any harm'. Even if that were true, however, it in no way legitimates a book which is presented to children who live in a totally different kind of society and whose responses are inevitably various

5

and quite unpredictable. Those who argued the case for *Little Black Sambo* and *Noddy* seldom bothered to search out the books and re-examine them in the light of contemporary conditions, but rather relied upon their own childhood memories. They deemed therefore that people who wrote against prejudice were going to extremes and indeed, those who criticize books can all too easily appear to rate all the negative aspects as equally important.

Thus, a female reader may reject a book because of its 'he-man' language, rather than looking at deeper issues like the characterization and the way in which girls are treated in the plot. Nevertheless, it is easy for people who have never themselves found language offensive to ridicule those who do. Some readers' reactions may seem excessive to those less concerned about language, and this probably accounts for the fears which many people have about censorship, although not even the most emphatic of those who sought out prejudice recommended anything so drastic. The idea that there were 'thought police' going around burning Blyton and *Biggles* often prevented some critics from even investigating whether perhaps there was really something wrong with these books.

Guidelines

Since it is clearly impossible to look closely at all the collections of guidelines about avoiding discrimination in literature, I will concentrate on a very influential set which came out in the mid-1970s and have been reproduced in a variety of forms since then. (See notes at the end of this chapter for details of the documents examined.) These were produced by the American Council on Interracial Books for Children, and were adapted by the World Council of Churches (1978) with the addition of specific points about religion (see Preiswerk, 1980) and also by Stinton (1979) and Hicks (1981). British guidelines against racism, such as those produced by the Inner London Education Authority (ILEA) in conjunction with the Centre for Urban Education (CUES) in 1980, and against sexism, like those of Rosemary Stones in 1983, were also inevitably influenced by the American ones. It should be noted that the Council was not recommending that books displaying sexist or racist characteristics should be burnt, or even necessarily removed from shelves. Rather the intention was to alert teachers and librarians to aspects of prejudice of which they may have been unaware, so that they could:

(a) look for better books, where possible, and not spend scarce resources on unsatisfactory books; and

(b) show children 'how to detect racism and sexism in a book [so that] the child can proceed to transfer the perception to wider areas.'

(Spare Rib, December 1980).

Gillian Klein, who was associated with the Guidelines produced by the Inner London Education Authority, emphasizes that these too were in no sense intended to be rigid (1985, p. 17).

If the Guidelines had always been read in the spirit in which they were put forward, it would have defused much of the controversy, but some teachers and librarians were perhaps over-zealous, and isolated cases which seemed to display uncritical adherence to the 'letter of the law' were inevitably seized upon by the media.

6

Rather than quoting the whole document, I am taking each of the points made and, where relevant, also citing the kind of objections which have been made, commenting on some of the reasons why people have been worried about them. The recommendations are as follows.

1. Illustrations

These should avoid *stereotypes*, such as the Native American 'brave' and his 'squaw', or the 'completely domesticated mother, the demure doll-loving little girl or the wicked stepmother; *tokenism*, like for example the depiction of racial minorities as looking just like whites except for their colour; and *passive or subservient roles* for ethnic minorities and females.

Objections which were made to this recommendation include:

1. the anxiety that women would never be permitted to choose domestic roles, or little girls be allowed dolls – a result which was not intended;
2. the fear that traditional tales, which abound in heroines waiting for deliverance and in wicked stepmothers, would be banned.

Counter to such objections is the movement, during the 1980s and 1990s, for presenting children with alternative tales, both traditional and newly written. The feeling articulated in the Guidelines also began to lead to an increase in the number of illustrators from ethnic minority groups, who have increased considerably since Errol Lloyd's *My Brother Sean* was published in 1973; additionally, several publishing companies, such as Tamarind and Mantra, devoted to the production of minority groups texts, were founded (See *Dragons Teeth*, No. 27, Summer 1987 and No. 32, Winter 1989 respectively for details of these companies).

2. Story line

The behaviour of white males should not be taken as the only standard for success, nor should females and members of other ethnic groups always be seen to rely on them for deliverance, or be encouraged to accept inequalities passively.

Objections could be made that in some societies, women *are* expected to act passively, and that to portray them in literature as doing otherwise is unrealistic. However, while it is difficult to combine proper respect for the traditions of other societies with resistance to women being put into a subservient role, I think many people are unhappy about such a situation being seen as an inbuilt, rather than a societal, norm.

3. Lifestyles

The manners, food and clothing of the white middle classes should not always be seen as a norm.

Objections to this tend to be made by those who have never tried to see their own culture objectively; since some of its customs are implanted in infancy, it is very difficult not to regard them as superior to alternative modes. An historical perspective can be very helpful here.

4. Relationships

Again, care should be taken that white males are not always portrayed as dominant, in society and the family. Due weight needs to be given to the effect of social conditions on family relations. Objections to this tend to be made by those who feel that in realistic terms, white males *are* dominant; here again, it can be claimed that writers of literature have a responsibility not to perpetuate unjust social systems.

5. Heroes and heroines

Not only should there be strong female characters and people from minority groups, but they also need to be shown opposing some of the power structures which Western society may take for granted.

Those people who object to this requirement imply that it would mean that individuals, such as revolutionaries, who oppose some social or religious institutions, might be depicted as models for children. One person's revolutionary, however, is another person's freedom fighter, and there is a good deal of relativism in the standards which are applied.

6. Effects on a child's self-image

There should be ample provision of characters with whom girls and ethnic minority children can identify.

This is a difficult area, particularly in relation to the literature of the past. It is also noteworthy that the child reader does not always identify, or fail to identify, with the characters anticipated; many girls have seen themselves as Jim Hawkins in *Treasure Island* or Mowgli in *The Jungle Books*, though both of these are boys and the latter is presumably Indian in origin.

7. Author's and illustrator's backgrounds

The creators of a book about a particular theme or culture should have some qualifications to portray it, either by background or acquired knowledge.

This recommendation has been particularly controversial, as it could be taken to exclude authors from writing or illustrating books about countries and peoples other than their own. It should instead be seen as a plea that writers and illustrators be accurate.

8. Author's perspective

Since all of us have our own sets of unexamined assumptions, it is worth trying to find out those which have influenced the creator of a book. People who query this suggestion have probably an unexamined but invalid assumption that they themselves are completely without prejudice of any kind!

9. Language

Sexist and racist language, and that which excludes females by using only the male pronoun, needs to be examined.

This is also an extremely contentious area. On the one hand, some writers, especially those of the past, have used terms to describe black people which are completely unacceptable today, so that their critics have sometimes asserted that their works should not be read by young children. On the other, some writers who are extremely anti-racist in their own attitudes have felt the necessity to portray racist characters in their books, which has led to them using offensive language, although it may be contextualized (but never sanitized) by being spoken by an objectionable person. Equally, such language might be spoken by a character, such as a child, who has not yet realized that it could give offence. Provided the book portrays such characters learning or being rebuked, where appropriate, some people would argue that the offence is mitigated.

10. Date

A recent date is not a guarantee of being informed about new perspectives; delays in publication mean that a book may transmit outdated attitudes.

This has been particularly criticized; Hoggart (*The Observer*, 22 January 1984) assumes that it means: 'If a book is even two years out of date, sweep it from the shelves.' While it is not impossible that excess of zeal could lead to such behaviour, it seems clear from the context that this recommendation applies more to information books than to fiction, and in any case, the recommendations are really directing adults to be careful and where appropriate to provide an historical context, rather than getting rid of specific books as such.

The relevance of the guidelines to children's books

All of these areas have remained controversial in the period since the guidelines were first published. One of the most important aspects is that although there is ample evidence of guidelines such as these being borne in mind by many teachers, librarians, authors, publishers and booksellers, they are less likely to be taken into consideration by parents and other people who buy books for children. There are also still in existence innumerable copies of books which do not adhere to any guidelines, and these are likely to be read by children without the guidance of a teacher. Children must be educated about such issues, and I would suggest that in many instances, books which preceded or have ignored such guidelines are themselves the most effective resources for such education. Insulating children from anything likely to mislead or to give offence would be as dangerous as failing to vaccinate them against, for instance, tetanus.

I shall be looking at many of these aspects in more detail in the next chapter, since some of the fundamental assumptions about the effect of literature on children need to be examined in more depth before the discussion in subsequent chapters of some books which have appeared since the mid-1970s.

One of the main limitations of guidelines like these is that by their nature they disregard literary quality and the appeal of books to children. Books which are on the right lines about racism and sexism need to be just as good and as readable as any others; they need to be enjoyed both by children and by adults. Only then will they have any chance of becoming part of the school culture, or being recommended by a child's peer group or by teachers and librarians; only then will they be bought for schools or by parents. If books lack interesting plots and attractive characters, or if the language, however non-racist and non-sexist it is, does not appeal to the child reader, then no adherence to sets of guidelines will cause the book to have a good effect.

It is important at this stage to establish that on the one hand, political commitment does *not* make a book inferior, and on the other that there *are* poor books whose adherence to the guidelines does not redeem them. An example of a strongly committed book, written out of a deep involvement with the socially deprived and racially oppressed black families of the Southern States in the 1930s, is Mildred Taylor's *Roll of Thunder, Hear My Cry* (1976), based on her father's stories about his childhood, but transmuted by her use of a young female narrator, Cassie Logan. I shall be discussing other aspects of this book in both Chapters 5 and 6, but an illustration of its power may be relevant here.

9

In the first chapter, the Logan children are walking to school, because the bus which transports the white children does not take 'coloreds'. Taylor skilfully incorporates a good deal of information and atmosphere about the economics of share-croppers and their difficulties in eking out a living ('a tall, emaciated-looking boy popped out suddenly from a forest trail and swung a thin arm round Stacey', p. 12), without at any point taking interest away from the characters. The 6-year-old 'Little Man', who is just starting school and prides himself on his neat appearance, is suddenly told by his brother to scramble up the steep bank into the forest:

'But I'll get my clothes dirty!' protested Little Man.
'You're gonna get them a whole lot dirtier you stay down there. Look!'
Little Man turned around and watched saucer-eyed as a bus bore down on him spewing clouds of red dust like a huge yellow dragon breathing fire. Little Man headed toward the bank, but it was too steep. He ran frantically along the road looking for a foothold and, finding one, hopped on to the bank, but not before the bus had sped past enveloping him in a scarlet haze while laughing white faces pressed against the bus windows. (p. 16)

This passage, chosen virtually at random, exemplifies the skill of Taylor's writing. Economically, she has conveyed the unequal situation and the way that the offspring of its perpetrators are conditioned to connive in and even to enjoy it; she has also shown the distress, albeit in a minor matter, which it causes to the victims. Little Man's running and hopping, as well as his anger and dismay, inevitably heighten the child reader's empathy. What is even more effective is the vividness and animation of the description of the bus: 'spewing clouds of red dust', 'like a huge yellow dragon breathing fire' and 'enveloping him in a scarlet haze'. The colours evoked here put into relief the 'white faces' of the schoolchildren, and complete the picture, yet there is nothing which departs from what, in the situation, is 'objective' fact. The details of the scene have both a metaphoric effect, and, since they come so early in the novel, a function in determining the reader's reactions. For the duration of reading this and other parts of the book, it would be very difficult for white readers not to feel as if they are members of the black community. Books like this show that in the hands of a skilled writer, it is possible for books to be well within any anti-racist and anti-sexist guidelines and at the same time to be literature as good as that from any period and place.

An earlier example of how intense political commitment does not necessarily detract from a book's appeal to young children is Anna Sewell's *Black Beauty* (1877). This book is not only a passionate denunciation of the fashion of the bearing rein, an aspect with which most young readers are likely to sympathize, since the first person narration inevitably makes them feel close to the horse; the book also shows intense concern with the wrongness of hunting (Chapter 2) and such aspects near to the heart of the Quaker author as the demon drink (Chapter 25), the importance of Sunday observance (Chapter 36) and the evils of electioneering (Chapter 42). Few of the child readers who have kept this book in print for the last 120 years will initially have cared much about any of these issues! Some adults have subsequently worried about its message of conformity and submission (see Stibbs, 1991, p. 110) but it would be difficult to contend that the child appeal of the novel has been diminished through its author's adherence to what could almost be described as 'political correctness' for the late Victorians!

Equally, there are many books which comply with these guidelines but which are unlikely to be of much appeal to either adults or children. An example is Patricia Quinlan's *My Dad Takes Care of Me* (1987, illustrated by Vlasta van Kampen); the simple story is about Luke, whose father has lost his factory job and is studying at home to be an accountant, while his mother leaves the home daily to work with computers. Luke is afraid to admit at school that his father is unemployed; he claims at one point, 'He's a pilot', though he is glad to have his father's home-made soup for his lunch. That the father is a 'new man', prepared to show his emotions, is clear:

> My dad gets sad too. One day I came home after school and he was crying. My mom said it was because he didn't get the job he wanted. I told him, 'It's okay, I love you, daddy!' My dad hugged me real hard. 'I love you very much, Luke,' he said.

This book would be unlikely to appeal much to children, as although a degree of natural sympathy is generated by the first-person narrative, little interest is created about what is going to happen next. Its weakness is in no way a result of its treatment of a contemporary issue. The book has probably been produced directly to speak to children who are in its narrator's situation, perhaps as a form of bibliotherapy (see Chapter 8), and its adherence to guidelines is not a cause of its lack of interest. Cassie's father in *Roll of Thunder* also loses his job and is capable of expressing his emotions, but that is in no way the cause of the success of this book, nor is the fact that it is addressed to an older reader.

Another well-intentioned book, Arvan Kumar's *The Heartstone Odyssey* (1988) also shows how commitment to a cause does not necessarily make for a successful literary endeavour. The book is neither written nor constructed very well, though apparently when it was mediated by teachers who were able to link it with dance and other creative activities, its limitations were less obtrusive (cf. Pinsent, 1990).

Guidelines are thus in many ways irrelevant to quality – they won't make a writer better or worse. But what is important is that a book written to deal with a problem or out of a deep commitment to a political cause should be a *good* book, or it may only do harm.

If what complies with guidelines may sometimes appeal to neither children nor adults, what of popular books which may be suspect because their non-compliance is very obvious? Much of the worry expressed in the late 1970s and early 1980s about possibly over-prescriptive rules was because books by Enid Blyton came under such strictures. I shall be looking further at Blyton in Chapter 4, so instead I shall touch here upon the phenomenal success of Rev. W. Awdry. *Gordon the Big Engine* was first published in 1953, but neither the title character's puffed-up pomposity nor the fact that he is basically good at heart seem to have changed over nearly half a century, in the many forms in which Awdry's stories have been reproduced. Like all the engines, Gordon is male, while the carriages are stereotypical females. In the story 'Down the Mine', Thomas (most children's favourite character) accuses Gordon of smelling of ditchwater, after the humbling previous episode when he landed in a stream. The carriages are in a 'typically feminine' flutter:

> Annie and Clarabel could hardly believe their ears!
> 'He's *dreadfully* rude; I feel quite ashamed.'
> 'I feel *quite* ashamed, he's dreadfully rude,' they twittered to each other.
> 'You mustn't be rude, you make us ashamed,' they kept telling Thomas.

But Thomas didn't care a bit.

'That was funny, that was funny,' he chuckled. He felt very pleased with himself.

Annie and Clarabel were deeply shocked. They had a great respect for Gordon the Big Engine. (1953, p. 36; a 1990 edition is virtually identical)

It is clearly impossible for these foolish females to detect Gordon's weaknesses; it needs a strong but somewhat cheeky male. This story seems to infringe at least numbers 1, 2, 4, 5, 6, 9 and 10 of the guidelines above, though I think the only one of these which is relevant to its popularity with young children is that of stereotyping; children know what kind of behaviour to expect from the engines and from the carriages, which makes for a ready enjoyment when they are in process of learning about the world. The question of stereotyping will be discussed in the next chapter. The success of books like these does not however invalidate the guidelines; it merely means that teachers and parents should be alert to children receiving too much of a diet of unadulterated Awdry. At the same time, it is worth analysing the factors behind the success of this series, such as young children's fascination with machines like these engines; the books are rather like a kind of alternative mode of animal fiction. Children's knowledge about the kind of behaviour which may be expected, and particularly their enjoyment of the deflation of pompous adults, are features common to a good deal of popular fiction for the young. These aspects need not in any way infringe reasonable norms about gender and race. Another attractive quality of these books to young children is the use of rhythmic language, in tune with the characteristic beat of steam trains.

The popularity of books like these, and the fact that they are well known to so many young children, means that they can be double-edged; on the one hand they can form part of the gender conditioning which very young children are constantly subject to, yet on the other they afford a readily accessible and easily understood means of introducing equality issues to the children. No doubt many young girls, who are often among the enthusiastic audience of this series, have already, even before Reception class, felt excluded from the 'macho' world of the engines!

Influential books about racism and sexism

Students who write essays about equality issues in children's books are, I find, most likely to use material from one of three books: Bob Dixon's *Catching Them Young 1: Sex, Race and Class in Children's Fiction* (1977); *Racism and Sexism in Children's Books* (1979) edited by Judith Stinton; and Gillian Klein's *Reading into Racism: Bias in Children's Literature and Learning Materials* (1985). These books all provide critiques of a range of well-known texts and have been influential in raising questions about such writers as Hugh Lofting, author of the *Doctor Dolittle* series, Captain Johns, of *Biggles* fame, and Enid Blyton. Because of their relatively early date, Dixon and Stinton inevitably tend to concentrate on the negative aspects of books already published; looking back at them today, the reader is likely, unfairly, to have a feeling of 'not again' when reading about *Little Black Sambo* and *Noddy*, but this is largely because these writers' works have made the issues so familiar. Writing a few years later, Klein, and Robert Leeson, in *Reading and Righting* (1985), were both able to begin to make an attempt to establish wider principles. In making any criticisms of Dixon and Stinton therefore, I should like to emphasize that the very reason that we can now see the limitations of some of the judgements expressed is because of their merits in making many teachers and students aware of their own prejudices.

My chief problem with Dixon's work is expressed most succinctly in his comment about gender, and in particular, the work of Alcott:

> These books are competently written and skilfully constructed. The values and attitudes so untiringly put forward in them, however, leave a lot to be desired. I can never see much in the argument which 'makes allowance' for the period when a book was written. If books are read now – and these are certainly very widely read indeed – then surely we have to apply contemporary standards in evaluating them. (Dixon, 1978a, p. 10)

The imprecision of language here makes it a little difficult to comment on, but presumably Dixon means 'contemporary standards' to relate specifically to 1977 attitudes about gender, rather than any approaches drawn from the area of literary criticism, though feminism and Marxism both have a good deal of relevance to the question at issue, and it is difficult to exclude these perspectives from the discussion. The complexity of Alcott's response to the situation of women in her day will be touched upon later (Chapter 5); while it would be inappropriate for the majority of young readers of her fiction (rather fewer, I suspect, today than when Dixon wrote) to be provided with an exhaustive account of her ambiguities, it is certainly oversimple to suggest, as Dixon goes on to do, that Alcott is deliberately influencing her readers against feminism (a word incidentally which the *Shorter Oxford English Dictionary* (1973) indicates was only used in its modern sense in 1895).

I would suggest that it is extremely illuminating for the young reader to see established works of literature within the social and intellectual climate in which they were written, and indeed, that understanding of them is very incomplete unless this is at least attempted. Certainly, by absolute literary standards, if such things exist, it may be possible to consider of works of *any* date whether their characterization or plot or imagery are effective, but unless the books are seen in the context of their period, much is lost. Books from the past may certainly be set against those of today on similar topics, but we must never reproach the authors of the past for being unaware of movements and ideas which came after them! My contention is that we gain a fuller understanding of what is involved in feminism, for instance, by looking at the works of Alcott in their own context, not by simply dismissing them as propounding out-of-date ideals. The answer to the popularity of books which seem out of keeping with modern standards about gender and race is to ensure that they have an audience of informed young readers, rather than discouraging children from reading them at all.

Similar remarks could be made about some of the contributions to Stinton's book, though inevitably, since it is a compilation, it is impossible adequately to take account of the variety of views expressed. I shall comment later in this chapter on the remarks that one of the contributors, Rae Alexander, makes about a specific text, but it is worth looking at her more general statement of principle:

> In evaluating multiracial books for pre-school through to sixth-grade levels, my major criterion was that no book would be listed if it was considered likely

to communicate to either a black or a white child a racist concept or cliché about blacks. Even one negative stereotype would be enough to eliminate an otherwise good book. (Stinton, 1979, p. 70)

Alexander's motivation appears to be her fear of a black child hearing a racist passage 'read aloud in the presence of white classmates'. I would agree that extreme care should be taken about this, but since good practice in literature classes does not normally include books being read around the class, the reading aloud would normally be done by the teacher, who would surely want to mediate any suspect passages and use them as a means of education for the class as a whole, black and white alike. It is also possible that small group reading could take place, but it is to be hoped that teachers would generally have already read any books presented to a group, and thus become aware of any potentially sensitive passages. The issue of the use of overtly racist language will be considered in the next chapter, and the pedagogic aspect will be considered in my final chapter.

Another interesting aspect of Stinton's collection is the fact that she includes four condemnations of Paula Fox's *The Slave Dancer* (1973), a book about which Dixon (1978a) says, 'It approaches perfection as a work of art' (p. 125). In *Now Read On* (1982, p. 109), he admits the divergence of opinion:

This is one of the best novels I have ever read and it was a shaking experience to read it, but should record that it has been condemned as racist by people whose views I respect.

This very difference of opinion from people whose attitudes on the subject are in many respects very similar is valuable when considering the use of controversial texts in the secondary school. It makes very clear to young readers the impossibility of reaching an absolute decision, or, in this case, even a consensus, on subjects so emotive.

Two of the contributors to Stinton's book, Albert Schwartz and Lois Kalb Bouchard, discuss how P. L. Travers and Roald Dahl respectively made amendments to *Mary Poppins* and *Charlie and the Chocolate Factory*; nevertheless, Schwartz and Bouchard still subject the authors to serious criticism. I am concerned that this is not the most positive way to improve the attitudes of those who admittedly need more understanding about what is involved in racism. As an educator, I know that I get better results from my students if I praise what they have achieved than if I condemn everything.

Neither Dixon nor Stinton give much attention to the intention of the author. This omission is quite valid, given how difficult it is to ascertain what authors have in mind or how influenced they may have been by their situations and upbringing. I would agree about the necessity of judging what has actually been written in the text, even if this is meant quite innocently and merely indicates what the author has taken for granted. But I think many critics tend to over-estimate the effect on the vulnerable reader. Children cannot be protected from all expressions of intolerance in literature or in life; what is more important is that they have enough self-esteem, and enough understanding of literature and society to contextualize such expressions. This is something which everyone has to do in some areas. For instance, Roman Catholic readers can be offended by the many expressions of intolerance in nineteenth century English literature, from Sir Walter Scott to Charles Kingsley, but this may not always prevent them from enjoying the work concerned; still less is it likely to make them lose their faith or their confidence in themselves.

Two controversial texts

I do not intend to devote much space to Helen Bannerman's *Little Black Sambo* (1899), as this book has become notorious in any discussion about racism in books, to a degree quite out of proportion to its merits. Despite all the controversy, copies of it are still obtainable, however, so some consideration of the reasons for its notoriety is probably necessary. Janet Hill (in Stinton, 1979, pp. 35–40) gives an interesting account of her own change of views about this book, influenced by the responses of black teenagers who compared it with Bannerman's equally poorly illustrated *Little White Squibba* (1966), which was published posthumously. Both books are about the eventual triumph of a young child over animals which want to eat them up, but Hill points out that Squibba's characterization is less of a caricature than is Sambo's, into which Bannerman has, perhaps subconsciously, put in some facets of a racial stereotype. It is interesting that Hill's secondary school pupils have clearly subjected both books to a full analysis and come to some informed conclusions, which must have been an exercise of considerable value to them. Because of its unfortunate use of the name 'Sambo' as much as anything else, this book may no longer be appropriate to children of the age for which it was originally intended, but this is difficult to ensure unless parents are made aware of the reasons for objecting to it. Analysis by older pupils could be a means of achieving eventual parental understanding; *Sambo* and the rest of the series can certainly be quite valuable resources for education against racism.

It is also worth drawing to the attention of adults providing books for children the aspect which has endeared this otherwise indifferent book to so many generations. This is surely the fact that the small child defeats the large and powerful predator. There are many other books which reflect a similar situation: from Hoban and Blake's *How Tom Beat Captain Najork and his Hired Sportsmen* (1974) and Maurice Sendak's *Where the Wild Things Are* (1967) to Tolkien's *The Hobbit* (1937).

An instance, however, where I feel that those who select books solely with an eye to their treatment of 'equality' issues may be going too far, and may as a result alienate their potential friends, is in Rae Alexander's remarks about Lucy Boston's *The Chimneys of Green Knowe* (1958). She says:

> Even such an imaginative and exciting story as L. M. Boston's *Chimneys of Green Knowe* [sic] . . . I excluded because of a derogatory description of a black boy's hair: 'Think of Jacob's crinkly hair, hardly the length of a needle. The most she could do with it [in her embroidery] was tediously to make knots.' In contrast the author refers to a white person's 'tresses': 'he was a vain man with hair he was proud of . . . There was enough of Caxton's hair to do the whole chimney.' (Stinton, 1979, p. 71)

I think that there are indeed some debatable elements about the portrayal of Jacob in *The Chimneys of Green Knowe*, but I do not think this is one of them, and if it was really the reason for Alexander rejecting this book, it shows an unfortunate lack of appreciation for the way the reader's sympathy works. Even in the part quoted, it is easy to see how Boston is alienating the reader from Caxton; the word 'tresses' as applied to a male character is at the least ambivalent, and when set against 'vain' it seems fairly clear that Boston is setting up a critical position against Caxton, who has already been revealed as one of the most unpleasant characters in the book, partly because of his mistreatment of Jacob.

Shortly after the quotation made by Alexander (Faber edition, p. 174) we learn that Caxton had dashed into a burning house to salvage jewels he had stolen, while Jacob rushed in to deliver the blind girl, Susan, from the flames. To clinch the matter, Jacob's short and troublesome hair seems to have been used in the embroidered picture to represent the blue–black eyes of swans, where Caxton's had been used for 'the old chimney'. The much more pleasant signification of the former is surely not accidental.

There are, however, a few slightly questionable aspects about this otherwise very admirable book, much of which is set in the eighteenth century and which was written in the 1950s, before attitudes towards ethnic minority groups were so clearly established as later. The antecedents for Jacob's use of the English language are to be found in literary portrayals of many earlier African characters rather than in real life. He says to Susan:

> When I come this morning with baby cuckoo, plant pot jump and squeak like now. Inside, small porcupine. I not ever put him there. Missy feel – all sharp thorns. (p. 114)

It is surprising that he manages to combine a large and vivid vocabulary with such inadequate syntax, but presumably Boston may not have had the opportunity for meeting many people of African origin. The passage quoted might also cause some readers to have reservations about the book, as it is about doing 'big ju-ju', tribal magic. Susan's rather narrow-minded grandmother finds the children performing this rite, and reacts: 'Oh! You wicked blasphemous obscene heathen! You savage! The altars of Baal in our own garden!' (p. 120). Here again, however, the reader has firm enough impressions of the characters to reject the negative terms. We already know, having met the 'magic' which pervades the whole of the Green Knowe series, that Jacob is not being fairly described by her.

Most readers, I suspect, would like Susan and Jacob to get married, but at the end of the book we are told that:

> she married Jonathan [her tutor] and Jacob . . . chose himself a wife from his own people and brought her back with him . . . . His wife was Nanny to Susan's children, and he and Susan were always devoted friends. (p. 184)

Marriage between Susan and Jacob would of course be impossible at that date, and this aspect, like many others in the book, would make for very interesting discussion. There is also much in the book about which many people could be ambivalent, including the word 'nigger' (p. 141), which is however only used by unpleasant characters. How much of the ambiguity of this book results from deliberate decisions on the author's part, and how much relates to her own unquestioned assumptions is impossible finally to determine. Discussing such matters is not, however, beyond the analytic abilities of those pupils who are capable of reading the book with understanding.

Conclusion

When I suggest that some of the pioneering work done in the late 1970s and early 1980s needs to be looked at in the light of the situation in society today, I do not mean to devalue the earlier studies. It seems to me that they have sometimes been misinterpreted by people who felt themselves threatened by criticisms of books which they remembered having enjoyed in their own childhoods. This has sometimes led to over-reactions, and charges of 'political correctness' rather than a more thoughtful taking on board of the criticisms, and a re-examination of the texts concerned in order to decide the best courses of action.

In the early and mid-1980s, a good deal of attention was given to the question of racism, culminating in the publication of the Swann Report(1985). In the references for this chapter, I have noted several other books and lists of recommended titles which came out around this time. In particular, the School Council project, 'Developing the Curriculum for a Changing World' helped to further the process of looking for ways to improve, rather than simply criticizing what already existed. An increasing emphasis on the dangers of sexism is also to be noted at this period.

Much has been done since the mid-1980s, and one of the most notable aspects is the increase in literature, for all age groups, which seeks to look positively at equality issues, representing people of all ethnic groups and both sexes as individuals. This interest has extended to a concern about how disabled people and the elderly are portrayed in literature. All these areas will be examined in subsequent chapters.

Another change which has occurred in the last 20 years is the considerable increase in the numbers of women, and black people of both sexes, possessing some power in society. Although their numbers are still commensurate neither with their numbers or their talents, at least today the criticism that it would be unrealistic to portray such people in positions of authority is no longer valid. In fact, in some respects, life is ahead of literature here.

Too many assumptions are made, without questions being asked about proof, concerning the way in which children are likely to be influenced by literature and the extent to which it can affect attitudes and behaviour. In the next chapter I go on to consider some of the many theoretical aspects which need to be discussed to underpin the critical considerations of specific books which follow it.

References

Note that an extensive bibliography is also given at the end of this book.

1. Guidelines

1. Council on Interracial Books for Children (n.d.) *Ten Quick Ways to Analyze Children's Books for Racism and Sexism.* New York: Council on Interracial Books for Children.
2. World Council of Churches (1978) *Criteria for the Evaluation of Racism.* New York: World Council of Churches. Includes material derived from (1).
3. Stinton, J. (ed.)(1979) *How to look for Racism and Sexism in Children's Books.* London: Writers and Readers Publishing Co-operative. These are derived from (1).
4. *Spare Rib* (1980) *Racism and Sexism in Children's Books. Spare Rib* 1980, December, pp. 49–50. These are derived from (1).
5. Jones, C. and Klein, G. (1980) *Assessing Children's Books for a Multi-ethnic Society.* London: ILEA, Centre for Urban Educational Studies.

6. Hicks, D. (1981) 'Ten Quick Ways to Analyse Children's Books for Racism and Sexism'. In *Minorities: A Teacher's Resource Book for the Multi-Ethnic Curriculum* London: Heinemann. This list is a shortened version of (1).
7. Children's Rights Workshop (1984) *Children's Books: A Statement and Lists from the Children's Rights Workshop*. August.
8. Stones, R. (1983) 'Questions to ask about Children's Books'. In *Pour out the Cocoa, Janet*. London: Schools Council. (Project 'Developing the Curriculum for a Changing World')
9. Equal Opportunities Commission (1984) *An Equal Start: Guidelines for Those Working with the Under-Fives*. London: Equal Opportunities Commission.

2. Lists of anti-racist and anti-sexist books

Adler, S. (c. 1989a) *Ms Muffet Fights Back: A Penguin Non-Sexist Booklist*. Harmondsworth: Penguin.

Adler, S. (c. 1989b) *Equality Street: A Penguin Multi-Cultural Booklist*. Harmondsworth: Penguin.

Elkin, J. and Triggs, P. (1986) *The Books for Keeps Guide to Children's Books for a Multi-Cultural Society, 0–7* and *8–12*, London: Books for Keeps.

Stones, R. (n.d.) *A Penguin Multi-Ethnic Booklist*, Harmondsworth: Penguin.

Stones, R. (n.d.) *Ms Muffet Fights Back: A Penguin Non-Sexist Booklist*. Harmondsworth: Penguin. (This is earlier than Adler, 1989a)

3. Children's books referred to in the text

Note. In this and later chapters details are supplied of books which have been discussed. This should be read in conjunction with the text and does not imply a recommendation of them for use with children. In most cases, the dates are those of the first English edition; in some instances an American edition may pre-date this.

Awdry, Rev. W. (1953) *Gordon the Big Engine*. London: Edmund Ward.

Awdry, Rev. W. (1992) *Your Favourite Thomas the Tank Engine Story Collection*. London: Dean.

Bannerman, H. (1979; 1st edn, 1899) *The Story of Little Black Sambo*. London: Chatto.

Bannerman, H. (1966) *The Story of Little White Squibba*. London: Chatto.

Boston, L. (1958) *The Chimneys of Green Knowe*. London: Faber.

Hoban, R. and Blake, Q. (1974) *How Tom Beat Captain Najork and his Hired Sportsmen*. London: Cape.

Kumar, A. (1988) *The Heartstone Odyssey*. London: Allied Mouse.

Quinlan, P. (1987) (illus. by V. van Kampen) *My Dad Takes Care of Me*. Toronto: Annick Press.

Sendak, M. (1967)*Where the Wild Things Are*. London: Bodley Head.

Sewell, A. (1954; 1st edn, 1877) *Black Beauty*. Harmondsworth: Penguin.

Taylor, M. (1977) *Roll of Thunder, Hear My Cry*. London: Gollancz.

Tolkien, J. R. R. (1937) *The Hobbit*. London: Allen & Unwin.

Children and Literature

Prejudiced attitudes have almost certainly existed since groups of people first distinguished themselves from one another. (David Milner, 1983, p. 5)

The power of books

There has always been a strong belief in the influence of literature on the actions and convictions of its readers. Distinguished writers from all periods, from Plato to Matthew Arnold, have held in awe the way in which narrative can move the emotions and affect the beliefs and motivations of its audience. The implication of this power, they concur in claiming, is that writers have an immense responsibility to express sentiments which are for the good of the human race.

When the Roman writer Horace or the great Elizabethan Sir Philip Sidney write about poetry, a word inclusive of the whole of what later ages would see as imaginative literature, they do not discriminate between literature for adults and that for children, because, other than Horn Books for learning the ABC, there were very few books designed specifically for the young. By the late seventeenth century, however, when authors, especially of moral tracts, began to see themselves as addressing either a young audience, or their parents, or both, the urge to influence them through story became more marked. Mrs Sherwood, whose *The History of the Fairchild Family* (1818) is one of the early landmarks of children's literature, is quite unashamed in her desire to influence the reader; in her Introduction, after telling about the idyllic rural background of Mr and Mrs Fairchild, she addresses the reader directly but disarmingly:

> You would perhaps like to hear the prayer which Mr. and Mrs. Fairchild used to offer up for their children as they knelt down of a morning with the three little ones kneeling before them. (p. 3)

Useless for the young reader to resist! Sherwood no doubt assumed that the parent would ensure that the child did not skip the lengthy prayers and hymns which follow each of her stories. Her tales include such unashamed religious propaganda as showing how a young girl's disobedience in playing with candles has not only led to her agonising death by fire but also to her presumed eternal death in hell (pp. 152–58).

There is equally little doubt about Dickens' designs on the adult reader when he attacks current educational thinking, in his well-known satirical description of the schoolroom at the beginning of *Hard Times* (1854). Mr Gradgrind demands:

> Now what I want is, Facts. Teach these boys and girls nothing but Facts. Facts alone are wanted in life. Plant nothing else, and root out everything else. You

can only form the minds of reasoning animals upon Facts: nothing else will ever be of any service to them. This is the principle on which I bring up my own children, and this is the principle on which I bring up these children. Stick to Facts, Sir! (Chapter 1)

How realistic are Sherwood, Dickens and the like in expecting literature to have an effect on the beliefs and attitudes of both young and old? At the conclusion of his psycho-analytically based exploration of what happens when readers encounter texts, *The Dynamics of Literary Response* (1968,1989), Norman Holland says:

> First, literature may reinforce or counter the defenses and adaptations our culture builds into us. Second, literature lets us experience those and other values in a more open, 'as if' way; it breaks down – for a time – the boundaries between self and other, inner and outer, past and future, and it may neutralize the primal aggression bound up in those separations. Yet, given the firmness of cultural structures and individual characters, it is very hard to see how the effects of literature can be more than small, local, and transient . . . . At most literature may open for us some flexibility of mind so that growth from it and other kinds of experience remains possible. (p. 340)

Holland's setting the power of literature against what the reader brings to it in terms of background and knowledge helps to account for the phenomenon that he describes earlier in the book, 'Different critics will get Christian or Marxist or existential meanings from the same text.' (p. ix)

As we have seen in Chapter 1, one person's anti-racist classic is another's racist diatribe, and throughout the examination of specific texts in subsequent chapters, it will always be necessary to remember that literature cannot act automatically, independent of what the reader brings to it. Nevertheless, I think that there are some texts which may help to increase the reader's 'flexibility of mind', thus breaking down hardened attitudes, or, in the case of children, assisting them in the process of establishing a positive view about the equality of everybody in society.

One of the most urgent needs is to ensure that readers understand what fiction is. As Hollindale (1988) says of *Huckleberry Finn*, 'You cannot experience the book as an anti-racist text unless you know *how to read a novel*' (p. 12). If we are claiming that story can be a very important agent of children's cognitive and emotional development, we need to ensure that they make a clear distinction between texts which claim to be factual and those which do not. Holland notes that, 'It is the expectation we bring [to what we read] that determines the extent to which we will test it against our everyday experience' (p. 68). Too many people seem never to have learned to read fiction; many inadequate responses to literature result from readers not applying the right kind of 'test . . . against . . . experience'. In the controversy about Salman Rushdie's *The Satanic Verses*, it became apparent that many of those who condemned the book were expecting it to be 'true' in an everyday sense – a surprising expectation for a book which begins with two men falling out of an aircraft at 29,002 feet and surviving!

Holland shows how imaginative fiction can be judged as 'safer' than real life: 'In everyday life, we feel it dangerous to respond to reality with as much affect from the massive, primitive depths of our earliest selves.' (p. 82) He goes on to say that one of the sources of enjoyment of literature is the fact that we think we will not have to act upon it (p. 98). The experience of deep-seated emotions within a safe, because hypothetical, context can indeed contribute to 'flexibility of mind' (p. 340), and I would go so far as to claim that sustained experience of literature from an early age can be a means of combining pleasure with the acquisition of tolerance, a combination less readily available from other sources.

I propose to go on to consider some of the theories which have been put forward about children's experience of literature. In the light of these I shall give some attention to the 'messages' which the adult authors, knowingly or unknowingly, insert into their books.

Children and literature

One of the phrases most often quoted in the area of literary education is the title of an article by Barbara Hardy: 'Narrative as a primary act of mind' (1968; in Meek *et al.*, 1977). In the period since this was written, the increased emphasis on narrative in education overall and in particular in literacy teaching has been considerable. Wells (1987) says:

> stories have a role in education that goes far beyond their contribution to the acquisition of literacy. Constructing stories in the mind – or *storying*, as it has been called – is one of the most fundamental means of making meaning; as such, it is an activity that pervades all aspects of learning . . . . Through the exchange of stories, therefore, teachers and students can share their understandings of a topic and bring their mental models of the world into closer alignment. (p. 194)

Margaret Meek (1982, 1988) looks at the evidence which shows how important the hearing and constructing of story is to children's understanding of their world. Bruner (1986) gives a closely argued rationale for the significance of narrative, which he sees as a vital part of children's cognitive development, particularly in the area of understanding human character. It could in fact be argued that those who do not have in their lives a place for story, whether by means of book, magazine, radio, film or television, are likely to find it more difficult to empathize with others because they may lack the imaginative ability to put themselves in the other person's place.

Since story is so important, the question of which stories are selected is also crucial. It is vital that the stories chosen, especially those for young children, are ones which will increase their ability to recognize the worth of all human beings, and of themselves.

J. A. Appleyard (1990) has put forward a reasoned account, supported by the findings both of psychologists and psycho-analysts and of literary and literacy theorists, concerning the way in which children's experience of fiction develops. His framework, 'The Five Roles Readers Take', to which I shall be referring at several points in the chapters which follow, may be summarized thus:

1. *The Reader as Player*. Listening to stories and playing with their themes in the pre-school years helps the child to sort out aspects of the world.
2. *The Reader as Hero/Heroine*. In later childhood the reader finds story a less ambiguous world than that of experience and uses it as a means to develop an understanding of how people behave in the real world.

21

3. *The Reader as Thinker*. In adolescence, readers use stories to further their understanding of the meaning of life, in a search for the best way to live their lives.

4. *The Reader as Interpreter*. Systematic study provides an approach to literature as a subject in itself, rather than simply a means of discovering about the world outside.

5. *The Pragmatic Reader*. Adults are able to choose the uses they make of reading.

(Summarized from Appleyard, 1990, pp. 14–15)

I have included Stages 4 and 5 for completeness, although they are not strictly relevant to children's experience of fiction.

Appleyard develops these ideas at some length and with extensive use of examples drawn from observations of young people's reading, made by himself and by others. While it is clear that no framework can be rigid about a subject which depends so much on the ability, development, and social situation of the individual, it does provide some useful suggestions as to how children's understanding of fiction develops, and this can be very helpful when thinking about the kind of literature appropriate to pupils of different ages, the strategies which they are likely to employ in reading it, and what motivates their search for meaning at any particular stage.

One of the authorities used extensively by Appleyard is Arthur Applebee's *The Child's Concept of Story* (1978) which is an invaluable source concerning children's responses to narrative at different ages. Particularly germane to the question of the child's development of understanding about the nature of fiction, is the study Applebee makes of how children begin to appreciate that not all stories are true (pp. 38–53). Although research which he quotes reveals that from as early as 2 years old, children begin to appreciate some of the conventions of story, they nevertheless take much longer to appreciate that the stories may not be true; he found that 50% of 6 year olds tended to think that story characters and events were probably real. As Applebee goes on to say:

> This lack of differentiation between fact and fiction makes the spectator role a powerful mode for extending the relatively limited experience of young children. The stories they hear help them to acquire expectations about what the world is like . . . without the distracting pressure of separating the real from the make-believe. And though they will eventually learn that some of this world is only fiction, it is specific characters and specific events which will be rejected; the recurrent patterns of values, the stable expectations about the roles and relationships which are part of their culture, will remain. It is these underlying patterns . . . which make stories an important part of socialization, one of the many modes through which the young are taught the values and standards of their elders. (pp. 52–53)

This passage makes several important points about the place which stories have in the cognitive and moral development of young children. If they are well chosen and well told, the stories children hear and the reading which they go on to do for themselves can help them towards an appreciation of their own worth and that of others, and about the kind of behaviour which best reflects these values. Literature is thus a major part of the education of children about the equality of all human

22

beings. Inevitably, however, stories derive from people who have told them or written them down, and it is obviously of supreme importance to consider the nature of the material to which children will be exposed.

Authors and ideology

One of the most important factors to be borne in mind when looking at literature for children is that no text can be written without the author's values being in some way significant in it. Even when writers are trying to be neutral, something not very frequent in the case of politically sensitive issues such as gender and race, their underlying assumptions will colour what they consider to be impartiality. One of the most important perceptions of recent theory is the fact that the term 'ideology' should not be confined to those on the political left. As Eagleton (1983) says of 'traditional critics':

> It is . . . difficult to engage such critics in debate about ideological preconceptions, since the power of ideology over them is nowhere more marked than in their honest belief that their readings are 'innocent'. (p. 198)

Hollindale's influential *Ideology and the Children's Book* (1988) emphasizes the importance of *passive* ideology, that which is taken for granted as a result of all the factors which have gone to make writers what they are. Some of this generally unrecognized cast of mind results from imbibing the attitudes of contemporary society and some of it is individual to each person. As Hollindale says:

> The individual writer is likely, as we have seen, to make conscious choices about the explicit ideology of his [sic] work, while the uniqueness of imaginative achievements rests on the private, unrepeatable configurations which writers make at subconscious level from the common stock of their experience. (p. 15)

Since ideology is so all pervasive, it would be both undesirable and unproductive for anyone to seek to banish it from books, even those given to children. What is needed in the teacher and subsequently in the young reader is an awareness of how the unexamined assumptions of both writers and society affect the books written.

Some years ago, before I became aware of the all-pervasiveness of ideology, I wrote a children's book, which remains unpublished, and I have found it interesting to re-examine the manuscript in the light of what Hollindale says about the effect of passive ideology. It is the story of a black girl and a white boy, aged about 10, whose families have moved in early to an estate being built on the site of an old house which has been demolished, and who are forced into each other's company in the absence of any other children. In looking at the manuscript from an ideological perspective, I feel that the story is, as I intended, impeccably anti-racist and anti-sexist; perhaps I should not have been surprised to observe, however, the extent to which I had, without intending to do so, also taken for granted middle-class values; for instance, the girl's father is a teacher, with a love of history and literature. My choice of setting and occupation was obviously partly governed by what I felt familiar with, but also by that which I felt to embody the 'good'. A similar process must underpin the choices about plot, characterization and language made by most writers.

The ways in which ideology is conveyed

Evidence of how writers are either directly seeking to influence their readers' ideas, or perhaps more insidiously but with just as much effect on their audience, incorporating their own unexamined assumptions, is to be found in their creation of character, their choice of narrative stance and plot structure, and their uses of humour, intertextuality, literary devices, and language. All too often, those who scrutinize books tend to confine themselves to fairly superficial aspects of language, with some attention to character. What is often ignored is the way in which other factors, such as point of view and apparently discrete images, may imperceptibly affect readers' attitudes just as much as the more obvious aspects.

The portrayal of character

Anxiety is often expressed concerning either the omission of black or female characters from many children's books, or the way in which, when they are included, they are often stereotyped and play less active roles than white males. The obverse of this is where complaints are made about tokenism and the inclusion of girls or ethnic minority characters where they may not be altogether appropriate. It is very difficult to determine how much children are influenced by the presence or absence of characters who are similar to themselves, since the aspects in which these characters resemble the reader may not be the obvious ones of race and gender, but more tenuous ones like hobbies or position in a family. Holland (1968,1989) gives some attention to the question of identification and concludes that we identify 'because the character satisfies a need for us' (p. 277). We take from the character:

> certain drives and defenses that are really objectively 'out there' and put into him [sic] feelings that are really our own, 'in here' . . . we incorporate the whole character, clothes, features, manners, physique, and the rest. (p. 278)

This implies that while we can never be sure which character in a book any specific reader may identify with, once having done so, he or she may well be disproportionately influenced by some of the features of that character, which could certainly include skin colour and sex.

Holland does not mention the *absence* aspect, where readers may find no characters with whom they want to identify, though if this is the case, young readers, given the choice, will probably reject the book as 'boring'. If the characters with whom they identify are always portrayed as inferior or powerless, it is likely to encourage them towards different kinds of book choices in the future. The survey carried out by the National Centre for Research in Children's Literature at the Roehampton Institute London, *Young People's Reading at the End of the Century* (Reynolds, 1996) does reveal some evidence that boys prefer to read stories about other boys while girls are less concerned about this (see Chapters 3 and 5 below), and that some children take skin colour or country of origin of the main character into account while choosing books; such factors, however, do not appear to be so important as far as *conscious* choice is concerned as aspects like the period in which a book is set or whether the character has similar interests to the reader.

While most adults would agree that children need to be weaned off dependence on stereotypical depiction of characters, it does seem that at an early stage in their development children gain reading confidence through the conviction that their expectations about a character will be fulfilled.

Applebee's influential study of children's understanding of narrative (1978) presents information about children's expectations about conventional story characters, such as cowboys, Santa Claus and witches, as well as animals: 'In children's stories dogs tended to be associated with boys and cats with girls.' Children interviewed in London for his study:

> were asked what such characters as lions, wolves, rabbits, foxes, fairies, and witches are 'usually like' in a story. At six, 41 percent of the children had firmly developed expectations about the roles of at least half of the characters; by nine, this had risen to 86 per cent of the children interviewed. (pp. 48–49)

Such expectations obviously resulted from the stories to which the children had been exposed, but their very strength suggests that the stereotypes have a function. Bettelheim (1976) argues that:

> polarization dominates the child's mind . . . A person is either good or bad, nothing in between . . . presenting the polarities of character permits the child to comprehend easily the difference between the two, which he [sic] could not do as readily were the figures drawn more true to life, with all the complexities that characterize real people. (p. 9)

Young children's predilection for the books of Blyton and Dahl suggests that it may be a necessary part of their development to seek out literature with stereotypical characters; Appleyard (1990) supports the idea that children in the second of his 'roles' (aged between 7 and 12) like to know exactly where they are in terms of characters:

> Characters tend to be ideal types of good and bad persons. Like the setting, characters are not described in much detail, but are tagged with easily recognizable traits that are mentioned whenever they appear in the story. (p. 62)

If children are likely to search out books which include stereotypical characters, it intensifies the need for such stereotypes, particularly if they are black or female, not to echo some of the out-of-date prejudices of society. Nor should their behaviour always be totally predictable; still less should their roles automatically be subordinate to strong white males.

A particular difficulty is the attribution to characters of traits which are generally seen as appropriate to white heroes, without any examination of whether a different set of qualities might for instance be relevant to heroines or to non-white heroes. Different ways of responding in relationships might be appropriate for ethnic minority or female characters, yet there is a danger that if these characters are portrayed as responding in these ways, they may be seen as weak. How can women be portrayed as strong without losing their femininity? This complex problem obviously cannot be solved once and for all, either by theorists or by the authors of children's books, as it depends so much on what is considered to be feminine, something which differs in different areas of our own society, and in different periods.

Kik Reeder (in Stinton, 1979) presents a critique of Astrid Lindgren's *Pippi Longstocking* books, in which as well as indicating the racially unfortunate fact that Pippi's father is the white King of Cannibal Island, she discusses how Pippi herself is sexist in her treatment of her friends. She suggests that, 'It is soon apparent that Pippi isn't a girl at all, even a tomboy, but a boy in disguise' (p. 115). Other readers might well query this last statement, for Pippi's strength is so considerable as to be absurd, an epithet which applies to a great deal in the books and no doubt adds to their attraction for the young. The criticism does, however, reveal that a book which is regarded by some as feminist, because of its very strong portrayal of a female character, can at the same time be seen as sexist for its rejection of 'feminine' qualities (which, of course, can be possessed by females as well as males).

Narrative, dialogue, point of view and intertextuality

The novelist and critic David Lodge (1990) quotes the Russian literary theorist, Mikhail Bakhtin, as saying, 'The writer is a person who knows how to work language while remaining outside of it; he has the gift of indirect speech' (Lodge, 1990, p. 7). It is this use of 'indirect speech' which can often confuse the reader unfamiliar with the conventions of the novel into not having the kind of perceptions about characters and situations which are intended by the novelist. Lodge presents Bakhtin's categorization of the voices which the novelist may use:

1. 'The direct speech of the author', in what seems to be an "objective", reliable, narrative voice'.
2. 'The represented speech of the characters' either directly or by reported speech or soliloquy.
3. 'Doubly-oriented . . . speech which not only refers to something in the world but also refers to another speech act by another addresser' (Lodge, 1990, p. 59).

Much earlier prose literature tended to make extensive use of categories (1) and (2), though sometimes venturing into (3); late twentieth century fiction, including a good deal addressed to children, incorporates a variety of perspectives, however; from this initial source of confusion, the young reader can begin to appreciate some of the difficulty in deciding precisely what the author's own opinions may be.

The result of this subtlety, as far as many readers are concerned, is that they may miss the condemnation of unsatisfactory attitudes which the author makes, and judge a book as racist or sexist where it may be really condemning racism or sexism. Of course it may well be that at a still deeper level, within what Bakhtin has termed a 'polyphonic' mode, the author *is* revealing subconscious prejudices. Readers of novels which make significant use of a variety of voices may feel deprived of an authority to tell them what to think and how to judge. But such writing has a validity to both ordinary life and everyday language, where it is seldom possible to indulge in the certitudes which can be found in some earlier novels. As Lodge says, 'For [Bakhtin], any discourse in which more than one accent or tone is brought into play makes apparent the dialogic nature of language itself' (p. 86). The child reader needs to become aware of the way in which, at any moment in the text, the narrative point of view is being positioned, to avoid a simplistic impression of what the author is doing, and indeed, to be able to recognize any ideological perspectives.

A recent book for the teenage reader which employs several voices is Berlie Doherty's *Dear Nobody* (1991), in which the narration is shared between Chris, a young man on the point of going to university, and his girlfriend, Helen, who has had to delay going to music college because of expecting Chris's child. Chris's narration is expressed in a straightforward introspective mode, recalling the past, but

Helen's takes the form of letters to her unborn child, whose existence she gradually comes to believe in more and more. Significant additions to the story are provided by other characters, notably Helen's aunt, who recalls the effect on her life of having had an abortion.

Young readers of this book sometimes feel the lack of an authorial stance on contemporary issues; they ask, for instance, why Doherty did not come out more explicitly for 'safe sex', and ponder her position about abortion, seeming to feel that they should have been given more information about the author's attitudes. Such a book can justly be termed 'dialogic', and while many examples of books using different voices exist from the past (such as Emily Bronte's *Wuthering Heights*), there are relatively few which make this kind of demand on younger readers.

Children's authors have frequently used the perspective of the first person narrator, and, even in some of the established classics, such as R. L. Stevenson's *Treasure Island*, it may not always be safe for the reader to assume that the narrative is always to be believed. Unreliable narrators are, however, much more common today than in the past, and this may lead inexperienced readers to fail to recognize where the author is directing their sympathies. Rosa Guy's teenage novel, *The Friends* (1974), begins, 'Her name was Edith. I did not like her' (p. 9), and many readers may well start from the expectation that they too are expected to dislike Edith. We learn that the speaker is Phyllisia, who has recently arrived in New York and finds the class she is in at school uncongenial:

> Of course there were many children in this class that were untidy and whom I did not like. Some were tough. So tough that I was afraid of them. But at least they did not have to sit right across the aisle from me. Nor did they try to be friendly as Edith did – whenever she happened to come to school. (p. 9)

It is soon apparent that Guy expects readers to be making up their own minds about the validity of Phyllisia's judgement about Edith, as we see how, despite herself, Phyllisia is forced to accept the poorer girl's friendship. We begin to realize that Phyllisia's expression of dislike may mask a combination of feelings: guilt at her own behaviour and fear that she too might find herself as 'low' as Edith appears to be. It is not until near the end of the book that we also learn that Phyllisia's opinions about a variety of things and people, most notably her father and his restaurant which she wrongly thinks is high class, are equally ill founded. It would be easy for inexperienced readers to assume that they were being encouraged to reject Edith, or uncritically to accept Phyllisia's snobbish attitude towards her. Confronted with ambiguous situations and attitudes, young readers often need guidance about the author's direction of the audience's sympathies.

Another device which has been popular with authors throughout the ages, though its effect on the reader has only been considered extensively in more recent literary theory, is that of intertextuality. By referring obliquely to a piece of another text, the writer brings into the reader's mind a different set of expectations, which may relate to a well-known story or to texts from a quite different kind of world, such as 'personal letters, publishing, the law, travel brochures and advertising' (Meek, 1988, p. 24). Meek goes on to say: 'On the surface, intertext can seem to be a kind of literary joke; underneath, it is a very serious business, part of the whole intricate network of words which mean more than they say' (p. 24). This too can often give guidance to the reader of the way in which the author wants to influence their judgement of character and situation.

There are many books on subjects related to equality issues which have not received the credit they deserve because readers have not realized the complexity of the different points of view which are being created. A notable example is William Armstrong's *Sounder* (1971) which was initially greeted with great acclaim and awarded the Newbery medal for children's literature; it was subsequently subject to a good deal of criticism, partly because it was not considered to present black language or black spirituality accurately, something about which I am not qualified to judge. (See Schwartz, in Stinton, 1979.) I would, however, dispute some of the other complaints which have been made, concerning the fact that the black characters do not show emotions or even have names; after all, none of the white characters have names either, the only named character being the dog.

Rather than dealing with specific points of negative criticism, it may be more useful to show the essentially dialogic nature of this text, and how it demands from the reader a response to the variety of different viewpoints given, all of which, however, add up to both an indictment of the cruelty of the white property owners towards the black share-croppers, and a deepened understanding of what it was like to be black in the Southern States in the latter part of the nineteenth century.

The novel is the story of how the 'coon dog' of the title is badly injured trying to prevent its master from being carried off to jail for having stolen a ham to avert hunger from his family. His son, through whose often incomplete perceptions the tale is told, though not in the first person, searches for his father, who has been sentenced to the Chain Gang, and incidentally finds a book, the *Essays* of Montaigne, and a teacher. Finally the man and then the dog die, the potentially pessimistic nature of this ending being defused because in the note at the beginning of the novel we have learnt that the author, although white, was taught to read by 'a gray-haired black man who taught the one-room Negro school' and, he says, 'It is the black man's story, not mine.' We therefore deduce that the boy in the story has become an able reader who is sufficiently competent and tolerant to teach a white boy.

This initial contextualization is already enough to alert the reader to there being more than one point of view presented in the novel, and this is clearly the case when the text is examined. Although we are never given any information which is not available to the boy, the beginning is certainly not from his perspective: 'The tall man stood at the edge of the porch. The roof sagged from the two rough posts which held it, almost closing the gap between his head and the rafters . . .' (Armstrong, 1971, p. 1). This straightforward passage of description nevertheless succeeds in conveying a sense of harshness and dire poverty, about which the boy, who has never experienced any other form of life, appears unaware. There is nothing here which would not be familiar to the reader of the nineteenth century novel. Almost immediately, we hear the boy's voice: 'Where did you first get Sounder?', to which the father answers: 'I never got him. He came to me along the road when he wasn't more 'n a pup.' Again, here, the dialogue is presented in a way familiar within the traditional novel. We soon find ourselves within the boy's consciousness, conveyed at first in the words of the omniscient narrator who is clearly adult: 'The boy . . . felt the importance of the years – as a child measures age – which separated him from the younger children.' The tone soon changes, however, and we are presented with the child's language, as he weighs up the question of whether, if he doesn't use all his energies in walking the 8 miles to school and the same distance home, his father will let him hunt with Sounder. 'Having both school and Sounder would be mighty good but if he couldn't have school, he could always have Sounder.' (p. 3). The distinction between different narrative voices becomes less clear cut as the story proceeds; there is frequently a quick transition between them, especially in the portrayal of the boy's thoughts:

> Sounder was well named. When he treed a coon or possum in a persimmon tree or on a wild-grape vine, his voice would roll across the flatlands. It wavered through the foothills, louder than any other dog's in the whole countryside. (pp. 3–4)

The perspective here is certainly closer than that of the initial description, but it seems to be only partly the boy's.

As the novel proceeds, we learn more about the religious background of the family: 'The boy liked to smell the oak slab. It smelled like the Mercy Seat meetin'-house picnic held every summer' (p. 15). Schwartz's criticism that what is portrayed in the book is White fundamentalism, not Black fundamentalism, seems a little pedantic; for most readers, I suspect, the impression of the importance of the 'Gospel' background to the boy is well enough conveyed – we know we are experiencing it through him by the tell-tale omission of the 'g' in 'meetin'. The stress on the sense of smell makes the effect all the more powerful. The same sense is also significant when three nameless white men come to the cabin and one says: 'There are two things I can smell a mile . . . one's a ham cookin' and the other's a thievin' nigger' (Armstrong, 1971, p. 21). As the men take away the father, the sheriff's command, 'Chain him up' is misunderstood by the boy: 'The boy thought they were telling him to chain up Sounder, but then he saw that one of the men had snapped a long chain on the handcuffs on his father's wrists' (p. 24). We are expected to deduce that it had never occurred to the boy that the men would chain up a human being in the way they might a dog.

Once the father is in jail and the winter comes on, the boy is worried about the fact that his father's overalls were torn as he was thrown into the wagon. He is a little consoled, however, in remembering a bible story:

> The boy wanted to ask who carried in wood to keep the people in jail warm. He knew they had big stoves in big jails. Once his mother had told him a story about three people named Shadrach, Meshach and Abed-nego who were in jail. Some mean governor or sheriff got mad and had them thrown right into the jail stove, big as a furnace, but the Lord blew out the fire and cooled the big stove in a second. And when the jail keeper opened the stove door, there stood Shadrach, Meshach and Abed-nego singing: 'Cool water, cool water; The Lord's got green pastures and cool water.' (p. 50)

The boy's thoughts and the intertextual use of the bible and of the 'spiritual' reveal how far his understanding of the world has been mediated through his religious background; given the status of these texts, the young reader is also firmly guided towards sharing the boy's compassionate engagement with his father's plight. We are also expected to appreciate the pathos of his naive expectation that people will be kind to his father.

29

The father is eventually sentenced to hard labour; "'Where's he gonna be at?'" the boy asked after he had swallowed the great lump that filled up his throat and choked him' (p. 74). Here we have an interesting shift from the boy's explicit consciousness to the narrator's presentation of his emotional reaction, of which, we may assume, the boy is only partially aware.

I have chosen only a few of the interesting shifts in perspective in this novel. Although we are never allowed to go beyond what the boy either implicitly knows or is consciously aware of at the time, a great deal more is conveyed through the variations in the narrative voice; this alternates between omniscience and the partial knowledge of the boy, which is sometimes expressed through his own limited vocabulary and sometimes through a sophisticated adult ability to generalize. A book then which at first sight is confined to an 'objective' narrator and a few, nearly inarticulate, speakers, has in fact a complexity of perspective which means that the judgement of it as not really anti-racist can be seen as over-simplistic.

As well as failing to understand the position in which they are put by the author, readers may sometimes, consciously or subconsciously, resist it. This sometimes occurs in the kind of popular fiction which relies on stereotyping and easy judgements. Meredith Rogers Cherland (1994) in her detailed ethnographic study of a group of seven sixth-grade Canadian girls, shows how they 'renegotiated' the rather conformist messages of the decidedly non-revolutionary *Babysitters Club* series to imagine themselves '*in conflict* with the roles that their families suggested for them . . . they saw girls of their own age acting as agents in their own right' (pp. 166–67). For slightly older girls, romantic stories and magazines may provide a cohesive bond with their friends and a means of exchanging giggles over the stereotyped behaviour of the characters, while the producer of the material may be expecting them to identify with these characters. The readers may be applying a greater degree of scepticism than the writer anticipates, and in Chapter 4 I shall be looking further at this stance in relation to popular magazines.

Plot structures

One of the difficulties of dealing largely with contemporary issues within a realistic format is that an author may be torn between fulfilling the young reader's assumed desire for a happy ending, and the fact that in the real world, such situations do not always end happily, and truth to life may demand either an unhappy ending or no real closure at all. Indeterminate endings are particularly difficult for immature readers to accept and Stephens (1992, p. 42) shows how young readers often interpret books as closed off, even when issues are left unresolved at the end. One problem which arises particularly in books about the elderly or the handicapped is that an important character dies; John Burningham's *Granpa* (1984) concludes with a picture of an empty chair, and young children are left free to interpret this to the extent that their own experience has made them ready for its implications, particularly in the light of the old man's illness a few pages earlier. As indicated above, Armstrong mitigates the sadness of the inevitable ending in *Sounder*, when both the father and the dog die, by means of the framing note from the author, who discloses indirectly how the 'boy' has grown up to be an educated man with a reasonable place in society.

Sometimes, what appears to be a defeatist ending may reflect the author's implicit ideology just as much as truth to the facts or to art; critics of Paula Fox's

The Slave Dancer (1973, 1979) might have been happier if the slaves had risen against the evil crew, whether or not such a revolt had been successful, but it would have been a different book from the one Fox wrote. It may be that her implicit and unacknowledged desire was rather to implicate *white* readers in the guilt of the slave-trade than to display to *black* readers the passivity of their forebears. Often, what is really needed is for children to put themselves in the position of the author who has created so complex and involving a situation that any determinate ending would be an over-simplification; this can help them to empathize with the writer at work, rather than always seeing books as finished products.

Humour

Children's humour is often fairly unattractive to the adult reader. Alison Lurie (1990) discusses the child's fascination with jokes, many of which are directed against teachers (p. 222) and evidence children's enjoyment in the 'putting down' of officious adults in positions of authority. Jokes and rhymes, whether part of children's oral traditions or contained in popular books and magazines, also frequently involve *risqué* language with lavatorial associations. Both the reversal of the order of society and the delight in the scatological come into the category of the 'carnivalesque', as defined in the influential work of Mikhail Bakhtin (ed. P. Morris, 1994). His thesis on the sixteenth-century French comedist Rabelais propounds the over-arching view that carnival, which turns society 'upside down' and embraces such forms as comic shows, verbal parodies, and various kinds of curses, has throughout history acted as a safety valve, allowing the common people to express their dissatisfaction with the established order while continuing to be subject to it in their daily lives, rather than revolting against it.

Carnival, which may also be an instrument of non-revolutionary change, involves the suspension of hierarchical precedence, since 'all were considered equal during carnival' (Morris, 1994, p. 199); its other features include travesties and profanations, images of the whole or part of the human body, with an emphasis on 'food, drink, defecation, and sexual life' (p. 199). It is easy to see how relevant this mode is to a good deal of children's reading, notably 'comics' and popular authors such as Roald Dahl. The possession by the child community of books which enable them to use 'rude words' and which can be seen as their own property rather that than of adults, recalls the function of carnival as a means for the oppressed sections of medieval society to 'let off steam'. Children's literature which includes such elements could be seen as performing a similar function; it recalls how Lurie's book about 'Subversive Children's Literature' is variously entitled: *Don't Tell the Grown-Ups* (hardback) and *Not in Front of the Grown-Ups* (paperback), both of which titles embody this sense of children being, as she says, 'an unusual, partly savage tribe'.

It is perhaps surprising how often the carnivalesque also occurs in some areas of children's literature which might be expected to be more serious, such as books depicting disability. Sometimes it seems to be there solely to amuse, but quite often it has a function which is strongly related to what the author probably sees as one of the purposes of the book. Morris Gleitzman's *Sticky Beak* (1993) is about Rowena Batts, who is born mute but can nevertheless communicate quite effectively through sign language; it begins with her throwing a large bowl of 'Jelly Custard

Surprise' into the blades of an air-conditioning fan at the school farewell party for Ms Dunning, who has married Rowena's father and is now heavily pregnant. As a result of Rowena's unpremeditated and apparently motiveless action, the headmaster's clothes are ruined:

> It wasn't just his sleeves that were dripping with jelly and custard, it was most of his shirt and all of his shorts and both knees. On top of his head, in the middle of his bald patch, were several pieces of pineapple. (p. 8)

The diminution of an authority figure, the abuse of food and drink and its wide dissemination by the fan, the way it recalls custard pie slapstick comedy – all these features of carnival are not, it eventually appears, present in the book merely as humour to encourage children to read on, but have a serious function associated with Rowena's disability. The 'accident' occurs at the moment that her father is on his knees, publically serenading his wife's eight and a half month foetus, an action which has brought to the fore his mute daughter's anxiety that she will be rejected if her step-mother has a speaking child. The wide spread of the custard, splattering the whole speaking community, of which in many ways she has been an involved member, presumably is a mode of expressing her suppressed resentment. There are many other similar elements in the book; the human brain is deprived of dignity by being described as 'like scrambled eggs when you don't wash the mushroom juice out of the pan first' (Gleitzman, 1993, p. 104), and at the end of the book Rowena's father is pelted with rubbish and discarded food (pp. 113–14). The cockatoo which is the 'sticky beak' of the title, displays another carnivalesque feature, the use of 'billingsgate', or abusive language. By contrast with Rowena, it can 'speak', and addresses her, 'Get lost, dork-brain. You smell. Go and fall off a rock.' (p. 44). In this book, then, it appears that the carnivalesque elements have a range of functions which may imperceptibly affect the reader's attitudes.

Stephens (1992) suggests that texts which use the carnivalesque may be categorised into three types:

1. 'Those which offer the characters "time out" from the habitual constraints of society, but incorporate a safe return to social normality';
2. those which question established ideas;
3. those 'which are endemically subversive of . . . received paradigms of behaviour and morality.' (p. 121)

Most of the books which seem to have a serious point to make seem to come into the second of Stephens' categories. While books about race, culture and language seem to be a little too cautious about these politically sensitive subjects to treat them with a light touch, there are a number of books written to emphasize the equality of females and disabled characters which make extensive use of carnivalesque elements and I shall be looking at some of these in the relevant chapters. Jokes involving parts of the body and near-explicit references to sex and defecation seem to particularly abound in books where one of the protagonists is near to death, and a part of their function is probably to relieve the tension. Their emphasis on the physical serves also to suggest subliminally that death is part of a continuum which also involves human waste products. Understanding the relationship between humour in children's books and the much wider ramifications of the carnivalesque can provide a further insight into the ways in which books influence readers.

32

Although the use of figurative language has always been one of the salient features of literature of all kinds, its importance within the realist novel is often insufficiently acknowledged; the author's use of imagery can be a subtle influence on the reader of which not enough account is always taken. David Lodge, himself a novelist as well as a distinguished literary critic, has done a good deal of work on the use of imagery within realist prose, and it may be helpful to quote his distinction (based on the work of Roman Jakobson) between the two most important and commonly used figures, metaphor and metonymy:

> Metaphor and metonymy (or synecdoche) are both figures of equivalence, but generated by different processes, metaphor according to similarity between things otherwise different, metonymy according to contiguity or association between part and whole, cause and effect, thing and attribute, etc. Thus if I transform the literal sentence 'Ships sail the sea' into 'Keels plough the deep', *plough* is equivalent to 'sail' because of the similarity between the movement of a plough through the earth and a ship through the sea, but *keel* is equivalent to 'ship' because it is part of a ship (synecdoche) and *deep* is equivalent to 'sea' because it is an attribute of the sea (metonymy). (Lodge, 1981, p. 21)

I have quoted this at some length because I have found that the term 'metonymy' is much less widely understood than 'metaphor', and because, as Lodge claims, 'Realistic fiction is dominantly metonymic' (p. 22). Stephens (1992) says, 'In this mode, a stretch of text means what it seems to mean, and that meaning is complete. But it also forms a part of a larger signifying structure' (p. 248).

In Chapter 1, I have already cited, from Lucy Boston's *The Chimneys of Green Knowe*, an example of an author employing metonym in this way; the curly hair of the little black boy, Jacob, has been used to embroider the eyes of the swan, creating a more positive impression than the 'tresses' of Caxton which have been sewn into a chimney, something which, in this book, tends to have associations with darkness and danger. Armstrong's *Sounder* includes many powerful examples of how the reader's feelings are affected by the use of metonym; when the boy takes to the jail a Christmas cake which his mother has baked, a:

> man with a red face squeezed the cake in his hands and broke it into four pieces. 'This cake could have a steel file or hacksaw blade in it,' he said. Then he swore and threw the pieces back into the box. (Armstrong, 1974, p. 59)

By the time the boy's father gets the cake it is nothing but crumbs. There is much that could be said about the way this passage acts as a signifier of the fragmentation of the black community; we have already seen how 'The white man who owned the vast endless fields had scattered the cabins of his Negro share-croppers far apart . . .' (p. 2). The fear of a hidden weapon is also evocative, but perhaps more than anything else, the passage reflects the destructive effect of white aggression on the life of the family. I am not in any way suggesting that such a passage should be read allegorically – the cake is *really* there in the novel – but that by a tissue of such passages, the author is in fact creating in the reader a strong degree of empathy with the black characters, together with condemnation of white hostility.

It would also be interesting to pursue in more detail the symbolic function of the large dog which provides the title of the novel, since Armstrong parallels the situation of the dog with that of the man, who dies slightly before it does. To claim this pairing is not to minimize the humanity of the man nor to regard the portrayal of the dog as in any way anthropomorphic. Rather, it is all part of Armstrong's technique of making the reader subconsciously sensitive to both. The book demands very close reading and could repay detailed study by secondary pupils, looking at the negative aspects (as highlighted by Schwartz) as well as at the positive ones.

Language

Language associated with racism, sexism or indeed outmoded ways of describing disabled people, is much easier to detect than some of the other elements which I am considering. It probably gives the most immediate offence, and deters readers from looking for any positive aspects in the books concerned. In the next chapter, I shall touch on the problems, in some of the 'classics' of children's literature, which are created by language acceptable in the past but no longer so today. Most books published within the last 30 years, however, avoid racist terms unless they are associated with unpleasant characters, whose malevolence is often in fact signalled by their use of language.

The problem is that young readers are more likely to notice, and sometimes to use, the unacceptable language, than to be aware of the author's techniques, which should be working to lead the reader to condemn such characters. Victor Watson (in Styles *et al.*, 1992) gives as an example a passage from a Robert Westall short story, 'The Bus', where 'a little balding bloke with a thin moustache . . . who had tears standing in the corners of his eyes' talks of what he sees as a happier past, 'A Brum without niggers. A Brum without Pakis. A *British* Brum. Every face a white face.' This is mediated through a focal character who is shocked by the illegality of the sentiments, but no indication is given as to whether this character rejects them, so that the reader has no explicit guidance in the text. It is easy to imagine how on the one hand passages like these could offend readers from ethnic minority groups, or indeed, concerned people of all races; while on the other hand, putting words into the mouths of potential racists. Nevertheless, the racist language has a function within the story, especially as the speaker is portrayed as apparently mild, rather than 'a great hulking member of the National Front.' Watson (Styles *et* al., 1992) says:

> I believe Robert Westall was irresponsible in writing that story – but I would defend his right to be irresponsible. We need irresponsible writers if the prevailing complacencies of our age – however benevolent – are to be challenged . . . However, if writers are to be allowed to be irresponsible, we must have responsible readers. (pp. 4–6)

This condition, he suggests, is best fostered by children having the opportunity to discuss their reading with fellow pupils and with teachers without fear of being made to feel that they will be in trouble if they do not follow a majority line.

It is impossible, however, to guarantee that in all circumstances children will have the opportunity to function in the way Watson advocates. In some instances, a book may seem to carry a racist message which is not contradicted until nearly the end of the book. Gillian Klein (1985) points out that with such books, many black readers may have been 'lost along the way', while some potentially racist readers may have had their prejudices reinforced (pp. 49–52).

Clearly, the situation in each book needs to be evaluated according to its merits, in the light of the class or child who may be exposed to the language. What does seem inappropriate is for any racist language in a book to be read 'around the class'; if it is actually spoken aloud at all, it needs to be through the voice of the teacher, who is in effect putting it into quotation marks. There is no easy answer, for such language is not only to be found in books which may easily be picked up by a child, but it also may be spoken, and it therefore demands discussion, not shirking. I shall return to this issue in the final chapter.

The visual aspect

There is a good deal of evidence from before 1985 that black children have often possessed an image of themselves as looking more like white persons than black. Milner (1983) refers to a number of investigations (p. 100 *et seq.*); particularly disturbing are his own studies set up in the early 1970s which revealed that as well as often selecting from photos white children as preferred companions, the children he questioned also often had a variant self-image:

> In response to the standard identification question, 'Which one of these two dolls looks most like you?' 48 per cent of the West Indians and 24 per cent of the Asians maintained that the white figure looked more like them. When asked 'If you could be one of these dolls, which one would you rather be?', 82 per cent of the West Indians and 65 per cent of the Asians indicated the white doll rather than their own-group figure. (p. 137)

This lack of valuing their own physical appearance may well have been related not only to the inferior social position of most blacks and Asians at that time, but also to the lack of images of ethnic minority characters on the covers of children's books. The situation has considerably improved since then, and there are now in this country a number of excellent examples of picture-books featuring black characters, who are also quite frequently depicted on the jackets of books for older children, and a number of these are discussed in Chapter 6. In the van of this movement were illustrators such as Errol Lloyd, the popularity of whose *My Brother Sean* (1973) influenced publishers and artists alike. Even so, Judith Graham, writing in 1990, was still able to say, 'When it comes to ethnicity, the black or brown protagonist is still rare' (p. 117). The solution she advocates is involving minority groups in book creation, something which has indeed happened to a certain extent in recent years. Nevertheless, a recent news item in *The Observer* (October 1996) is disquieting; it reports that although British publishers appear relatively enlightened about the desirability of portraying children from ethnic minority groups on their book-jackets, 'their European counterparts "are shocked by" or "do not like"' these non-white images, because they are convinced that parents in their countries will not buy these books. Some British publishers, dependent as they are on co-editions, therefore change the book-jacket for European sales, but others choose instead to market such books in the USA.

The chief reason for anxiety is not so much the blatant commercially based attitude of the European publishers, as the fact, which presumably is supported by market research, that many parents on the Continent are still so racially prejudiced as to react against books depicting black children, with the consequent effects on the self-images of the many ethnic minority children in their countries.

That children's attitudes to books can be influenced by covers and illustrations is certain; the Roehampton Survey (Reynolds, 1996) reveals that these were the most important factors governing choice at Key Stage 1, and even at Key Stage 4 the cover ranks as the second most important feature for girls and the third for boys (pp. 1–2). How much children's attitudes to themselves are influenced by these factors is less easy to determine; Judith Graham (1990) says:

> Obviously if large numbers of minority-group children never see positive images of themselves and their group reflected in the printed or televised images in their society then all the well-documented problems that accompany low self-image become a reality. (p. 58)

The featuring of black children in picture-books which may be used to introduce children to reading is particularly important, especially since children from some minority ethnic groups may not yet be fluent in English so that 'reading the pictures' becomes even more valuable to them than to their English-speaking classmates.

The illustrations in a number of contemporary books portray ethnic minority children where the text makes no specific mention of their colour. Perry Nodelman (1988) suggests that:

> apparently superfluous pictorial information can give specific objects a weight beyond what the text suggests . . . . That the boy who goes out to play in Ezra Jack Keats *The Snowy Day* is black implies an attitude of tolerant unconcern for such matters in a text that never mentions the boy's color; the apparently superfluous information in the picture gives the text a meaning it would not have on its own. (p. 106)

Whether or not research can prove that the visual presence or absence of ethnic minority characters is significant to the self-image of black readers, it remains a matter of importance to white readers, who need to see that the multi-racial society which in most cases they experience in the classroom is also given a place in the books they read. If they do *not* live in an area where this is true in the classroom, it becomes still more important that it should be imaged in the books, or school can be a rather unrealistic introduction to life in our multi-ethnic society!

Conclusion

My intention in this chapter has been to highlight some of the reasons for claiming that books can influence children's attitudes, and to examine the means used by authors to express their conscious beliefs or subconscious assumptions about the position in society of such groups as females, people of African or Asian origin, and the elderly or disabled. It seems to me that if such people are usually depicted, in words or pictures, as less important, or alternatively are not there at all, every child is done a disservice. We must, however, remember that children will experience reading, not only in the classroom, but also in the home, where they may be exposed to very far from acceptable images, in books of the past or in popular magazines. Ultimately, what is needed is for children to be alerted to all the means authors use to create in the reader particular attitudes towards the characters, so that they are not passive recipients of someone else's ideology but active participants in the creation of their own.

References

Note that an extensive bibliography is also given at the end of this book. The inclusion of a book here does not in itself imply recommendation, and should be seen in the context of discussion in the text.

Armstrong, W. (1971) *Sounder*. London: Gollancz.
Boston, L. (1958) *The Chimneys of Green Knowe*. London: Faber.
Burningham, J. (1984) *Granpa*. London: Cape.
Dickens, C. (1961, 1st edn, 1854) *Hard Times*. London: Dent.
Doherty, B. (1991) *Dear Nobody*. London: Hamish Hamilton.
Fox, P. (1973;1979) *The Slave Dancer*. Basingstoke: Macmillan.
Gleitzman, M. (1993) *Sticky Beak*. Basingstoke: Macmillan.
Guy, R. (1974)*The Friends*. London: Gollancz.
Lindgren, A. (1947; 1st English edn, 1954) *Pippi Longstocking*. Oxford: Oxford University Press.
Lloyd, E. (1973) *My Brother Sean*. London: Bodley Head.
Sherwood, M. M. (1st edn, 1818) *The History of the Fairchild Family*. London: Ward Lock.

Have the 'Classics' Had Their Day?

He hath disgrac'd me and hind'red me half a million; laugh'd at my losses, mock'd at my gains, scorned my nation, thwarted my bargains, cooled my friends, heated mine enemies. And what's his reason? I am a Jew.
(Shylock, in Shakespeare's *The Merchant of Venice*, III, i, 45)

The word 'classic' is by no means a precise one, but I do not intend here to enter into controversy about either the history of the term or its accuracy as applied to some of the major texts of children's literature. Popular usage tends to regard classic texts as those which are relatively universal in their appeal, transcending barriers of both place and time; here I shall therefore discuss some of the major texts which have survived from the past and have also been translated into a number of other languages. It seems valid also to make some kind of fairly arbitrary distinctions on grounds of quality, though these are likely of course to be tendentious.

In this chapter, I am generally considering works which teachers and librarians are likely to advocate children reading, while in the chapter which follows, I shall look rather at books which children tend to find by themselves, especially through recommendations from friends. I am well aware, however, that such a distinction cannot be rigid, and I am governed also by affinity between texts, so that it is convenient to put Blyton, Captain Johns, many of the writers of school fiction, and, a little less certainly, Lofting and Dahl, into the next chapter, and to confine myself here to the kind of texts often to be found in large quantities in school stock cupboards, or which have at some point received critical acclaim in the 40 or more years since they were originally published. All of the books I discuss have, as far as I know, remained in print for most of the period since their original publication.

On the whole I want to confine my discussion to 'children's' classics, but it is notoriously very difficult to find any satisfactory definition of children's literature; in particular some of those works written for adults which are, today, more often to be found in the children's section of the library or bookshop cannot be excluded from discussion. Notable in such a group are *Robinson Crusoe* (1719) and *Gulliver's Travels* (1726), two of the eighteenth century works written with an adult audience in mind but which sustained generations of young people when all too much that was written directly for children was very explicitly didactic, particularly about religion and morals. The third of the trio of adult classics appropriated by past generations of children, Bunyan's *Pilgrim's Progress* (1678), seems however to be relatively little read today so it will not be given attention here. Certain novels of Dickens, especially *Oliver Twist* and *A Christmas Carol*, sometimes appear in editions, often abridged, which are aimed specifically at children. Even Shakespeare cannot realistically be excluded from discussion, since his plays are to be found on the English National Curriculum at Key Stage 3, for pupils from 11 to 14; many teachers of younger children, however, see no point in waiting until secondary school to introduce pupils to some stories and scenes from the plays, especially since there are short and simplified television versions.

The question of whether it is legitimate to talk about a 'canon' of children's literature is somewhat peripheral to my focus, though there seems little doubt that the books which I am discussing would be part of such an entity. To that extent, they raise the issue as to whether canonicity by its nature tends to exclude females and minority groups. 'Classic' children's literature probably includes more books by female authors than does the adult canon, but this in no way exempts it from controversy about gender, as will be seen. The problem however with many of these classics lies less in the prejudiced attitudes which can be detected in them than in the background knowledge needed to appreciate or even to understand them. Children feel distanced from them; in some instances there might seem little point in worrying about unacceptable attitudes in books which young people are unlikely to choose to read of their own accord. After all, if the only experience they have of such books is in school, the teacher is able to discuss any difficult issues and mediate to the children the kind of attitude which seems appropriate today. One of the reasons why such books need to be confronted, however, is because the 'orthodoxy' of the 1970s about race and gender often took issue with them, as instanced by Dixon's comments (1978a, p. 10) about Alcott (see Chapter 1).

Even if children might not want to read these books in the original, they often will have been presented with the Disney version of, for instance, *Peter Pan* and *The Jungle Books*, and either they themselves or their teachers may want them to have the experience of the original texts. Such books, without any sanitizing expurgations or introductions, may in any case be found on their parents' or their grandparents' bookshelves, and in some instances are still to be found in bookshops, libraries and book club magazines.

Questions about any elements in these books which might seem unacceptable today really arise most with the ones which the children might actually read by themselves. There are fewer problems about any books from the past which children will only encounter when they have mature reading skills; by this I mean not only the ability to cope with difficult language, but also the literary awareness which enables them to see something of what the author is doing in creating the characters and attributing them with language which at times may be judged to be sexist or racist. As mature readers, they may also begin to understand the way the author has been affected by society's attitudes on such subjects.

Ultimately, the only really effective action against bias in books is to equip readers with the abilities to detect it and contextualize it in what they know of the author's social and personal background. This does not mean 'making excuses' for the authors because as poor ignorant people of the past they did not know any better, but rather helping young readers to realize how present-day attitudes which might seem beyond question have themselves evolved from those which seem less acceptable, and may, indeed, be superseded in the future.

Before judging whether or not such books should be taught, we need to examine our motives in teaching them, and if any specific book we are considering actually adds to the experience of the child. It is easy to be swayed by the feeling that children need to be made aware of their 'literary heritage'. The first Cox Report, *English for Ages 5 to 11* (1988) put forward a number of possible models of English teaching (Section 3.19–3.26, p. 12): the 'Personal Growth', the 'Cross-curricular', the 'Adult Needs', the 'Cultural Heritage' and the 'Cultural Analysis'. The stress on texts from the past in the 1995 revision of the English National Curriculum suggests that the Literary Heritage view dominated in the group responsible for that document. It is, however, worth considering whether or not it is really the best policy to give children 'classics' before they are able to appreciate them properly; it is easy for adults to telescope the process of growing up and think that they were, for instance, reading *Alice in Wonderland* when they were only 5 years old. In many instances, the supposed problems about texts vanish if they are presented to pupils old enough to appreciate the social context and aspects of the writing style such as irony and the adoption of a variety of points of view.

It is, however, impossible to deny that some of the classics of the past are, by current standards, intolerant on matters of race, culture or gender, as my discussion below will admit. Sometimes it may be necessary to question whether or not children today will really be deprived of anything worthwhile if they never meet them. There can be no absolute answer to such questions, and teachers are inevitably aware that if some children do not read these books at school, they probably will never experience them at all, at least as books; in many cases, they may well encounter them in film and television versions, which, because of the need to attract a wide audience, will often play down the aspects which might seem repugnant today.

A criticism which may with some justice be levelled against a good many of the 'classics' of English literature is that many of the villains have a tendency to be foreign, black, Arab, or Asian. While this stereotyping is bad, it must be admitted that it would be equally racist to remove from such groups the chance of being villains at all!

The debate on some of these issues has suffered from people taking extreme positions. On the one hand, those who are rightly worried about racism have sometimes reacted equally strongly against a book which, because of when it was written, uses terms like 'nigger' or 'redskin', as they might against pernicious National Front propaganda. On the other hand, those who parody any kind of hesitation about past texts as 'political correctness', tend inaccurately to claim that all the books which they remember reading in their childhood, from *Robinson Crusoe* to *Noddy*, have been outlawed by 'loony left' teachers and librarians; their characteristic stance is, 'these books never did me any harm'. What has in fact happened over the last 20 or so years is that people concerned with book buying policies have become more discriminating, and a good many other people have become aware about the arguments on both sides and increasingly anxious about both choice and use of books.

People who love books are generally torn between on the one hand a horror of censorship, with recollections of the Nazis burning books, and on the other a loathing of any kind of material which spreads racial hatred, or advocates abhorrent practices such as pederasty. We may sometimes take refuge in the concept that books which are racist automatically lack literary merit, but as the examples which

I shall go on to consider make plain, this is an oversimplification. There is no easy way out; each book needs to be considered on its merit in relation to the child or children who will read it, and the way it will be mediated to them. A book which accepts the values of the past without question, when these are radically different from those of today, may easily have high qualities, as surely is the case with some of Shakespeare's plays, and novels by Defoe and Dickens. Many such books may not really be accessible to young people, but that way out is not available in the case of books like *Oliver Twist, Tom Sawyer* and *Robinson Crusoe.* Children will continue to read these books, often in a form which provides no contextualization for the aspects about which we might feel unhappy.

Naturally, the debate remains as to the extent to which children are likely to be influenced by such books, but in the long run, the only possible answer is to make children into critical readers, able to detect and withstand all forms of prejudice, however subtly they are conveyed. Paradoxically, one of the most effective ways of doing this is to help them to work through books which may not always be perfect in their adherence to contemporary views about equality.

Race and culture

Rae Alexander (in Stinton, 1979) in compiling a list of recommended books proposes a simple criterion for de-selection:

> no book would be listed if it was considered likely to communicate to either a black or a white child a racist concept or cliché about blacks. Even one negative stereotype would be enough to eliminate an otherwise good book. (p. 70)

While this may well have been appropriate for her purposes, I would contend that it would leave children without the chance of examining the very different kinds of negative depictions in books, and confuses language (likely to be determined by the period in which the books was written) with theme, which needs to be examined, since it may be either positive or negative in its effect, independently of language. Alexander admits herself to be particularly concerned about the hypothetical situation of a black child involved in the reading round the class of such books. Most educators today, however, would consider that such a teaching technique is not to be recommended, though the teacher may still need to exercise caution about the choice of books for small group reading.

Alexander's limitation seems to me to be likely to deprive the young reader of most texts from the past, and to preclude the possibility of their working out for themselves, guided initially by the teacher, either what their authors really thought or how they were influenced by society. It would also mean omitting some great literature and sounds dangerously near to censorship; policies like this have given rather too much ground to those who deny that there is any need to worry about racism in literature.

I propose to go on to consider some texts by major authors which would not pass the Alexander test. I am in no way automatically recommending these for use in the classroom; rather I am trying to indicate some of the positive and the questionable qualities which need to be taken into account when deciding whether or not to use a book with a group or a class, or to recommend it to an individual pupil. Most of these books furnish ample opportunities for the development of understanding

41

about the way in which race or culture is treated; what sometimes becomes apparent is the way in which, beneath a very obvious disparagement of black people, there is often a kind of admiration – the fear of and fascination with the other, well discussed by Edward Said (1987, p. 30) in his study of Orientalism.

Shakespeare and Dickens: anti-semitism and the need for a villain

It is difficult to start any consideration of English 'classics' without at least briefly mentioning Shakespeare, for his work acts as a cultural icon against which others are judged, and even young children may have imbibed, from teachers, parents or peers, some form of attitude towards his work. *The Merchant of Venice* could be seen as a key text, for it combines story elements which are likely to interest the young (such as the casket scenes) with the powerful expression of prejudice. Shakespeare's portrayal of Shylock is often located as a site of anti-semitism, yet unlike his contemporary Christopher Marlowe's portrayal of Barabas, the title character of his *The Jew of Malta*, as a stage villain, enjoying poisoning a conventful of nuns, Shakespeare seems to have been unable to avoid showing Shylock as human and sharing our basic humanity : 'Hath not a Jew eyes? Hath not a Jew hands, organs, dimensions, senses, affections, passion . . .' (III, i, 50). In the play we undoubtedly see a portrayal of the anti-semitism of the gentile characters, but the dramatic form should prevent us from taking this as the final viewpoint of the play.

In fact, it could be argued that in most productions, the audience is left with a good deal of sympathy for Shylock, having lost his daughter and much of his wealth, being forcibly baptised a Christian and dependent for his very survival on the charity of Antonio, whom he loathes. I am not claiming that Shakespeare was an exponent of racial equality ahead of his time, but merely that complex texts demand deeper analysis than simple rejection because of the uncomfortable elements. Another difficult scene in this play is that where the Prince of Morocco chooses the wrong casket, followed by the racist remark of Portia, a character with whom we are generally in sympathy, 'Let all of his complexion choose me so' (II, vii, 79). This needs, however, to be set into the context of her adverse but humorous comments in an earlier scene (I, ii) about her English, Scottish, German and Neapolitan suitors, highlighting their 'national' characteristics. While use of stereotypes as a source of comedy is undoubtedly a risky business, which demands discussion, outlawing it would be impossible; again, we cannot assume that Shakespeare's attribution of a remark to a character necessarily means that he endorses it, a fact which could provide a valuable lesson about drama.

We see this particularly in *Othello* where a number of unpleasant racist remarks are made in the first scene (lines 67, 89–90, 113) by Iago, who turns out to be one of Shakespeare's most evil villains. By contrast, Othello is portrayed as intensely noble, but at the same time credulous. What is more at issue than the language is the question of how far his credulity is to be regarded as in any way resulting from his race; this question is far too complex for a simple answer, though it would certainly reward informed discussion in the light of the beliefs of the Elizabethan age. It is surely far preferable that issues such as these be faced in the classroom, rather than simply assuming that the text will determine the audience's reactions.

For various social and economic reasons, the stereotyped portrayal of the Jew as evil and avaricious has been very strong in England, in both literature and life; one of the most unpleasant instances in major literature is to be found in Chaucer's 'The Prioress's Tale', where a group of Jews are seen as responsible for the murder of a devout little boy who sings a hymn while going through the ghetto. I suspect that Dickens in *Oliver Twist* (1837–38) took the stereotype on board for literary purposes without a great deal of intellectual consideration. It has been suggested that many of Dickens' early novels are a kind of reworking of his own childhood experience of poverty in the city of London. Hobsbaum (1972) says: 'Dickens's entire career was an attempt to make sure that no one was going to put him back into the blacking factory of his nightmares' (p. 112). His dependence for his stories on the child within himself probably helps to account for their appeal to children, who may not initially be capable of reading the text but will have met Oliver, David Copperfield and Pip through film and television. Of these books, probably *Oliver Twist* is the one which young people are perhaps most likely to attempt to read, and unfortunately, it is the one which includes the most blatant example of racial prejudice, in the depiction of Fagin. After the Artful Dodger has taken advantage of his ignorance of London ways, Oliver wakes up in a sordid room to see, standing over a frying pan: 'with a toasting fork in his hand . . . a very old shrivelled Jew, whose villainous-looking and repulsive face was obscured by a quantity of matted red hair' (Chapter 8).

Fagin does not improve upon closer acquaintance, despite his initially friendly remarks to Oliver, and the situation concerning prejudice is worsened by his constantly being referred as 'the Jew'. The character was apparently modelled on a notorious Jewish fence, Ikey Solomon, whose evil characteristics were regarded as being typical of Jews throughout the country (*Oliver Twist*, ed. Fairclough, 1966, p. 487–88). The anti-semitism here seems to me to create a much more difficult problem than does Shakespeare's Shylock. It is in the section of *Oliver Twist* most accessible to children, and because of the use of caricature which is heightened by Cruikshank's illustrations, represents a high degree of what appears to be deliberate stereotyping. Recent adaptations of the text for young children are likely to make Fagin's Jewishness less emphatic, a 1990 version, abridged by Lesley Baxter, seems to change all of Dickens' references to 'the Jew' simply to 'Fagin'. His character has also been softened in the musical *Oliver*.

Nevertheless, the problem of the young reader encountering the original text remains. There would be no point in attempting censorship, as libraries and bookshops abound with copies of it. For the adult to claim, 'It did me no harm' is disingenuous; which of us can say with certitude that we are not affected by this kind of view? In the post-Holocaust world it is difficult to be complacent about the time-dishonoured impression which Dickens gives of Jews as evil and avaricious. The only answer, again, must be the education of the sensibilities, so that the reader can take this kind of caricature as a reflection of what Dickens, perhaps without thinking, accepted from the long-standing anti-semitic literary tradition. Obviously books like this should not be read around the class, but there is no way that teachers can or should stop them being read at all. Therefore at some point the creation of villains who are stereotyped into racial or religious moulds (we might think of some of the monks and Jesuits in Scott and Kingsley, for example) needs to be questioned and set into context. Books which appeal to young children, like *Oliver Twist*, can provide an excellent source for doing this.

Daniel Defoe and Rudyard Kipling: the myths of empire

I have already mentioned the significant place which *Robinson Crusoe* (1719) has in any study of racial attitudes. Defoe's automatic assumption of the white man's right to take possession of the island, and to expect subservience from the natives, who are by nature ignorant and barbarous, though in some instances capable of education, means that this is a very contentious text.

Although Defoe's language is not so latinate as some of his contemporaries, the book in its original version, for adults of the eighteenth century, still presents a challenge to the young reader, and it surely must be one of the texts most often presented in an abridged format. Since the racist and colonial attitudes in this book are not at the relatively superficial levels of language but are totally integrated with the plot, they are unlikely to be reduced in later versions. A children's edition of 1986, although it is abridged, nevertheless includes in its entirety the passage (p. 175) about 'the poor savage' submitting himself to his rescuer which I have quoted as the epigraph to my introduction (see p. 1). Shortly after this scene, Crusoe begins to teach him English: 'I made him know his name should be Friday . . . I likewise taught him to say Master, and then let him know that was to be my name' (p. 176). It is apparent that Defoe intends no criticism of Crusoe for regarding another human being as his possession, but rather applauds Crusoe for his clemency and desire to educate the poor untutored savage. A simplified 'read it yourself' version intended for children of 6 omits the episode of Friday kneeling beneath Crusoe's foot, but still seems to have no hesitation about the white man's right to name him: 'As it is Friday, I shall name you Friday' (Ladybird, 1993). This version is certainly less objectionable, but its accessibility for younger children is a little disquieting, since it makes so many tacit assumptions about the superiority of Crusoe's culture, and by implication, his right to be in charge.

Personally, I would advocate that this book only be read by older pupils who are able to contextualize it within the history of colonialism, and can judge Defoe's attitudes by the standards of both his age and ours. It would, however, be impossible to ensure that younger children had no access to it in some form. In addition to the text, there are numerous film and comic versions still extant, and by no means all of these present an acceptable picture. Stinton (1979) rather facilely says:

> As for Defoe's novel, an end to abridgements of such 'classics' would mean that children would be unlikely to read the novel until they were old enough to judge it for themselves. (p. 1)

This sounds suspiciously like censorship, and in any case would be difficult to apply to the hosts of second-hand outlets such as car-boot sales, not to mention copies still to be found in grandparents' lofts. We are faced with the real situation of the existence of countless copies not only of *Robinson Crusoe*, but also of *Gulliver's Travels* (1726) which makes similar assumptions though in a rather less objectionable way. Subsequent 'Robinsonnades' such as Marryat's *Masterman Ready* (1842) and Ballantyne's *The Coral Island* (1858), which also assume the natural superiority of the white man, proliferate and may be found and read by young children. Even if they don't read these, they will be faced with the other numerous descendants of the desert island tradition, which involves much that seems immediately attractive, particularly to young males: adventure, triumphing against savage hordes, building one's own secret place.

There is no easy answer; a pious hope that such books will cease to exist does not even begin to tackle the problem. It seems to me that the school has some responsibility for helping even young children to recognize that one individual assuming possession of what could be another's land or property, deeming that the behaviour of the owners is so uncivilized that they have no rights, and subjugating them by superior technology (all of which could be seen as the attributes of colonialism) is at the very least extremely uncertain morally. Looking at easy texts which problematize some of these issues, or dramatizing similar scenarios, might provide an acceptable way to present them to young children, and would give the basis for discussion, rather than automatic assumption about the rights of the more powerful.

The later nineteenth century near-contemporaries, Rider Haggard and Rudyard Kipling, are important contributors to the British imperialist tradition, basing their writings on their experiences in Africa and India respectively. Both authors have often been subject to attacks which sometimes seem to have resulted from reading about the themes of their books rather than reading the texts themselves. The narrative of *King Solomon's Mines* (Haggard, 1885) is set within a distancing framework which makes it impossible to determine precisely Haggard's views about the subjects described, which include a romantic relationship between a white man and a black woman and the regaining of an African kingdom for the rightful ruler, Ignosi, alias Umbopa. When first encountered by the narrator, Allan Quartermain, he is described thus:

> slipping off the long military great coat which he wore, and revealing himself naked except for the moocha round his centre and a necklace of lions' claws. Certainly he was a magnificent-looking man: I never saw a finer native. Standing about six foot three high he was broad in proportion, and very shapely. In that light, too, his skin looked scarcely more than dark, except here and there where deep black scars marked old assegai wounds. (p. 41)

Haggard's device of concealing himself in a role of 'editor' alerts the experienced novel reader not to regard this description as necessarily representing his own perspective. It certainly reveals a strong admiration for the physique of the 'native', reinforced by the way he is soon set against the equally impressive form of the white hero, Sir Henry Curtis. This recalls Quartermain's earlier claim (p. 3) that he has known natives who were more truly gentlemen than were many white men, and leads to the well-justified expectation that the nobility of Umbopa's character will accord with his appearance. Nevertheless, the narrator's description of his skin as 'scarcely more than dark' reveals a possible prejudice, though we have no indication as to whether or not it is shared by the author. The racist perspective here is by no means crude, though possibly all the more insidious as a result; the attitude towards colonialism is also somewhat ambiguous. Despite the heroics which would appeal to many young readers, it probably demands to be read by someone mature enough to have a background knowledge of the complex history of the British involvement in southern Africa.

Kipling's work is also liable to be heavily criticized rather than being given the close examination it deserves; simply to dismiss it as racist and therefore not to be read is to ignore the ambiguities it presents, which result from the writer's own ambivalence towards both India (where he was happy as a child and later as a young adult) and England (associated with his unsatisfactory foster-parents as well as his schooling). The works most accessible to children include *The Just-so stories* (1902), for reading to the very young; *The Jungle Books* (1894, 1895), a rather variant version of which has been screened by Disney; and *Kim* (1901), a demanding read for anyone and not originally intended for children, yet constantly in print in editions for young people.

The Just-so stories are not in most respects problematic to most people. (Except for Marcus Morris, who is described by Carpenter and Prichard (1984, p. 285) as complaining in 1957 that they gave an unrealistic picture of animals!) The only story which might perhaps attract some attention concerning prejudice is 'How the Leopard changed his spots'; this also involves an Ethiopian changing his skin from an unsuitable white to a new black skin which is described in positive terms; he has changed to 'a nice working blackish-brownish colour, with a little purple in it, and touches of slaty-blue. It will be the very thing for hiding in hollows and behind trees' (p. 31). However, opposite a picture and in no way part of the story, we have in small print: 'the Ethiopian was really a negro and his name was Sambo' (p. 32). As in Bannerman's *Little Black Sambo* (1899) (see Chapter 1) much of the offence lies in the name, and it seems quite likely that Kipling was capitalizing on the popularity of this slightly earlier book. I suspect that few adults reading this story to the very young children who form its implied audience pay much attention to the text associated with the pictures. At least one recent edition (1994) omits this sentence.

The Jungle Books occasionally pose problems for adults who are able to detect some of Kipling's imperialist subtext, but probably fewer for a child audience. Dixon (1978a, p. 96) in his adverse criticism focuses rather on the tendency towards militarism, here and in *Stalky and Co.* (1899), though readers with a knowledge of the British rule in India are also likely to see the difficulty which the more sensible animals have over controlling the monkey-people, the bander-log, as being reminiscent of the problems the colonial administrators had with the 'natives'. I think it would take a very unusual child reader to detect this or most of the other questionable aspects of this book; to interpret the animals as standing for any other groups demands the kind of literary sophistication which would probably render the reader immune from being influenced by such implications. It is true that the villagers are not depicted as favourably as are the animals, but I think this merely comes over, especially to the young reader, as an antagonism to humans, rather than anything directed against the Indian people as such. After all, Mowgli must be an Indian himself.

Edward Said (1987) has provided a scholarly critique of *Kim* in which he claims that the book falls into the nineteenth century stock depiction of the 'Oriental' as both fascinating and unreliable. Here and elsewhere, like his forerunners and contemporaries (cf. Said, 1987, p. 30), Kipling accepts without question that imperial rule was the best thing for India. Said (p. 28) claims: 'If one were to read *Kim* as a boy's adventure story, or as a rich and lovingly detailed panorama of Indian life, one would not be reading the novel that Kipling in fact wrote.' Many writers find Said's persuasive analysis far too subtle; J. Jones, in the *Financial Times* of 22 September 1996, complains of 'American academics, who have made such a meal of a classic adventure story'. Even if the analysis is accepted however, the question arises as to how far the child reader is likely to be influenced by any such imperialistic motifs. The difficulty of the style and the unfamiliarity of the allusions (the first short paragraph demands six explanatory notes in Said's edition) would certainly repulse all but the most able. Unlike *The Jungle Books*, however, where a child able to read it would probably not understand the allegory, in the case of *Kim*, the very rich but inevitably dated picture of India conveyed would, I feel, go some way to creating attitudes inappropriate to modern India. This does not mean that the book should not be available to the able young reader; merely that the context which could be supplied by a brief note on Kipling's background might avoid the formation of misleading impressions.

Harriet Beecher Stowe and Mark Twain: slaves and 'Indians'

Knowledge about the phenomenon of slavery and the responsibility for it is an essential part of the education of young people, and one of the most effective ways of providing this, especially because of the emotional involvement, is undoubtedly through reading the powerful and historically significant indictment of it to be found in Harriet Beecher Stowe's novel, *Uncle Tom's Cabin* (1852). Although in many respects this book is quite accessible to the younger reader, there are some problems which result from the very highly committed stance of the author. Passionately caring about the sufferings of the negro slaves, she wanted to get across to her white readers the knowledge about the inhumanity displayed by other white people in dealings with the slaves. Perhaps inevitably, the slaves therefore are depicted as making little attempt to do anything about their own situation – after all, her intended audience was white and it would if anything strengthen her message if the white reader became involved in trying to prevent cruelty by white perpetrators. As a result, the black reader today can become incensed at the passivity of Uncle Tom, whose very name has become an abusive label for the 'wrong kind of nigger'.

Contextualization within the historical background is again essential for the young reader of this book. It is also worthy of note that the style makes heavy, and justified, use of irony, a literary device notoriously difficult for the less sophisticated reader. The following passage from Chapter 12 highlights the problem. A black woman has just learnt that her child has been taken away, sold by a man who says of negro babies: 'they is raised as easy as any kind of critter there is going: they an't a bit more trouble than pups'. When she learns about the loss of her child, she is so distressed that she cannot talk:

> Tom had watched the whole transaction from first to last, and had a perfect understanding of its results. To him it looked like something unutterably horrible and cruel, because, poor, ignorant black soul! he had not learned to generalize and to take enlarged views. If he had only been instructed by certain ministers of Christianity, he might have thought better of it, and seen in it an everyday incident of a lawful trade – a trade which is the vital support of an

institution which some American divines tell us has no evils but such as are inseparable from any other relations in social and domestic life. But Tom, as we see, being a poor, ignorant fellow, whose reading had been confined entirely to the New Testament, could not comfort and solace himself with views like these. (pp. 154–55)

It is necessary to understand the strongly Christian perspective of the author to appreciate the significance of Tom's reading, 'confined' to the New Testament, being set against the ironic 'praise' given to 'certain ministers of Christianity' and 'some American divines'. It is easy to imagine an inexperienced reader thinking this to be a criticism of Tom's ignorance rather than a presentation of him as a much sounder authority; by his death in Chapter 40, 'The Martyr', forgiving his enemies, he is very clearly established as a Christ figure, whose sufferings mirror Christ's passion (a word whose origin is of course the same as 'passive'). It is likely to be difficult for some readers in today's very different society to be aware of the effect of some of the religious allusions.

Mark Twain's great American novel against slavery, *The Adventures of Huckleberry Finn* (1884), does not seem to me to be very appropriate for readers below 16. In any case, most younger children would probably find the extensive use of dialect a formidable barrier. Again the author's employment of irony presents problems to the younger reader, and, I suspect, is misunderstood even by older readers unfamiliar with the novel form. One of the irritants to many people is Twain's use of the word 'nigger', though it is difficult to see how avoidance of it could have been allied with authenticity. The situation concerning this kind of usage in some American States is described in Nat Henthoff's *The Day They Came to Arrest the Book* (1988), and this could be a useful introduction to both *Huckleberry Finn* itself and some of the issues concerning racism and censorship which are involved.

Gillian Klein (1985) quotes, with tacit approval, John H. Wallace's claim that *Huckleberry Finn* 'maligns all black people', a statement I find hard to reconcile with the way in which Huck recognizes the qualities of Jim as far exceeding those of his own loathsome racist father. Nor does it really help Klein's case to cite the criticisms made of the book by Alcott, for Alcott's anxiety about the fact that Huck did not always tell the truth, and her remark (quoted by Carpenter and Prichard, 1984, p. 5) that 'If Mr Clemens cannot think of something better to tell our pure-minded lads and lasses, he had best stop writing for them,' reveals a large gap between her sensibilities and today's audience.

Personally, I am far more anxious about the treatment of racism in Twain's earlier book, *Tom Sawyer* (1876), partly because this certainly *is* a book for children. There are few problems about the depiction of black people; the way Huck describes another character, Jake, as a 'good nigger', with whom, despite society's censures, he has actually eaten meals (p. 174), may well have been the genesis of the later adult novel. Twain seems, however, to have had much less sensitivity to the situation of 'Indians'; the character of Injun Joe is one of unmitigated evil, especially in the scene where he kills the doctor in the graveyard, and makes his accomplice Potter think that he has done it himself (pp. 69–71). His implacable and disproportionate hostility to the doctor is attributed to his ancestry: 'The Injun blood ain't in me for nothing'; in a way not dissimilar to Dickens' constant tagging of Fagin as 'The Jew', he is always described as 'Injun', and often referred to as a half-breed.

Later in the book another character says that this kind of intensity about revenge 'notching ears and slitting noses' is not characteristic of any white man (p. 185). We have here as evil a stereotype of an Indian as anything to be found in literature concerning ethnic minority characters. Injun Joe's malice is intrinsically linked with his race and it is so integral to the plot that it is difficult to see how the book could exist without it. The only answer again must be to set the book in its period, to present Twain as someone blind about his own prejudices, despite his very positive attitude concerning the evils of slavery and even, as far as he could appreciate it, racism.

The depiction of 'Red Indian' characters is an element which could be regarded as somewhat problematic in Barrie's *Peter Pan* (1911, from the play of 1906). Some may find it offensive that the 'Redskins', like most non-native British in earlier literature, find it impossible to speak proper English: 'Me Tiger Lily. Peter Pan save me, me his velly nice friend. Me no let pirates hurt him' (p. 112). What is more concerning is Barrie's taking on board some of the negative stereotypes of the 'oriental' (despite the Indians coming from America). The Indians are seen as wily and untrustworthy:

> By all the unwritten laws of savage warfare it is always the redskin who attacks, and with the wiliness of his race he does it just before the dawn, at which time he knows the courage of the whites to be at its lowest ebb ... With that alertness of the senses which is at once the marvel and despair of civilized peoples ... with almost diabolical cunning ... (ch. 12, pp. 130–31)

Of some Indians who are defeated, he writes: 'No more would they torture at the stake' (p. 132), and throughout the book, it would be difficult to detect from the descriptions that the strange savages are fighting against the villain of the piece, Hook. Offence is, however, largely at the verbal level, rather than the thematic; many are massacred after showing great bravery, but a small remnant, with Tiger Lily, fight their way out and are not heard of again in the book.

As well as seeing the Indians as savage and treacherous, Barrie seems also to have absorbed something of an eighteenth century stereotype, when he refers to how 'the noble savage must never express surprise in the presence of the white ...' (p. 132). Again, we have an extremely complex set of images, reminiscent of earlier depictions of non-European characters. In fact there is an affinity between depictions of such people, naive, untrustworthy and yet possessing the potential to be educated into 'good' adults, and the attitude often taken to the figure of the child in eighteenth and early nineteenth century literature; 'native' people are often seen as being like children, as indeed, in some eighteenth century writings, were women (cf. Lord Chesterfield, quoted in Chapter 10 below). Only white Englishmen are truly grown-up! This has a curious relevance to the figure of Peter Pan himself, the child who will never grow up, and it might well be asked whether the prejudice in the book really matters, since it is a text which in its unabridged version is unlikely to be read by the really young child. In fact, many adults are surprised by it, with its clear appeal to the older reader, over the shoulder of the young listener.

Unfortunately some recent versions abridged for much younger readers still seem to show insensitivity in the depiction of 'Indians'. The Disney (1993) edition has: 'Without warning a group of Indians leaped out of the bushes and grabbed the boys! . . . At the village the Indian Chief was waiting for them. He was very angry. "Where is my daughter, Princess Tiger Lily?" he asked the Lost Boys.' The picture depicts him as a hostile and threatening figure, but the whole mode of illustration of the book is caricature, and Tiger Lily's picture is not unattractive by comparison with those of some of the other females. In this book, it is the pirates, not the Lost Boys, who have captured her, and after her release by Peter Pan, they all celebrate with the Indians, a scene not in Barrie. Probably the only objectionable aspect is the language. However, this is not as offensive as that in the original.

The Ladybird (1994) edition has pictures which are less caricatured; the Indians are fairly indistinct and it is hard to be certain whether Tiger Lily is in the picture at all. The text is rather confused, and the Indians are consistently described as Redskins, which is not the case in Disney; it may well be that the Disney Corporation, in producing the film on which the book adaptation is based, have had to research to avoid the elements which could cause offence to readers.

Among the other well-known children's books which have been criticized on grounds of the incidental portrayal of minority groups in a negative way are also Jean de Brunhof's *Babar* books, which have the kind of view of Africa valid perhaps in the 1930s but not today, and some of C. S. Lewis's *Chronicles of Narnia*. The Calormenes (particularly featured in *The Horse and His Boy* (1954)) seem to be darker in colour than the rest; their culture is described in terms redolent of the exoticism of the *Arabian Nights*, and they seem distinctly less civilized than the average Narnian. Few child readers, however, are likely to be aware of the extent to which the author's attitude to them is allied with the strongly Christian ethos of his books, resulting at times in what has been seen as an ill-informed anti-Moslem prejudice. Lewis himself would probably have pointed to the scene in *The Last Battle* where it is made clear that devout worship even of the heathen god, Tash, is acceptable to the Christ-figure, Aslan. The Calormene noble, Emeth, describes his encounter with Aslan: 'I said, Alas, Lord, I am no son of thine but the servant of Tash. He answered, Child, all the service thou hast done to Tash I account as service done to me.' (p. 149)

Exception has also been taken by Holbrook (in Fox *et al.*, 1976) to the militaristic and frequently prejudiced stance of the *Narnia* books. C. S. Lewis undoubtedly accepted uncritically many of the prejudices of his class and period, especially as far as gender stereotypes were concerned, though it should not be forgotten that his ideal of human spirituality is represented by a female character, Lucy. It is unlikely that the expression of his prejudices has any more impression on young readers than his fairly explicit (to the adult) traditional Christian framework and moral didacticism, which are often ignored by children reading the books.

Gender in boys' and girls' books: Alcott, Coolidge and others

The vast majority of the books which are now seen as 'classic' children's literature, from the Perrault and Grimm fairytales to *Winnie the Pooh*, are likely either to portray all-female characters in stereotypical gender roles or to omit them almost completely. Certainly most of the books already discussed in this chapter are not notable for the portrayal of strong female characters, but their very absence, provided it is compensated for in the rest of children's reading by plenty of books which do feature girls, gives ample material for discussion and for the development in child readers of an understanding of the periods depicted. I do not propose here to enter in any detail into the debate about boys' and girls' books of the later nineteenth century, since this subject has already been fully explored, notably by Reynolds in *Girls Only: Gender and Popular Children's Fiction* (1990). I shall simply consider a few of the books which are especially popular with girls, to the extent that boys often feel they will be ridiculed if found reading them; in these books there are many female characters, and the depiction of these naturally conforms to the expectations about womanhood of their period.

Notable amongst such books are Alcott's *Little Women* (1868) and Coolidge's *What Katy Did* (1872), and the many successors written both by them and by others. As Dixon (1978a, p. 7) says of these and other well-known stories: 'Nearly all the stories have, as a prominent character, a girl who is, in the course of the story, made to conform.' It would be difficult to dissent from his exposure of the way in which traditional feminine values are extolled throughout these texts, but I doubt whether the enthusiasm which generations of girl readers for the books has really led to their taking on these values.

The reason for this is I think to be found in the old D. H. Lawrence adage, 'Never trust the teller, trust the tale'. The young reader today does not read these books because she is won over by the figure of Jo at the end of *Little Women*, when she is well on her way to becoming her father's ideal of 'a strong, helpful, tender-hearted woman' (ch. 22, p. 216). Nor is the reader likely to be particularly touched by Katy's conversion, facilitated by the over-perfect Cousin Helen. Rather it is the boy-like Jo and the pre-accident Katy from the early chapters of these classics who have already won the young female reader's sympathies. I suspect the fascination of the tomboyish heroines partly results from the fact that in both cases, beneath their authors' deliberate didacticism in putting forward desired female values, the books reveal how Alcott and Coolidge, perhaps subconsciously, craved after a different kind of role: one which, to some extent, they had already adopted by writing. The strong similarity between Alcott and the character of Jo is made clear by their writings; Alcott's 'adult' novel, *The Chase*, published from manuscript for the first time in 1995 is described on the cover as:

> Remarkable for its portrayal of the sensuality and spirit of its Victorian heroine, *The Chase* tells a compulsive tale of love, desire and deceit.

It is not difficult to recognize the affinity between this and the kind of stories which Jo is portrayed as writing. *Little Women* also features Mrs March's surprising admission, 'I am angry nearly every day of my life' (ch. 8, p. 78), which perhaps reflects something of the author's suppressed feelings; anger is an emotion which does not form part of the ideal picture of the woman of the period. Such aspects probably have more effect on the modern reader's enjoyment of the book than Mrs March's extolling 'To be loved and chosen by a good man is the best and sweetest thing which can happen to a woman' (ch. 9, p. 95). There is much scope in this book for 'oppositional' reading, with the female reader taking from the text what she wants, without being led to endorse an over-conformist feminine role.

A similar clash between what is explicitly said about feminine roles and the way the children actually behave is to be found in Nesbit's *The Railway Children*

(1906), where Roberta (whose name, usually shortened to Bobbie, perhaps makes her one of the first androgynous heroines) at one point says, 'I wish I was a boy' (p. 199). After Bobbie's brave behaviour throughout the book, the doctor's lecture to Peter about the differences between males and females ('girls are so much softer and weaker than we are', ch. 13, p. 217) is not totally convincing; here again we have a strong heroine who may have to live in a male-dominated world but nevertheless comes over as the most memorable character. The effect of this and several of Nesbit's other books, such as *Five Children and It*, is to convince the reader that females are as capable of adventures as males, whatever limitations society of the time seeks to impose on them. Statements like the doctor's sometimes give the impression that the author is trying to convince herself, despite her subconscious reservations, about the proper kind of female role; in her own life, Nesbit often transgressed against society's conventions.

There has been some recent criticism of Frances Hodgson Burnett's *The Secret Garden* (1911) because of the change in focus late in the novel away from Mary, the bad-tempered and sallow girl who discovers the garden, to Colin, her weakly cousin. Both children grow in strength but at the end of the novel it is Colin who we see walking 'as strongly and steadily as any boy in Yorkshire'; Mary is not even mentioned at this point. Nevertheless, I think that for most readers the very way in which we have been led since the beginning of the story towards an empathy with Mary, despite her imperfections, supersedes the relatively late appearance on the scene of Colin. In spite of his key role as son of the house, he hardly overcomes his initially somewhat negative presentation. Throughout the book, Mary has been the active agent of his recovery, aided by the mysterious mother-nature figure of Mrs Sowerby and her Pan-like son, Dickon. The garden itself, with all its symbolic significance, is immutably associated with Mary rather than Colin, partly because of her priority in time, partly because of our implicit acceptance, even without the intertextual knowledge of the literary and biblical antecedents, of a garden as a figure for a female rather than a male.

Disability and children's classics

There are perhaps few issues about which attitudes have changed more in recent years than that of disability; I will be giving some attention in a later chapter to a range of more recent books which deal positively with this subject. The problem in past texts is partly that of language; until recently no one had any scruples about the use of the word 'cripple'.

Much more important than the term used is the role generally assigned to disabled people, and this seems to reflect a good deal of polarization, in a way not dissimilar from that in which authors of the past often treated women as angels or whores. Disabled people are seldom portrayed simply as themselves; instead they are either saintlike in their patience or evil and sinister, though sometimes instead they may merit derision. Some of this negative portrayal seems to derive from the tradition that the good are beautiful and the bad, like Shakespeare's Richard III, are ugly and deformed. In John Donne's 'First Anniversary' the world is seen as deprived by the death of the ostensible subject of the poem, Elizabeth Drury; we have in fairly close proximity:

She, she is dead; she's dead: when thou know'st this,
Thou know'st how lame a cripple this world is. (ll. 237–38)

and

She, she is dead; she's dead: when thou know'st this,
Thou know'st how ugly a monster this world is. (ll. 325–26)

In Stevenson's *Treasure Island* (1883) one of the most sinister figures is Blind Pew (Chapter 3). He introduces himself as 'a poor blind man, who has lost the precious sight of his eyes in the gracious defence of his native country,' yet before the reader can take this as a signal for pity, we learn the reactions of Jim Hawkins, who as first person narrator is the strongest influence on the way we interpret behaviour:

> I held out my hand, and the horrible, soft- spoken, eyeless creature gripped it in a moment like a vice. I was so much startled that I struggled to withdraw; but the blind man pulled me close to him with a single action of his arm. (pp. 32–33)

Surely every reader rejoices in Pew's death shortly afterwards, even though it might have been expected to have created in us some sympathy, because it is caused at least partially by his lack of sight. His blindness is constantly emphasized, and he is portrayed as both continually demanding pity, yet not really needing any, because of his 'incredible accuracy and nimbleness' (p. 34); he is also strongly evil. The description quoted above is strangely reminiscent of Tolkien's Gollum who is not blind but lives constantly in the dark (*The Hobbit*, ch. 5); in both cases, being unable to see can be regarded as a metaphor for darkness of soul.

The more notable nasty character in *Treasure Island* is of course the one-legged Long John Silver. He certainly doesn't partake of the ugliness tradition, but his jovial exterior masks evil and treachery, and it is difficult to be sure of the textual function of his disability, unless it is to mark him out as potentially untrustworthy. This is certainly the way it works for the reader, though not for Squire Trelawney and Jim Hawkins. In most situations, we are scarcely conscious of any difficulty he may have in moving, as his mental agility more than compensates for it. One wonders how much Stevenson's own ill health led to his depiction of this one-legged character as enjoyably wicked rather than pitiable; perhaps it gave him a means of expressing the part of himself which had to be kept repressed in respectable society. A similar element of comic evil pervades the description of Barrie's one-armed Captain Hook.

A particularly interesting treatment of what seems at first to be disability is in Burnett's *The Secret Garden*. When Mr Archibald Craven is presented as a figure of fear to Mary, he is thought of as a hunchback; as he becomes more congenial, and less a figure of terror, she meets him and discovers that 'he . . . was not so much a hunchback as a man with high, rather crooked shoulders' (ch.12, p. 95). Colin, his son, is initially seen as indulging in unmanly weeping and tantrums, and we learn that it is because he not only fears an early death, but also thinks that he too is a hunchback: '"I felt the lump – I felt it," choked out Colin. "I knew I should. I shall have a hunch on my back and then I shall die."' It takes Mary's angry inspection to refute this belief, and from this point on, Colin becomes a 'beautiful child', healthy like his cousin who has also become far more attractive, so mirroring the fact that her character too is becoming much more pleasant. Presumably it would have been impossible for Burnett to have portrayed Colin as a fundamentally good and attractive character had he *really* been 'deformed'.

Disabled people who excite derision are also frequent, at least in adult literature; the blindness of old Lancelot Gobbo in Shakespeare's *The Merchant of Venice* provides humour for the audience, as does the deafness of Jonson's Corbaccio in *Volpone*. Disabled children, however, are more likely to excite pity. I suspect many disabled people would prefer depiction as active characters, even those who are villainous, rather than them always being presented as objects of pity.

An instance of this sentiment being evoked for a 'cripple' is in the character of Tiny Tim in Dickens' *A Christmas Carol* (1843); he is an important part of the process of Scrooge's conversion by the Spirits of Christmas Past, Present and To Come. Pathos is abundantly created; his father recounts:

> He told me . . . that he hoped the people saw him in the church, because he was a cripple, and it might be pleasant to them to remember on Christmas Day who made lame beggars walk and blind men see. (Stave Three, p. 52)

In his perfect patience, it seems never to occur to him that perhaps Christ might also cure him! We hear his 'plaintive little voice' singing a song about a lost child travelling in the snow (p. 57) and the Spirit's answer to Scrooge's query about his future is 'I see a vacant seat in the poor chimney corner, and a crutch without an owner, carefully preserved' (p. 55). Dickens employs this sentimentality to ensure that the reader shares Scrooge's concern about the plight of the poor; it is probably also a factor likely to enhance the sales of the book. To most modern readers it is distasteful, and it is liable to cause embarrassment if any children using crutches are in a class to whom such an excerpt be read. There is probably a case for some judicious cutting, but the use of such characters demands some attention, so typical is it of an era when those without full mobility were seen as objects of charity. One suspects that Dickens here is projecting his ever-present image of himself as a victim-child on to an even more deserving object of pity.

While Katy's positive use of her temporary disability as a means of character reformation is admirable in Coolidge's *What Katy Did* (1872), the situation of Cousin Helen is a little more complex. The evocation of pity is secondary to the message of positive acceptance of disability, even to the extent of living next door to her former fiancé who could not marry her because of her accident, and enjoying visits from his wife and children. Coolidge's stress on creating a pleasant environment in the sick-room could almost be acceptable, but for what the modern reader is likely to find Cousin Helen's excessive piety. It has been suggested that the very real phenomenon of invalidity in Victorian women (such as Anna Sewell and Florence Nightingale after her Crimea exploits) is a means of escape into a world they could control from a world which they could not (cf. Reynolds, 1990, pp. 128–32).

Most of the crippled victims in both children's and adult fiction of the past are female, and Tiny Tim could be seen as a feminized character; all of them are highly idealized. In Laura Ingalls Wilder's *By the Shores of Silver Lake* (1939), the narrator's sister Mary, who is rapidly losing her sight, suffers from an even more acute case of over-idealization; as the preacher, Brother Alden says, 'Mary is a rare soul and a lesson to us all' (p. 217). Since readers inevitably identify with Laura, as first person narrator, they are more than likely to feel impatient at Mary's angelic patience. There is no hint that the author intends the reader to regard Rev. Alden's somewhat sanctimonious words as ironic; what is quite likely is that, since this book was based on her real experiences, something of Wilder's own repressed irritation at her sister always being shown to her as an example of virtue is subconsciously being shared with the reader.

Depictions of disability which are not intended to excite pity, horror or derision are fairly rare in the 'classics', and none of these are likely to win favour in today's classrooms; they could prove offensive to children now included in mainstream education and considerable care needs to be taken. Seldom in fiction are visually or otherwise handicapped characters allowed simply to be themselves, or to figure as the main interest of the text. It could be argued that the omission of disabled characters is less harmful than their depiction, which all too often seems to result from authors projecting on to them aspects of their own personalities which have not yet fully matured. Invisibility is less harmful than negative portrayal; presumably children who are partially sighted or lack mobility will generally identify with leading characters in the same way as other readers, though they should certainly be given the opportunity to read some of the much more enlightened texts written since 1950, especially by Rosemary Sutcliff. When disabled characters do occur in books from earlier periods, it requires a great deal of tact from the teacher or librarian, to set it in its period. Appreciation of the problems which faced disabled people in the society of the past could prove quite illuminating to all children.

Conclusion

I do not share the pessimism of those who think of the 'classics' of children's literature as so steeped in the prejudices of their age as to be unsuitable in today's classroom or library. Rather, providing a proper background is given, in some cases they may prove an integral part of the process of helping children to be aware of the way in which attitudes towards 'race', gender and disability have changed over the years. But they demand even more close preparation from an adult wanting to use them with young people than do more contemporary texts.

There is a particularly acute need to show that using the vocabulary of the age does not imply that an author had the kind of prejudices which that kind of language would imply today. It is important to realize that thematic aspects may be much more significant than vocabulary in reflecting attitudes. Given the care that needs to be taken, study of these texts from the past can be very rewarding, not least in providing the foundations for understanding both literature and society today.

References

Note that an extensive bibliography is also given at the end of this book. Since most of the books referred to below appear in a variety of editions, references have only been given where a text has been quoted. Note that this list is not intended to imply recommendation.

Alcott, L. M. (1994; 1st edn 1868) *Little Women*. Oxford: University Press.
Alcott, L. M. (1995) *The Chase*. London: Random House.
Barrie, J. (1951; 1st edn 1911) *Peter Pan*. London: Hodder.
Barrie, J. (1994) (retold by Joan Collins) *Peter Pan*. Loughborough: Ladybird.
Coolidge, S. (1982; 1st edn 1872) *What Katy Did*. Harmondsworth: Penguin.

Defoe, D. (1986)(Puffin edn abridged by Robin Waterfield) *Robinson Crusoe*. Harmondsworth: Penguin.

Defoe, D. (1993)(adapted by Fran Hunia) *Robinson Crusoe*. Loughborough: Ladybird.

Dickens, C. (1966; 1st edn 1837–38) *Oliver Twist*. (ed. Fairclough, W.) Harmondsworth: Penguin.

Dickens, C. (n.d.; 1st edn 1843) *Christmas Books*. London: Collins.

Disney, W. (1993) *Peter Pan*. Connecticut: Grolier (Note that Barrie's name does not appear in this text.)

Haggard, H. R. (1994, 1st edn 1895) *King Solomon's Mines*. Harmondsworth: Penguin.

Henthoff, N. (1988) *The Day They Came to Arrest the Book*. Harmondsworth: Penguin.

Kipling, R. (1975; 1st edn 1902) *Just So Stories*. London: Pan.

Kipling, R. (1994) *How the Leopard got its Spots*. London: Pavilion Books.

Lewis, C. S. (1964; 1st edn 1956)*The Last Battle*. London: Harmondsworth.

Nesbit, E. (1960; 1st edn 1906) *The Railway Children*. Harmondsworth: Penguin.

Stevenson, R. L. (1946; 1st edn 1883) *Treasure Island*. London: Studley.

Stowe, H. B. (n.d., 1st edn 1852) *Uncle Tom's Cabin*. London: Nelson.

Twain, M. (1950; 1st edn 1876) *Tom Sawyer*. Harmondsworth: Penguin.

Wilder, L. I. (1961) *By the Shores of Silver Lake*. London: Lutterworth.

Prejuduce and
Children's Popular Fiction

Their skin began to drop off their bones and, as I stared open-mouthed, they crumbled to powder and dissolved to the ground, their clothes disintegrating with them (*Goosebumps: Welcome to Dead House*, Stine, 1992, p. 121)

What do children choose to read?

When we talk about 'Children's Literature', we often have in mind the 'literary heritage' from the past, or contemporary 'quality' children's fiction which has received a literary prize. Young people, however, are likely to spend more time, and possibly be more influenced by, less 'worthy' reading matter, some of it fairly ephemeral. The Roehampton Survey (Reynolds, 1996) reveals that a high proportion of the reading of young people today takes the form of what might be described as 'non-quality' fiction, such as Series Romance and Horror, and magazines, the amount increasing as they get older. To the question, 'Do you ever look at magazines?' the percentage of those who answered 'Yes' was:

	Girls	Boys	
Key Stage 2 (7–11 years)	80.3	68.4	
Key Stage 3 (11–14 years)	95.8	80.8	
Key Stage 4 (14–16 years)	98.5	90.0	(p. 34)

In this chapter, I shall be considering the extent to which some of the books and magazines most popular with children and adolescents may justifiably cause anxiety to parents, teachers and librarians, whether because of either their prejudiced portrayal of any group of characters, or their inclusion of elements which do not seem to many adults to be suitable reading for the young.

Most adults today are prepared to admit that their own childhood reading did not consist solely of children's classics, but was more likely to be made up of surfeits of Blyton or *Biggles*, or a diet of comics which ranged from *Beano* and *Dandy* to football or pony magazines. Such adults would be prepared to endorse what Dickinson (1970, in Fox *et al.*, 1976, p. 74) has to say about the value of 'rubbish', which he defines as 'all forms of reading matter which contain to the adult eye no visible value, either aesthetic or educational'. He claims that such reading helps a child to feel a sense of identity with the rest of a group; it also provides a form of both reassurance and relaxation while enabling children to work out for themselves their own critical standards. Most important, perhaps, relatively undemanding material can encourage the activity of reading among those who might otherwise not indulge in it so frequently. Most parents and teachers today would probably endorse these points, and we tend to see less of the kind of puritanism, nigh to censorship, which banished non-quality material, notably Blyton, from respectable libraries, and discouraged parents from buying it for their children.

Nevertheless, many of these otherwise approving adults might still have to admit that they are not always happy with the variety of 'rubbish' which children today are consuming. If, however, adults are too overt in their expressions of disapproval of any books or magazines, the more likely it will be that young people will read them, for adolescents in particular need to feel that their reading is their own, recommended by their peers rather than by some 'ancient' teacher. While about 30% of Key Stage 2 (7–11 years old) children admit to often or very often being helped in choice of reading by their teachers or librarians, the figure shrinks to about 23% for Key Stage 3 (11–14 years old), and about 15% for Key Stage 4 (14–16 years old) boys, who unlike the girls of the same age also claim to be little helped by their friends (Roehampton Survey,1996, pp. 9–10). This seems to tally with the impression which many teachers have of girls reading collaboratively and boys reading in a more solitary manner.

While there may indeed be some cause for anxiety about the nature of young people's reading, we should not automatically assume that a work which is popular with them is necessarily of inferior quality. Weaknesses of style and characterization may be all too apparent to some sophisticated adult readers, but we should be prepared to recognize the skilful way in which popular writers succeed in retaining the reader's interest with effective plotting. Some contemporary writers who deliberately set out to attract young readers and deal with everyday life are just as competent as more acknowledged major writers, but have a better grasp of the contemporary idiom of their chosen audience; this very quality may at the same time distance them from adult readers.

A matter which does legitimately cause concern, however, is whether this non-quality reading may foster attitudes which are unacceptable, especially concerning sex or violence. Adults are likely to think that the books and comics which they themselves read as children were far more innocent than those which their children buy or borrow from their friends. Looking back at some of the literary loves of their childhood might disabuse them of this belief; comics and the favourite writers of childhood have always been subversive, taking the side of the children and satirizing pompous adults. In the past too, they have constantly been partisan, extolling the virtues of the British or Americans and the vices or follies of everyone else, to an extent which might well not be appreciated by most adults today. What some of the teenage magazines of today possess, however, is a frankness about sexual matters which can horrify the parents of their readers, who naturally want to retain the idea of childhood innocence (disregarding the fact that their own childhood recollections might show this to be a myth!).

Naturally parents fear the way in which information about arcane varieties of sexual experience is provided for the young. The teenage magazines most likely to cause anxiety are usually aimed specifically at girls, though evidence in the form of letters to the problem pages reveals that their male coevals often also find them a source of useful information. Before looking in more detail at such magazines, however, I want to examine some of the other kinds of reading favoured by young people today, and any of the attitudes which, explicitly or implicitly, these seem to endorse.

Apart from the question of explicit sex, the aspects most likely to be considered unsatisfactory in popular reading for young people may be categorized as follows.

(a) Gender stereotyping

In this kind of material, there is little of the depth characterization which can be found in quality literature; in some of it, for instance, girls are more likely to be seen as craving for the attention of boys rather than having a 'proper' range of interests. The importance of this is increased by the fact that there is a very considerable degree of gender division in young people's choice of popular reading. Girls often associate together and recommend books to each other, so that other girls are driven to reading more 'girly' topics than they might otherwise choose, in order to be in with the group. Equally, boys find themselves stereotyped as readers into what seems to be 'macho', and can only feel free to read their sisters' books if they claim to be doing so to ridicule them.

In fact, like most sweeping generalizations, it is only partly true that the female characters in girls' comics, magazines and popular novels are shown as strongly feminized, and even in some of the Romance series, girls are seen to do active things rather than simply waiting to be chosen by a male. Cherland(1994, p. 167) suggests that girls' purposes in reading may be different from the messages ostensibly conveyed by authors, so that material which seems to cast them in a conventional role may speak to the girl reader about female agency. If anything, contemporary material is more likely to portray the girls as thinking for themselves than it was when today's parents were young readers.

(b) Racial stereotyping

Because of legislation and changes in society, not least because a multi-ethnic readership needs to be considered, contemporary material gives rather less cause for concern about racism than do some of the older books, like those by Blyton, which are still being published and read. As will be seen, however, many of these books have been changed to allow for changes in society's attitudes.

(c) Violence

This is still to be found in today's preferred adolescent reading (cf. Sarland, 1991), especially in some of the imported comics, but it was prevalent, often to a greater extent, in some of the classics of the past such as Thomas Hughes' *Tom Brown's Schooldays* (1857) or Kipling's *Stalky and Co* (1899).

(d) Insensitive treatment of age or disability

Again, this is more likely to be found in non-quality literature than in major writers, but probably less so today than in the past.

Continuity and change: popular authors, past and present

Although by far the majority of children today attend day schools, it is surprising how long the attraction of boarding school literature has endured. While comics portraying this setting have long vanished, the main source of the tradition, Thomas Hughes' *Tom Brown's Schooldays* (1857) has constantly remained in print, and it is still possible to buy such perennial favourites as Elinor Brent-Dyer's *Chalet School* books (1925–1970). A popular supplier of books by post, The Book People, advertises the *Jennings* series by Anthony Buckeridge in one of their 1996 catalogues; although this is a fairly late example of the genre, the world of prep school is as unchanged as ever. In *Jennings Abounding* (1967), a French boy cannot understand the rules of cricket; in his dense Gallic ignorance, he is reminiscent of the rather earlier world of Blyton's non-sporting French teachers. In *The O'Sullivan Twins* (1942), for instance, we learn that:

> Mam'zelle would never have dared to behave in such a free and easy way at her school in France when she had been a girl. She had worked much harder than any of the girls at St. Clare's. She had played no games, had been for hardly any walks, and had never even seen the inside of a gym until she had come to England. (p. 42)

She is duly reproved by the headmistress who says: 'It is just as important to know how to have good fun – as to do good work, you know' (p. 43). The pro-English prejudice here is relatively harmless, and many contemporary readers are just as likely to sympathize with the foreigners and regard the public school fixation with organized games as futile, thus reacting in a way contrary to the authors' intentions. Blyton also emphasizes the kind of values which both girls' and boys' schools wanted to further by means of the games. In *Claudine at St. Clare's* (1944) the little French girl who is the title character is meant to gain the reader's approval for her dawning recognition of English superiority when she says:

> You English girls, you are so serious and solemn and so very, very, honourable. I too have my own honour, and although it is not quite like yours yet, perhaps one day it will be. (p. 135)

Blyton's chauvinism, to which I will return, is matched by her advocacy of traditional values. The matron in *The O'Sullivan Twins* gives advice which may surprise today's readers: 'You hope to be happily married one day, don't you – and run your own home? Well, you must learn to take care of your own linen and mend it then' (p. 13). Such statements are likely to amuse rather than condition today's female reader, and in general, such books can provide a really valuable education about the cultural values of the past; children are likely to enjoy searching for outmoded points of view like this in books by people like Angela Brazil, Dorita Fairley Bruce, Frank Richards of Billy Bunter fame, as well as the books named above. It is likely that the readers will generally prefer to identify with the girls whose activities are least conformist. Blyton is an instance of a writer whose attraction to the young is in the subversive qualities she seems to display; she gives the impression of being on the side of the children rather than the adults. Although her final message may often be one of conformity, the impression derived by the child reader is likely to be one of independence.

The hostility towards foreigners which seems fairly harmless in Blyton's school books takes on rather more sinister forms in some of her other work. Given the length of time since their first publication, her *Famous Five* and *Secret Seven* books remain enormously popular: '[in Key Stage 2] 132 children chose *Famous Five* titles (77 girls, 55 boys) and a further 79 opted for *Secret Seven* titles (41 girls, 38 boys)' (Roehampton Survey,1996, p. 73). Both sexes also picked children from these series as their favourite characters. Her other books, such as fantasy and those for younger children, also remain popular. Blyton is far too marketable a product to be abandoned simply because of her prejudices against black people and foreigners, which have been fully demonstrated by Dixon (1978a, pp. 96–100, 107–12). Instead, her work has been adapted to omit the material which is most suspect.

The area of Blyton's writings which has perhaps excited most controversy is that of the *Noddy* books. On the one hand, a number of adults have remembered their own enjoyment of these books when they were children, and have ridiculed what they saw as the extremes of 'political correctness' which made them fall into disrepute, especially because of the 'golliwogs'. On the other, many readers, not only those who are black, have been perturbed at what they saw as racist elements. The name 'golliwog' could provide an offensive term to be used by children, but what is worse is the way in which the golliwogs, already confined to their own sector of Toytown, are demonised because their actions are worse than merely normal mischief.

The most notorious example of this has been extensively quoted and discussed by Dixon (1978a, pp. 96–99). Noddy is forced by a golliwog to drive into the 'dark dark wood' where not only his car but also all his clothes are taken away from him, a scene unpleasantly sado-masochistic even if the potentially racist elements are ignored. In the more recent version, *Noddy and the Goblins* (1992), however, as well as the golliwogs being metamorphosed into non-racially specific goblins, this scene is much abbreviated. Noddy is forced to drive into the wood, and loses his car and his hat, but there is no hint of any further assault. Sympathy is just as clearly with Noddy as in the original, but the goblins do not come over as so malign as the golliwogs; while the story can still act as a warning to children not to go off with anyone they are not sure about, it fortunately loses most of its unhealthy undertones. Comparing the original with the adapted version could make a very informative exercise for pupils older than the readers for whom the book was originally intended.

Blyton's treatment of ethnic minority characters in her fiction for older readers has also been altered in recent editions. In the original edition of *The Island of Adventure* (1944), the children are met at the station by Jo Jo, the servant of Philip's uncle:'[They] saw a coloured man coming towards them. His skin was black, his teeth were very white, and he rolled his eyes in a peculiar way' (p. 32). His use of language also recalls the distinctive inability of nearly all the black characters in English literature before the mid-twentieth century to speak English properly: 'They coming to Craggy-Tops? Miss Polly, she didn't say nothing about any friends, no she didn't' (p. 33).

At first, the children consider Jo Jo to be thoroughly stupid, but as the book goes on, they discover he is in fact a villain. In 1988, a revised edition was published which has Jo Jo replaced by Joe, who in all ways resembles him but does not appear to be black. In the description above, 'strange' and 'lined' replace 'coloured' and 'black', and his eyes now 'dart' rather than 'roll'; the English of his speech does not, however, seem to have improved at all! Young readers today would probably be unaware of how his language and even the sanitized form of the description form part of the typical stereotype of black characters in literature; again, there seems little reason to prevent children having the chance to get 'hooked' on to a story which may lack depth but provides plenty of excitement.

Changes like these can, according to the point of view of the reader, be ascribed either to 'political correctness' or to the combination on the part of the publishers of a legitimate desire to prevent unnecessary offence and the natural wish to continue selling a popular product. The question arises as to how legitimate it is to modify an author's text in this way. In past ages, the process of 'bowdlerization' was applied to Shakespeare, so there seems no reason why Blyton should be exempt from it; I suspect she herself would have been happy if it meant that her books kept on selling and were thus available to continued generations. I am only a little concerned that in the 1988 edition of *The Island of Adventure*, no hint is given about this process, other than the small print indicating that it is a revised edition. We need also to realize that copies of the original edition still exist in many attics; adaptation can never be the complete answer while books which display prejudice are still extant. The process of education about the evils of prejudice can however be much assisted by comparisons between editions. The way the book has been changed offers scope for (probably secondary age) pupils to study the relativism of different cultural attitudes.

Similar reservations apply to a number of other books from a period before the greater sensitivity to such issues of the 1970s. The *Biggles* books(1932–70) by Captain Johns, have also recently been revised, though inevitably the British characters remain far superior to those of any other nation.

Hugh Lofting's *Doctor Dolittle* books (1920–52) have also remained popular, despite legitimate criticisms (Dixon, 1978a, pp. 105–107; Suhl, in Stinton, 1979, pp. 19–26) of the attitude shown to the African ruler in the first of the series. As Carpenter and Prichard (1984) indicate, this seems to have been something of a lapse by Lofting and is not so characteristic of the later books in the series, which display an attractive kinship with animals and sympathy with nature. In the light of this, the revision which has been undertaken with the authority of Christopher Lofting seems valid. In the Afterword to the 1988 American edition, reference is made to the problem created by 'incidents depicted that, in the light of today's sensitivities, were considered by some to be disrespectful to ethnic minorities and therefore, perhaps inappropriate for today's young reader.' In the conviction that the author would have 'been appalled at the suggestion that any part of his work could give offence', the revisers claim that he would have been the first to alter such passages. 'The message that Hugh Lofting conveyed throughout his work was one of respect for life and the rights of all who share the common destiny of our world.' (pp. 137–39).

In most cases, removing questionable elements in books like these is relatively simple and does not do violence to the plot or characterization, though surely any changes of text ought to be acknowledged. Writers more recent than Blyton, Johns and Lofting have sometimes made their own changes once they have come to recognize the potentially racist nature of material in their books. Both P. L. Travers, author of the *Mary Poppins* books (1934–82) and Roald Dahl (in *Charlie and the Chocolate Factory*, 1964 and 1973) have revised their books in order to omit elements found objectionable, but in both instances the revision has not satisfied all their critics. The problem is that the implicit assumptions which gave rise in the first instance to the offending passages also led to a number of other, less obvious, indications of a belief in white superiority.

It is difficult to change the underlying impression of a book by making cosmetic alterations, especially if the book is set in a place strongly affected by the colonial past, such as Africa. Many of the criticisms of the revised versions (Stinton, 1979, pp. 27–34, 41–44) are, however, of aspects which would be unlikely to be noticed by young readers. I think most adults are likely to be glad that explicitly offensive material has been omitted from more recent editions of these still popular books. I would, however, emphasize that there must be many copies still extant of the unmodified versions, so that, as ever, the only effective action against racism is to educate children to perceive it and reject it, a process in which the co-existence of original and 'expurgated' versions can be extremely useful.

Authors may of course act on objections of this kind by writing subsequent books in a way which shows that they have considered the matters raised. Richard Adams's *Watership Down* (1972) has been criticized for its militaristic bias, its chauvinism in confining all the heroic action to male rabbits, and its conservative view of society. More recently, Adams's *Tales from Watership Down* (1996) at least partly redresses the balance by including a story about a burrow controlled by a female rabbit.

The attraction of Blyton and Dahl, as well as of Richmal Crompton's *Just William* books, seems to lie to a considerable extent in the young characters showing themselves as cleverer than the adults. Not everyone would agree that this is a good thing; as one of my mature students says: 'education in school is surely meant to lead children to better, kinder, more considerate ways of living, and how can stories which portray the opposite do this?' I would, however, suggest that many of the stories of these writers are far more conformist than they appear; the children's rebellion is in fact really exposing the hypocrisy of adults whose theoretical values, indicated by what they tell the children to do, are contradicted by the way they themselves act. As a result, the actions of the children in the end really support the traditional values of society, while their superficial disobedience and riotous behaviour has the additional advantage of wooing the child reader.

It is interesting in this context to recall the work of Bakhtin (see Chapter 2) who shows how the controlled riot of the carnivalesque has often been permitted in societies of the past, to ensure that rebellion did not get out of hand. Much of the apparently 'subversive' material of Dahl, as well as comics for all ages, could be seen as fulfilling something of this function.

Comics and magazines for the younger reader

The history of comics for young children has been bound up, at least since 1914, with the world of entertainment, when *The Favourite Comic* featured 'Ragtime Rex' (Gifford, 1975, p. 28). Characters from film and radio, like Laurel and Hardy (Gifford, 1975, p. 61) and Big Hearted Arthur (p. 100), are to be found in their pages, though probably the greatest landmark of this symbiotic relationship was the link with Disney in the *Mickey Mouse Weekly* (1936) 'the first comic in full-colour photogravure' (Gifford, 1975, p. 82). It is therefore hardly surprising that there is a high degree of interdependence today between periodical material for young children, television programmes, and books featuring the same characters. Most of the journals for the young child might more appropriately be termed magazines; of the older type of 'comic', the most notable survivors are *Beano* and *Dandy*, the former of which still features among the top five choices of the Key Stage 1 children interviewed in the Roehampton Survey (1996, p. 28). The rest of the top five, *Mightly Morphin Power Rangers*, *Sonic the Comic*, *Barbie*, and *Tots tv*, together with other magazines clearly also addressed to young children, such as *Rosie and Jim*, *Fireman Sam*, *Postman Pat*, *The Lion King* and *Thomas the Tank Engine and Friends*, also have very apparent connections with films and television series aimed at the same age group. The commercial angle is strengthened by the large number of products linked with all of the characters in these magazines/books/pro-grammes. Children may read, bath and play with, sleep in, paint and model, and eat and drink from, products embossed with their favourite TV characters.

The attraction to parents is emphasized by the words 'Compatible with the National Curriculum' which appear on at least five of the titles named above, which are among the Redan Group's 'Fun to Learn' educational magazines. The attraction to children is enhanced by the provision of a 'free' gift, such as Plasticine or sweets, and the excitement of the possibility of seeing their name in print on a published letter, picture or birthday greetings. (Details of the specific issues of these and other comics and magazines examined are to be found in the references at the end of this chapter.)

Much about these magazines is admirable, though it is difficult not to feel concerned about the commercial aspect; very young children are being inducted into consumerism, and their parents are inevitably being pressurized to buy by the fear that their own child will not only feel underprivileged but will also lack the educational stimulus of their friends. The contents are unexceptionable except for one aspect, the very gendered nature of the material. An analysis of the readers' section of one issue of each of the following magazines, where it is possible to learn the sex of the children featured, shows that the audience reflects the compilers' expectations, and thus the gender expectations of society.

	Children named	
	Boys	**Girls**
Rosie & Jim	5	11
Fireman Sam	15	4
Thomas	14	3
Tots tv	–	4
Sonic	5	2
Barbie	1	14

The gender distribution is if anything even more clear-cut when the stories are examined. Only in *Rosie and Jim* and *Tots tv* is there a balance between the sexes, and it is interesting to note that both of these also feature black characters. A simi-lar gender division obtains in the *Beano*, where the majority of the strips feature male characters such as 'Dennis the Menace' and 'Joe King' (both of whom meet some exceptionally naive females). The masculine dominance is, however, broken by the somewhat assertive females, 'Minnie the Minx' and 'Ivy the Terrible', both of whom, like most of the male characters, succeed in defeating some rather stupid adults. Puncturing adult pomposity seems to be the main theme of much of the material, and is undoubtedly the reason for the long survival of this comic (the first issue was on 30 July 1938, shortly after the *Dandy* on 4 December 1937) which is also significantly cheaper than the rest; it lacks the impression of many of the other periodicals for younger children that the parent is looking over the shoulder of the child and approving the activity!

The predominance of males amongst *Beano* characters may be not unrelated to the predilection of boys, even at a young age, for having male characters with whom to identify, whereas although girls can become deeply committed to Cindy or Barbie, they are often prepared to identify with male heroes in books where there are no significant female characters. The Roehampton Survey (1996, p. 63) showed that, at this age, a higher proportion of boys than girls objected to the main character being of the opposite sex (53.2% as against 39.5%). Publishers and TV producers have made attempts to redress the balance by series which do feature at least some girls; there may be no female Teenage Mutant Turtles but there are female Power Rangers, who generally claim the loyalty of the young girls among their viewers.

Animal characters are in fact even more popular with both girls and boys of this age group than are characters from film or TV (Roehampton Survey, 1996, p. 62), though in many instances, as with Sonic the Hedgehog and the Lion King, and the two aspects come together. A new (November 1996) comic, *Ace Ventura, Pet Detective* capitalizes on this interest, and provides some useful information, also involving a good deal of stress on the environmentally friendly aspect (which has a mention in several of the other periodicals mentioned, including *Beano*). Amongst both books and magazines, however, it seems that, as often the case in quality reading, the animal characters are very often male.

While there is no reason why young girls should not enjoy books featuring male characters, the proportion of representation of the sexes seems very unbalanced, and publishers might well look to see whether it is really impossible to find positive and active female characters, whether animal or human. After all, the female lead in Robert Westall's *Blitz Cat* (1989), for somewhat older readers, certainly appeals to both boys and girls.

Books and magazines for the pre-teens

The enthusiasm of children who have arrived at a certain degree of reading autonomy for either authors they know well or for books in series is well known. It is as if they want to have the support of a familiar author or a plot which follows a formula, within a variety of slightly different characters and story lines. J. Appleyard (1990; see Chapter 2) who presents a framework of 'Five Roles Readers Take' describes the reader of this age as:

> The Reader as Hero and Heroine. The school-age child is the central figure of a romance that is constantly being rewritten as the child's picture of the world and of how people behave in it is filled in and clarified. (p. 14)

He goes on to claim that as part of this process of constructing their world:

> Conventional values, type characters, simple plots and one-sided ideals are exactly what 10– or 11-year-olds expect to find in stories . . . . Not only is one

book very much like another in the series, but the true fan may reread the same book 'at least a dozen times' (p. 85)

The favourite authors named by children between 7 and 11 in the Roehampton Survey (1996) were Roald Dahl, Enid Blyton and Dick King-Smith, and the top five individual titles were all by Dahl, little real difference being apparent between the sexes. Dahl is sometimes criticized for his intolerance of some adult characters; they are portrayed as unpleasant and needing punishment, encouraging children towards a simplistic view of morality. Provided, however, that his books are not the only ones read by children, they are unlikely to have an excessive effect. His humour too is of much the same type as that of many boys of this age group and is likely to be more attractive to children than adults. In the single most popular title, Dahl's *The BFG*, some adults may be embarrassed at a prolonged discussion of what is termed 'whizzpopping', the result of the bubbles in the giants' fizzy drinks going downwards instead of upwards (when they would issue, a little more politely, in a burp). As Sophie, the little girl snatched by the BFG, admits about human society:

> Everyone is whizzpopping, if that's what you call it. Kings and Queens are whizzpopping. Presidents are whizzpopping. Glamorous film stars are whizz-popping. Little babies are whizzpopping. But where I come from, it is not polite to talk about it. (p. 72)

Many children are likely to feel that for the first time they have an adult author who is prepared to include the earthiness so characteristic of playground jokes!

By contrast with the non-gender specific popular authors, many comics, maga-zines and popular series are very clearly aimed at either the boys or the girls of this age group. In some instances, the publishers seem to have become aware of the insatiable appetite of young readers for predictable material, and series initially aimed at older readers have given rise to younger variants. Children who are not quite ready for adolescent horror can be safely chilled by *Goosebumps* or *Sweet Valley Twins Super Chillers* (which sounds rather like something from the super-market deep freeze!). As one 12-year-old interviewed in connection with the Roehampton Survey (see Hunt, in Collins, 1997, Chapter 8) says, 'They aren't re-ally scary, but it's nice to think they are'.

Other children may seek material more concerned with family and school mat-ters; the first of the *Sweet Valley Twins* series for younger readers, *Best Friends*, is explicit about the relationship of this series with that about adolescents: 'Meet Jessica and Elizabeth before they reach Sweet Valley High'. That the readership and nearly all the characters are female might concern parents and teachers, espe-cially when the books are seen in the context of magazines addressed to the same age group. Certainly the author, whose somewhat androgynous name, Jamie Suzanne, is not on the cover where only 'created by Francine Pascal' appears, is aware of the readers' likely interests in ballet classes, what to wear, and the behav-iour of teachers and classmates. Nevertheless, the endorsement of an activity to which, no doubt, many of the readers of the series are partial, is not whole-hearted. When Jessica, one of the twins, wants to join the Unicorn Club, its leader tells her:

> 'A lot of times we talk about people, like who's going out with who and who's breaking up with who.'
> 'Oh,' said Jessica, feeling slightly disappointed.

Ellen took over. 'And,' she whispered dramatically, her blue eyes flashing, 'we talk about boys.'

Jessica straightened up. 'Oh,' she said with a knowing smile. (p. 15)

Much of this book is devoted to revealing the hollowness of the activities of the club, shown both by the members' unwillingness to have Elizabeth, Jessica's much more conformist twin, as one of them, and Elizabeth's rejection of its activities, which include a cruel joke on a less attractive girl. The other main moral message of the book seems to be that its readers should not be afraid to be individuals. Elizabeth's realization that her own style and hobbies may be distinct from those of her identical twin has something to say to readers who are unlikely to be in precisely the same family situation but are of an age where it can be difficult to be prepared to diverge from group values.

Far from limply taking on the kind of values which seem likely to please its readership, this book at least seems to proclaim the importance to young females of having interests other than simply make-up and boys. It could, however, be faulted on grounds of the very comfortable middle-class values it takes for granted; the girls have their own rooms which can be furnished and decorated in whatever manner they prefer, with no questions being asked about costs – many readers might find their life-style enviable. It has also been suggested (Daly, 1989, quoted in Cherland, 1994) that the split between the law-abiding Elizabeth and her more daring twin, Jessica, allows the young reader safely to indulge in less socially acceptable impulses.

Sweet Valley Kids also appears as a cartoon-strip in a magazine for girls of this age, *Girl Talk*, which unlike some of the others for slightly older girls mentioned below (*Big* and *Shout*) seems clearly aimed at the pre-adolescent reader. All the letters are from girls (not surprisingly in view of the title!), aged 11 and under. There is some emphasis in the features on animals, a major interest of girls of this age, which also provides the theme for popular series. One of the consistently alliterative titles in the *Animal Ark* series, *Cub in the Cupboard* (1994) has Mandy, who helps in her parents' veterinary practice, taking a stronger role than her brother James in rescuing a fox cub and agitating against either hunting or trapping foxes.

Books like this would not be adequate if they were all that girls read, but since they generate an enormous appetite for reading more of the series, they can only serve to encourage plenty of reading. Values propounded are unexceptionable: be nice to people, even those who are less attractive, be yourself, be honest.

The magazines for this age group which were found in the Roehampton Survey to be the most popular were *Big*, *Shout* and *Fast Forward* for the girls, and *Shoot* and *Match* for the boys. The gender divide is very marked, and boys from about 8 upwards seem to choose magazines which reflect their interests, especially football and cars, and increasingly with age, computing. Examination of an issue of *Match*, for instance, reveals just what might be expected. Attempts are made to show that the leader writer, Matchman, is one of the boys, with vogue spellings and expressions like 'coz', 'woz', 'alwaze', 'he's coppin' nuff boos'. There is some provocative English chauvinism, with 'Scottish football is so bad, we don't actually know who anyone is up there.' Advertisements for shirts of leading football clubs abound, there are give-away stickers, and a football board game. The reading demands could be potentially fairly high, but presumably the reader is likely to be selective about the clubs and stars which interest him. While it gives no signs of welcoming the female reader, there is little she, or indeed any adults, could object to.

This is not the case with *Action Man*, a publication too new for the Roehampton Survey and probably addressed at boys not quite ready for the specialized football magazine. It features macho males in combat uniform and places a good deal of focus on weapons. The central spread is the Amazon jungle where the reader is invited to choose two weapons from a list including hand grenades and a 'combat L. S. V.', in order to destroy Dr X's chemical weapons factory, and finally is encouraged to answer the question: 'Did you defeat Doctor X in the way he deserves?' with 'Yes, I blew him away'. The adult reader may suspect the compiler of this activity of being 'tongue in cheek', but the already belligerent tendencies of pre-teen boys could well be encouraged by it.

The girls' magazines, *Shout* and *Big* are both filled with spreads and photos about pop-stars, but in other respects they are quite different. *Big* gives little attention to its readers' lives, has no problem page, though there are readers' letters, as well as little messages from the readers to groups: 'Please come to Clitheroe' or 'I will love you forever'; these convey a very innocent impression. There are pull-out posters of stars, and a good deal of reading material, based on what the stars have to say, such as whether or not they have girlfriends. Some of the reading is potentially quite challenging, but here again, presumably readers exercise selectivity in choosing their favourite stars to read about. Throughout the magazine, the dreams of the readers are being fuelled. *Big* is also very popular with young teenagers, and it could be criticized as leading the pre-teens on to aspects of life they might not all be ready for, to keep up with their group. Even if they wanted to, however, there is no way that publishers could restrict sales only to an older age range.

An incidental positive aspect of both the pop and the football magazines is the furthering of inter-racial harmony; many of the pop stars and the football stars are black, and they seem to exert as much appeal on their fans as the white stars.

The style of *Shout* is far more reader centred. Though the pop-stars are featured, there are no posters; instead readers contribute their experiences of life, such as 'The worst job ever!' Fashion also ranks high, and beauty tips abound; problem letters focus on anxieties of early puberty like menstruation and being ready for a bra, and difficult relationships with parents. Advice is given not to sleep around, and there is information about eating disorders. The reader's likely love of animals is acknowledged, and in general there is much of interest for a girl not totally into pop-stars. A keynote of many of the letters and stories is 'I felt embarrassed', which seems characteristic of the growing self-consciousness of the readership addressed. There is an open and sensible feel to the approach; for instance, although not many black girls appear in the pictures, the fashion page includes comments from a black adviser about style. If then there is indeed a gender divide in the material read by boys and girls on the verge of puberty, most of it need cause little anxiety to their parents and teachers.

Teenage reading

There is a considerable and perhaps surprising degree of continuity between pre-teen and adolescent book reading, with Dahl ranking as most popular author among secondary school pupils as well as junior children; he was named in the Roehampton Survey (1996, p. 74) about four times as often as his nearest rival, Enid Blyton. When, however, adolescent readers answered the question about the kind of books which they preferred (p. 71), a rather different situation occurred, with horror being the most popular genre for both girls and boys. Humour and adventure were also popular choices overall; romantic fiction and animal stories are consistently popular with girls, while fantasy and science fiction seem consistently to interest more boys than girls.

Table 1 below gives the figures for those who said they 'very often' or 'often' read these kinds of fiction. (See figures at end of my Introduction for total numbers of pupils surveyed; here the average percentage of non-respondents was 11.2% for Key Stage 3 and 15.6% for Key Stage 4.)

Table 1   Percentage of readers reading fictional category

| | Keystage 3: 11–14 | | Keystage 4: 14–16 | |
	Girls	Boys	Girls	Boys
Adventure	34.9	54.0	15.4	35.0
Fantasy	22.5	37.2	16.2	28.6
Mysteries	38.3	43.5	27.5	26.3
Horror	68.1	57.1	56.4	42.3
Humour	50.8	54.0	33.1	36.3
Science Fiction	8.9	32.4	7.3	32.9
Romance	34.2	11.0	38.6	4.8
Animals	36.8	25.1	14.2	8.9

There is much that could be said about these choices, but the most relevant aspects here are the areas which might cause anxiety to adults: the girls' consistent interest in romance, which traditionally is thought to be a genre portraying females in passive roles, and the dominance of the genre of horror, one which is also very popular with children from 7 to 11 (49.8 % of girls, 59.3 % of boys).

In the past, the source of much of the reading about romance done by teenage girls would have been magazines, such as *Jackie*, which ceased publication during the 1980s. Today's teenage magazines are very different, and some consideration will be given to them below; if girls choose to read romances, they are now more likely to find them in series fiction, like *Point Romance* or *Making Out*.

It is easy to recognize the continuity between the stereotypes of fairytales and those of the romantic fiction found in comics, magazines and series targetting the female reader. This kinship is acknowledged by Walkerdine (1984) in the title of her article, 'Some Day My Prince Will Come', where she examines two girls' comics, *Bunty* and *Tracy*, which were popular at that time. *(Bunty* still exists, and with its focus on school makes a strong contrast with, for instance, *Big*, likely to be read today by the age group on which Walkerdine focused.) Walkerdine's findings are that traditional virtues such as patience and selflessness are propounded in these magazines, while in many instances the girls are put forward as victims who nevertheless win, through their passivity and helplessness.

To assume automatically that large-scale reading of this material necessarily encourages girls to model themselves on such behaviour would, however, be oversimplistic. Martin Barker (1989) supplies a critique of Walkerdine's views and dissents from some of her interpretations of the material. Perhaps most significant is his point that the stories may give voice to the frustrations of the readers, whom he suggests are often from a working-class background, with all its limitations (p. 233). Thus the girls are using the stories for their own needs, rather than being 'used' by the writers of them. He found that not all stories necessarily portrayed the male as the solution to all problems; one of the most popular was in fact a tragic story (Barker, 1989, pp. 234–38).

This did not however mean that the magazine was seeking to influence girls to a passive acceptance of their limitations, and Barker also shows that it is wrong to consider the stories alone without some examination of the context of the rest of the magazines. Within such features, he detected a good deal of stress on improvement, both in working hard at school, and about appearance and social contacts. Despite the qualities identified by Walkerdine, stories as well as articles tended to portray females who were in many cases more independent minded than most of their readers. (Barker, 1989, p. 249, citing Sarby's research based on an earlier sample.) Clearly it is dangerous to make assumptions about the reasons for girls' attachment to the genre of romance, but it still seems legitimate to hope that the stories they enjoy will at least mirror some of the qualities and attainments of real women today. In the last 10 years or so, there has been a considerable increase in the number of romance series addressed to young readers (as against those which have for long been available to adult women). Linda Christian-Smith (1993) has made a study of Teen Romance novels and the responses of their readers, and found that a powerful motive for their attraction was that: 'The novels operated at a distance from young women's own lives and provided a comfort zone where there were no consequences for risking all for love' (p. 53).

The novels which are most likely to be problematic are those where there is a real gap between the position and aspirations of women in society, and those depicted in the romances. What seems apparent is that for all age groups, the complexity of the relationship between the fictional world, the reader's demands and expectations, and the real situation of women today, need a good deal of discussion, in school and outside it. This does not mean that teachers should attempt to take ownership of this kind of reading, which would only be likely to serve to alienate the pupils who feel it to be their property, not that of their teachers who are so clearly 'past it'. Rather teachers need to be aware of their pupils' reading, accept it as a given, not to be deplored but sometimes, perhaps, to be talked about openly.

A similar openness needs also to obtain about the area of contemporary series fiction which is perhaps the most popular with both boys and girls, that of horror. Most of the popular series are far more lurid on the cover and in the blurb than they turn out to be within the story, though of course some young people gravitate fairly early to adult horror; Hunt (in Collins, 1997) talks of a 12-year-old girl enjoying, with parental approval, *The Silence of the Lambs*.

Issues of stereotyping also arise in this area, and certainly the expectation that the active role is more likely to be taken by the boy is worth discussion. Cherland (1994) suggests that 'the gender-specific threats of violence amounted to the prevailing culture's *counter*-move to the girls' resistant desires for agency' (p. 179). It seems to me, however, that this suggestion in itself makes the girl readers appear as passive victims of the publishers of these series. It under-estimates the extent to which girls read about violence and horror not only for the pleasing frisson which it creates, but also in order to enjoy laughing at it with their friends (Sarland, 1991, pp. 54, 72).

Both romance and horror series can arouse anxiety because of the assumptions which they make about the comfortable social status of the characters and the expectation of male–female bonding from an early age. These could lead to a feeling of failure in young readers of both sexes who are not blessed in these ways, but they could also increase the sense of unreality, thus allowing young people to explore relationships in a setting very far removed from their everyday scene.

The popularity of series fiction with all age groups is a phenomenon not without precedent in the past, but certainly more marked today. Partly this reflects marketing and packaging; books are grouped together even when they have relatively little apparently in common. In a recent issue of *The Book People*, readers are offered 'Five unabridged classic novels' (Nesbit, Montgomery, Barrie and two by Burnett) – an easier purchase, needing less selection, than single texts. As well as the series which have already been named above, others, such as *Baby Sitters Club*, *The Boyfriend Club*, *X Files*, *Ravenhill*, *Ballet School* and others are popular with a range of readers from about 10 to 14.

Magazines for the adolescent reader also exhibit a good deal of continuity with those for the pre-pubertal child. Boys are generally offered material related to their interests, such as computers, football, fishing, cars and bikes, while girls have a choice of a large range of periodicals which very much reflect the aspects of life which can be counted upon to appeal to all their readers: relationships, with friends, the opposite sex and parents; fashion and looks; pop stars and groups.

One worry often expressed by parents and teachers is that such magazines reveal a decline in literacy by the young; while it is true that comics and magazines of the past, from *Eagle* to *Girls' Crystal*, certainly had many quite long stories which are absent from their counterparts today, it is not true to say that teenage magazines and comics are easy reading. In fact they generally demand different kinds of reading skills, which may be more in tune with a computer-literate age; pictures and their captions need to be read in a certain order, text is often printed in and on different colours, and the adult reader may often long for a more traditional approach to print, without giving enough credit to the high degree of a specific kind of literacy which this medium demands.

One of the aspects about the girls' magazines which tends to cause parents the most anxiety is the explicitness of their treatment of sex. This is probably one of the major concerns of parents who may have been shocked to find their teenage children being told things in the magazines which they themselves didn't know! I shall give some attention below to this aspect. As against this, however, teenage magazines have what might seem a surprising number of responsible things to say about for instance, not having sex until you're ready for it and using precautions when you do, and about avoiding drugs; they also provide a number of sensible health tips.

Also of concern is the way in which they foster a consumer mentality. The free gifts, the advertisements, the stress on fashion, the encouragement given to the desire to collect the singles from a particular pop star or group – all these could all be rightly accused of generating previously unfelt needs. It must be recognized that the young people live in a commercial world, and exposure to these inducements is likely to alert young readers to the hazards, even if it means that to start with they learn by the experience of losing out financially! The obverse of this is that, perhaps responding to the feelings of young people, the magazines show attention to ecological aspects and animal welfare.

The magazines vary from those most concerned with the music scene to those which focus particularly on their readers' queries. The most popular with the secondary school pupils in 1995 when the Roehampton Survey (1996) was completed were *Just Seventeen* (attracting twice as many readers as its rivals), *Big*, which has already been discussed above and which is concerned with music, *Mizz*, *Sugar* and *Smash Hits*. Others also popular with girls of this age are *Bliss* and *More*, the last named of which is sometimes regarded as the most explicit.

The issue of *Smash Hits* examined (see references at the end of this chapter) exemplifies some of the qualities. Kate, the Editor, tells the readers about the qualities of the revamped version of the magazine:

> More gossip, more posters, more interviews and brand spanking new features. Plus a ruddy fabulous FREE tape . . . check our flashy new bedroom-wall-friendly, extra glossy, politically-correct wood free new paper . . . and you – yes YOU! – can challenge Peter Andre, Louise and smart arse Andi Peters in our regular new cosmic pop quiz thingy, Star Wars.

While the language here uses the register of the pop scene, it also shows interesting features like the awareness that the readers are concerned about the planet, an understanding of the gap they feel to exist between them and their pop heroes, and a willingness to use words which not very long ago would not have been felt appropriate in any form of written English, especially in material being sold to teenagers from reputable newsagents ('ruddy', 'smart arse'). In addition to the emphasis on stars, which includes free posters (including one of a girls' group), parents might take heart from an advertisement for child-sponsorship, which must at the least imply that the charity concerned has some reason for expecting some of the readers to respond to the appeal.

The language of the editorial ('Ed's letter') of *Just Seventeen* is also quite revealing:

> Y'know the feeling, he walks in the classroom and yer stomach turns to mush. You're a wreck, girl. You've never even spoken to him, but you know it's lurve [sic] . . .

It's very clear that the girl-reader who needs the 'Crush 'n' burn' guide which is the central feature is likely to be well under the eponymous age of the magazine!

Featuring large in most of the magazines are the letters from readers. Some of these occur on the many problem pages, to some of which boys are encouraged to contribute, often being answered by experts, such as doctors. The advice which probably occurs most often is not to rush into having sex too soon. Letters also include, in a number of instances, confessions about misdemeanours causing

72

embarrassment to friends or family. The frequency of such sections suggests that teenagers feel the need both to admit their own shameful exploits and to read about those of others – a kind of confessional function which absolves the guilt. The readers' craving to ensure that they conform to the standards of the group may also account for the provision of numerous questionnaires, which sometimes also ask the boyfriend to complete his section, with the object of seeing if both partners have the same feelings.

There is inevitably a good deal of material about appearance – hair, make-up, and clothes, with an emphasis on the latest fashion – and this could be regarded as one of the most debatable areas of these journals, encouraging their readers to spend money. It has to be remembered that a good deal of the revenue of these journals comes from firms which need their products to be publicized, either through advertising or in editorial material; a good deal of the attention given also seems to be quite responsible, presenting a sensible appraisal of the offers in the light of what is really suitable for a specific girl's needs.

The aspect which is most likely to be queried by parents and educators is the inclusion of some fairly explicit sex stories. The journal which includes most of these is *More*, where in issue 223 we have 'I had sex on stage', 'My boyfriend became a woman' and advice on how to have sex in the bath. This magazine is the only one to include 'erotic fiction' (a fairly harmless story in this issue). From the advertising and some of the features, however, it is clear that this magazine is not really directly addressed to the under-16s, though many of them in fact read it; the tacit assumption that many of its readers will be in a sexual relationship is therefore not so reprehensible as it might seem.

All of the magazines seem to be providing the kind of information which girls today are likely to need, for instance about male anatomy and the consequent dangers of arousal, precautions against AIDS and conception, and an understanding of health matters which it might not be easy to find elsewhere. Material from the Roehampton Survey (1996) indicates how helpful young people often find magazines in understanding their own physical development and some of the pressures of society about sex and drugs (see for instance p. 124 and p. 226 of the report). While both the topics and their presentation in the magazines may often seem distasteful to an older generation, it is apparent that they are, by and large, performing a useful function, which more adult-friendly material would be unlikely to achieve.

Conclusion

My discussion in this chapter, frequently based on what nearly 9000 young people have to say about their reading, suggests that some of the fears voiced about popular fiction and magazines may not be entirely substantiated. The popularity of certain authors is surprisingly long enduring, and some of the more objectionable features, particularly on the subject of race, which marred the original versions of their stories, have been modified without, I would claim, any deleterious effects. The phenomenal popularity of series fiction with all age groups also need not lead to excessive anxiety – often the covers promise far more horror than the text delivers. Once allowance is made for material placed prominently to attract readers, many of the magazines aimed at teenage girls are also seen to provide a good deal of helpful advice.

73

The element common to all these areas of popular reading is the commercialization; publishers are aware that even from pre-school, there is a market available where the consumers feel the need to be part of a group, whether it be of owners of a range of Barbie dolls or Action Men, or followers of a particular pop-group. Perhaps the most important service teachers and librarians can do for young people is to help them to make informed judgements about the books and the magazines, and about the products they are extolling. They will succeed in doing this more effectively if they are non-judgemental in their expressed attitudes towards the voluntary reading of their pupils – whatever their own opinion of its merit may be!

References

Note that an extensive bibliography is also given at the end of this book.

Children's books quoted

Blyton, E. (1944) *The Island of Adventure*. London: Macmillan.
Blyton, E. (1988, revised edn) *The Island of Adventure*. London: Pan.
Blyton, E. (1942) *The O'Sullivan Twins*. London: Methuen.
Blyton, E. (1944) *Claudine at St. Clare's*. London: Methuen.
Blyton, E. (1992) *Noddy and the Goblins*. London: BBC Enterprises.
Dahl, R. (1982) *The BFG*. London: Heinemann.
Lofting, H. (1967; 1st edn 1922) *The Story of Doctor Dolittle*. Harmondsworth: Penguin.
Lofting, H. (1995) *The Story of Doctor Dolittle*. London: Random House.
Stine, R. L. (1992) *Goosebumps: Welcome to Dead House*. London: Scholastic.
Suzanne, J. (1987) *Sweet Valley Twins: Best Friends*. New York: Bantam.

Magazines and comics

The discussion in this chapter was based on the following issues:

Ace Ventura, November 1996; *Action Man*, 16 October, 1996; *Barbie*, 18 December, 1996; *Beano*, 12 October, 1996; *Big*, 2–15 October, 1996; *Bliss*, November, 1996; *Bunty*, 26 October, 1996; *Fireman Sam*, 17 October, 1996; *Girl Talk*, 4 September, 1996; *Just Seventeen*, 16 October, 1996; *Match*, 12 October, 1996; *Mighty Morphin Power Rangers Chronicles*, No. 7, 1996; *Mizz*, 9–22 October, 1996; *More*, 9–22 October, 1996; *Rosie and Jim*, 10 October, 1996; *Sonic the Comic*, 15 October, 1996; *Smash Hits*, 9–22 October, 1996; *Shout*, 11–24 October, 1996; *Sugar*, November 1996; *The Lion King*, No. 42, 1996; *Thomas the Tank Engine and Friends*, 10 October, 1996; *Tots tv*, 3 October, 1996.

Anti-Sexist and Emancipatory Books

By the time they enter the primary school, many children have already formed a clear view about the roles of women and men in society and about their own role in relation to other children.

(Equal Opportunities Commission, *An Equal Start*, 1984, p. 6)

Male and female central characters

In British society today, males slightly outnumber females, though the discrepancy between the sexes in positions of power in industry and commerce is considerably more than this. Even in education there still remains an imbalance, though it is being gradually altered as more female professors and head teachers are appointed. It would, however, be a mistake to think that the situation in society only disadvantages females; more recently there has been an increased understanding of the extent to which society's expectations may discriminate against men, in areas such as expression of emotions, spending time with young children, and suitability of jobs. There has also been recent evidence of boys' underperformance at school, not only in the initial stages where young boys seem to take longer to acquire reading competence but also at GCSE. Therefore in considering the kind of images disseminated by books for young people, I will also be giving attention to the portrayal of male characters and the ways in which boys' reading of literature is affected by this.

In examining the 'classics' (Chapter 3) it was apparent that while there was no shortage of female characters in earlier children's literature, there was from the mid-nineteenth century onwards, a high degree of polarity between fiction for boys and that for girls. The roles of female characters were also often very gender-related; and even in books written by women, female characters have often not been depicted as particularly powerful. Criticism has arisen of the way in which even female authors have often preferred to make their more interesting characters males.

Female characters have never been significantly present in boys' school and adventure stories, but even among the considerable output of quality children's fiction written since the second world war, dealing with subjects such as family relationships, some major women writers have still chosen to focus on male characters. Lucy Boston's *The Children of Green Knowe* (1954) and Philippa Pearce's *Tom's Midnight Garden* (1958) and *A Dog So Small* (1962), are amongst the most notable examples of this emphasis: though it could be argued that the vulnerability of Tolly, Tom and Ben respectively, means that the male reader, possibly enticed into the book by the presence of a male protagonist, can learn some valuable lessons about relationship and the expression of feelings. In the same period, Mary Norton's creation of the strong female character of Arrietty in *The Borrowers* (1952) perhaps circumvents the problem of encouraging the male reader by awarding her otherwise subordinate young male character the consolation prize of at least being full human size, unlike the miniature Borrowers!

The Roehampton Survey (1996) reveals that boys are more influenced by the appearance of the cover of a book and by the illustrations than are girls, and also that for primary age boys the most important single factor concerning preference for characters is that of being the same sex. Part of the reason for this seems to be peer pressure, which may be exerted by both boys and girls. Fiona Collins (1997) quotes a 12-year-old girl who says to a boy who picks up Judy Blume's *Are You there God? It's Me Margaret*, 'No you can't read that, I'm sorry', to which he replies 'I see what you mean.' He goes on to say, 'Sometimes you really want to read a book, but you have to read it at home because if you took it into school someone would laugh at you for reading it.' (Collins, 1997, ch. 5).

Many male authors, including such significant writers as Robert Westall and Dick King-Smith, have continued to appear reluctant to place females in a leading role, as the following figures indicate. Table 2 is based on a collection of 112 works of quality children's fiction written since 1990, most of which were chosen because they were by leading authors or illustrators and showed a particular concern for equality issues. It reveals a strong tendency for male authors not to choose female protagonists, though female writers show more willingness both to write about males and to use a mixed cast of focal characters.

Table 2 Male and female protagonists in a selection of books published since 1990

	Focal character(s)		
	Male	**Female**	**Mixed**
Books: male authors	16	5	–
Books: female authors	12	33	7
Picturebooks: male authors	9	1	1
Picturebooks: female authors	8	17	3
Total	45	56	11

Given the fairly equal numbers of male and female authors involved, the discrepancies are quite striking, though opinions will inevitably vary about their effect, or indeed their cause.

It is difficult to find agreement about whether it is important for readers, of either sex, to meet strong female characters in books. Many women, talking about their own childhood experiences of reading fiction, admit to an androgynous ability to identify with interesting characters of either sex. Certainly books should not be rejected simply because the only interesting characters are all males, nor indeed if they are all females. Yet the reader can experience a special feeling of identification with an interesting character of the same sex. This is probably particularly important at the stage when children display a strong preference for adventure stories, approximately seven to twelve, as suggested by the work of Appleyard (1990, p. 60). He also refers (p. 91) to research which shows that boys prefer stories featuring male heroes involved in adventure and mystery and girls prefer stories about female characters in home or school settings, though such preferences become less marked in the secondary school age range, a finding also borne out by the Roehampton Survey of Young People's Reading, where the 53.2% of boys at Key Stage 1 (4–7 years) who say they dislike having a girl as central character, declines to 10.3% who express such feelings at Key Stage 4 (14–16) (1996, pp. 63–65).

It could even be that if male readers' reluctance to read books featuring female heroes can be overcome, they will have more to gain than female readers from this situation. For boys to admit to the 'feminine' side of their nature can be liberating, allowing them to acknowledge tender feelings and the need to express emotions. A number of recent children's books are beginning to take the risk of showing males who display emotions and vulnerability; some of these will be discussed below.

Nevertheless, as ever, the objection can be raised that literature by itself isn't going to change society. How much then does the gender of strong central characters matter? I would claim that books which omit females or only portray them in subservient or limited roles can be disempowering to female readers and are likely simply to confirm the unconscious prejudices of the male reader.

Literature which does portray females in a reasonably equal way can help make females aware of their own potentialities, and can prepare males in imaginative terms for their likely real adult experience of having to cope with women on equal terms. It can open up their horizons and represent society more accurately; it is notorious that even children whose mothers have positions of responsibility and authority at work are likely to expect females in books to have traditional roles. More women are working outside the home than ever, so it is inaccurate if women are seen only as wives and mothers.

It may well be asked how far we should we go out of our way to portray women taking roles in society that in general they don't occupy as yet. While questions obviously occur about differences between fantasy and realism, and the extent to which it is acceptable in the latter to portray a society which does not exist as such, it can at the same time help girls to try to see themselves in situations which they may not otherwise have thought of; it can also let boys play with the idea of females doing the kind of jobs in which they may not yet have seen them.

The dilemma about the portrayal of female characters reflects the ambiguity of women's situation in society. Should women be portrayed with markedly feminine characteristics? If they are too much like males, we are not really finding a place for the female but rather expecting women to become surrogate males. This tends to result in complaints that we want women to have more authority in our society but not to exert it in a masculine way. It is notorious that many successful women have attained power by taking on male qualities and consequently have little sympathy with, or indeed from, women who haven't wanted or been able to do this. Yet if women are simply going to behave exactly like males, there may be little point in demanding proper representation at all levels of society for them. We need equality in the full sense for all the qualities which have been regarded as traditionally female, even to the extent of admitting that many of these have been displayed just as fully by men. Books which emphasize female characters may run into the danger of making them indistinguishable from males, though it could be argued that even doing this achieves the object of making females visible.

Before discussing in more detail some books which attempt to challenge male and female stereotyping, however, I want to examine a category of children's fiction which seems particularly slow to give female characters their full rights, that of animal books.

Animal fiction

There are many reasons (cf. Pinsent, 1993, pp. 34–43) for the continued popularity of animal fiction, especially among the youngest children, who are likely to experience the books through being read them by an adult. Part of the appeal clearly derives from children's fondness for animals as such, particularly the small and cuddly ones. The feeling of being in control, the opportunity to 'try on' adult roles within the safe context of identification with an animal, and, not least, the enjoyment that such books give to the adult who is sharing them with the child, are all significant factors which mean that publishers are encouraged to produce books for all ages featuring animal characters.

As well as its popularity with the implied reader, however, animal fiction has an additional advantage for the publisher: it avoids issues of race, and indeed, in showing animals of different species co-operating (often in a most unlikely fashion), it presents an ideal which images interracial harmony. Yet in avoiding one evil it often runs into another. Even in relatively recent books written for children, including a large number of picture books, the number of male animal characters considerably exceeds females, in a proportion far outnumbering that of other juvenile fiction and totally different from the situation in society at large, or, indeed, in the animal kingdom itself.

The results of a small investigation, based again on a collection of quality children's books but not confined this time to recent fiction, are displayed in Table 3.

Table 3   Animal protagonists in some children's books

	Focal characters		
	Male	Female	Mixed
Books: male authors	25	3	3
Books: female authors	9	1	3
Picturebooks:male authors	9	–	1
Picturebooks: female authors	4	5	–
Total	47	9	7

The table does not include the work of Beatrix Potter, as the large number of her books might distort the figures; approximately twice as many of her books have male as female protagonists, mixed being less common. In the case of picturebooks, there are many instances where the author of the text and the illustrator are not the same person. In these cases, for the purposes of the table, I have generally taken the sex of the author, though it is interesting to note that there is a strong tendency for both to be of the same sex.

These figures, when compared with those in Table 2, reveal a large discrepancy between the overall numbers of principal female characters, and those in books with animal characters. There are roughly six times as many male leading animal characters as females. While it could be argued that this partly results from including books from earlier periods, it is still noteworthy that a number of fairly recent books have a preponderance of male characters, something which also occurs in animal texts which form part of Reading Schemes, such as *Open Door*.

Animal books from the past seem to have retained their popularity to a considerable extent both with publishers and with those responsible for the commercial use of feature characters on other products. These in turn tend to be male, such as Winnie the Pooh, Peter Rabbit and the animals from Kenneth Grahame's *The Wind in the Willows*; although Carroll's Alice does her best for her sex, it is also noteworthy that the animal characters she meets in Wonderland are also predominantly male, and these are likely to feature on products nearly as much as she does. Incidentally, as has been seen in Chapter 1, the same is true of the Reverend Awdry's trains, which could well be counted as honorary animals; the engines are all male and the carriages female and Thomas the Tank Engine has enjoyed considerable commercial success in the area of linked merchandise!

Some recent books about animals have made a real attempt, however, to portray non-stereotypical males, who are vulnerable and sometimes open to receiving advice from females. Jill Tomlinson's *The Owl who was Afraid of the Dark* (1968) is advised by his own mother and helped by a range of humans, including an old lady and a little girl, to discover that dark is exciting, beautiful and fun. Plop's fear overcome, he is free to join his family's night life; no doubt this book has been an agent in overcoming night-fears for many children since it was first published. More recent is a picture book by Phil McMylor, *This Way Little Badger* (1996), where the title character's fears are quieted by his big sister, Belle.

Stereotyping and the reader: folk and fairy tale

One of the complaints often voiced by middle-aged feminists today is that girls and young women, while happy with the results of women's political activity, notably equal salaries and employment opportunities, often refuse to call themselves feminists. They are as addicted as were their grandmothers to the kind of romantic fiction which suggests that a woman's chief fulfilment is to be found in marrying a handsome and wealthy 'Prince Charming'. The area of romance in contemporary books and magazines has been considered in Chapter 4, but it is interesting to look at some of its earlier literary antecedents and at recent attempts to alter them.

There has been a good deal of discussion of the ways in which fairytales in particular tend to stereotype female characters, so that most of them are presented as either the beautiful but helpless young girl who needs to be delivered by the handsome prince, or the evil stepmother who is seeking her downfall. *Snow White* is perhaps archetypal here, but similar characters are to be found in a wide range of the traditional tales collected by Perrault and Grimm.

The stereotypical male character who is likely to win the allegiance of many male readers is surely the handsome and brave prince, often the youngest of three sons, who from an initially unfavourable beginning goes on to rescue the damsel in distress. It would be difficult to prove any lasting damage done by these tales; nevertheless it is worth remembering that their text is by no means sacrosanct but has been adapted in every period to enshrine cultural aims which seem appropriate at that time. Jack Zipes, in *The Trials and Tribulations of Little Red Riding Hood* (1983; 1993) and his other works, and Marina Warner, in *From the Beast to the Blonde* (1994), have been among the foremost in showing how many changes this genre has been prone to. Tales which may once have celebrated women's rituals and growth of independence have been adapted in periods of women's dependence in accordance with the views of society. Personally, I think that children need to have a knowledge of the traditional tales to appreciate fully their cultural heritage, and it is certain that if they do not know at least some earlier versions, they will not enjoy to the same extent many of the current adaptations and parodies of them. For the intertextual references in recent parodic versions of the tales to be really effective, children need to have some understanding of the stereotypes which are being challenged.

There are various possible ways of counteracting the traditional stereotypes. *Changing Stories* (Mellor, 1984) is a stimulating collection of material suitable for the secondary classroom on the way these stories have developed over the ages; the earlier version of 'Red Riding Hood', with its scatological elements will come as a surprise to many. The little girl, realising quite early that the wolf is posing as her grandmother, does not passively wait to be eaten or to be delivered by a male woodcutter, but relies on her own wits, tells the wolf she needs to 'go', rejects his suggestion to 'do it in the bed' and flees outside to escape homewards (see Zipes, 1993, pp. 21–23).

Alternatively, Alison Lurie, in *Clever Gretchen* (1980) has selected a range of stories with strong heroines. Additionally, Angela Carter edited two collections of fairytales as well as using their themes extensively in her short stories, reminding us that these stories were not originally intended specifically for children.

Children who are familiar with traditional versions of some of the tales may well be ready to discuss whether life today is really like that. They may enjoy versions which present the victims, not necessarily all female, in an active role, such as *Clever Polly and the Stupid Wolf* (Storr, 1955), *The True Story of the Three Little Pigs* (Sczieska and Smith, 1989) and *Three Little Wolves and the Big Bad Pig* (Trivizas, 1993). Older pupils are more likely to enjoy *Politically Correct Bedtime Stories* (Garner, 1994), which in its provocative changes designed to send up all possible 'isms', presents some fertile material for discussion, such as the description of Grandma as being optically challenged and the wolf having a tendency towards cross-dressing. Finally the 'woodcutter-person' is rejected for assuming that 'womyn' cannot solve their own problems!

Another interesting treatment of such stories, which also lends itself to a good deal of discussion, is that which assumes knowledge of the stereotype but challenges it in an original story. Robert Munsch's *The Paper Bag Princess* (1982), Martin Waddell's *The Tough Princess* (1986) and Babette Cole's *Princess Smarty Pants* (1986) are popular examples of this genre. Fremantle (in Pinsent, 1993) shows however how children below about 8 years old may find it quite difficult to understand what is being done in challenging stereotypes. Maybe children need to start with accepting these, however unrealistic we, and later they, may find them, to form a basis for looking at gender roles.

An alternative approach to a traditional story is to be found in Babette Cole's *Prince Cinders* (1987), who is 'small, scruffy and skinny' with three big hairy brothers. After temporarily being changed to a big hairy lout, he loses his trousers on reverting to his normal size at midnight. Princess Lovelypenny searches for someone the trousers will fit, discovers and marries Cinders, while the brothers are all changed into house fairies (a role with which, judging by their expressions in the final picture, they are somewhat discontented!). Comic though it is, this book seems to be making a serious point in its defiance of the stereotypes, and like the rest of Cole's work, is well suited to children's sense of humour.

Non-sexist and anti-sexist fiction

Sue Adler (in Claire *et al.*, 1993, p. 111) puts forward three categories of children's books which attempt to avoid sexism, and, in some instances, also to remedy some of the ills of society: non-sexist books, anti-sexist books, and feminist books. She defines non-sexist fiction as either (a) that portraying a society in which discrimination on the grounds of gender does not exist, or (b) where 'men and women, girls and boys, are shown in equal numbers, performing similar tasks and behaving similarly'. Category (a) is likely to be confined to science fiction; Adler cites Piercy, *Woman on the Edge of Time* as an example and I am not familiar with any comparable books written specifically for younger readers.

There are, however, a number of children's books which, it could be argued, belong in her category (b), since they are fairly oblivious of gender differences as far as providing opportunities for characters of both sexes to function autonomously. The female characters of writers such as Nina Bawden, Penelope Lively, Jacqueline Wilson, Anne Fine, Ruth Thomas, Diana Wynne Jones, to name but a few, do not seem particularly handicapped by their sex, in fact, probably less so in the fiction than in society at large. The same could of course be claimed for *some* of the female characters in Enid Blyton's adventure books, notably the androgynous George, but as we have seen in an earlier chapter, the situation is more complex than this.

Contemporary picture books, even where the author/illustrators do not seem to have made a particular effort to redress the sexism of society, frequently portray a reasonably equal world. John Burningham's Shirley, despite her conventional parents, seems to have a rich fantasy life, and Shirley Hughes' Trotter Street is a non-sexist as well as a non-racist space.

In the last 20 years there have been a number of anti-sexist books for children, which have set out, with more or less success, to 'challenge sexist assumptions [and in these] the subtext "gender" becomes the subject of the book.' (Claire, 1993, p. 111). Notable among such books are Gene Kemp's *The Turbulent Term of Tyke Tiler* (1977), Anne Fine's *Bill's New Frock* (1989), some picture books, and the anti-sexist fairytales discussed above.

Gene Kemp (1977) has revealed that the major surprise of *Tyke Tiler*, the disclosure of the gender of Tyke, the active, 'loud-mouthed ruffian' (so described by her long-suffering headmaster (p. 30)), was not in Kemp's original plan for the book. It arose from her decision to change the sex of the protagonist after protests from her own daughter (*TES*, Septmember 1983, p. 41) that the boys got the best parts, and after attending a feminist workshop. The question certainly arises as to whether Tyke, as a result of the facts that she is indistinguishable from a male in behaviour, appearance or language, and that her best friend is a boy, Danny, really does anything for femaleness.

It could be argued that Kemp accepts the stereotype of the male and thus portrays Tyke as a very atypical female. But this I think is to lose sight of the chief value of the book, at least for those who have not had its impact diminished by being told about the end. The revelation that Tyke is in fact a female has its major effect on the *readers*, who in spite of a few clues, like Tyke being described at one point as a mermaid, and the fact that her role *vis-à-vis* Danny certainly includes a nurturing aspect, have in nearly every case automatically assumed that such a daring character must be male. Many supposedly enlightened female readers have found themselves guilty of making sexist assumptions.

Part of the problem of the novel lies, however, in the area of credibility. Why is Tyke so alienated from the female classroom community that she seeks friendship from a boy whose low ability and severe speech impediment have also isolated him from his peers? Is this degree of alienation in itself the reason for Tyke's behaviour being in many respects anti-social? What is going to happen to Danny in the more challenging milieu of the secondary school? Why do the other female characters, such as Tyke's sister and her mother, have such traditional views about female roles? Why are the characters who have the most contact with the outside world, the father with political ambitions and the head teacher, both male? Why is the student teacher, Miss Honeywell, so stereotypically feminine, in name and appearance? Tyke describes her as 'like looking at sunshine' (Kemp, 1977, p. 46).

These questions might appear to indicate taking the book too seriously, but in such issues it is perhaps possible to detect some of Kemp's implicit ideology, which may also include the suspicion that females are more caring. The climax, where Tyke falls off the school roof because she has been climbing too high certainly could be felt to suggest metonymically that as a female she is aspiring too high in attempting to rank with males: pride comes before a fall. It could also be seen as suggesting that with puberty, her female side will have to come to the fore.

In raising these questions I don't mean to undervalue Kemp's achievement, but merely to suggest that there are limits to what is possible in anti-sexist fiction. In the classroom, boys are often angry to have been 'misled' into assuming Tyke to be a boy; perhaps their reaction to this may make them think a little more about respective gender roles, but it can only be partially successful unless it leads them to a further stage of awareness of the potentialities of females.

Alienation of the key character from the group is also evident in Anne Fine's anti-sexist work, *Bill's New Frock* (1989). Bill Simpson wakes up one morning to discover that 'he' is a girl, but no one, at home or at school, notices anything untoward in his new gender identity. This means that he (or she!) is in effect newly born, with no continuity from his existence of the previous day, in spite of knowing the other pupils and not apparently being a new pupil. Fine seems to be taking for granted that the situation of a girl is worse than that of a boy, but wanting teachers and male pupils alike to be aware of their sexist attitudes and behaviour.

Much of the message of this book seems to be against specifically female dress, both as a sign of gender identity and as a disabler in everyday tasks. The dress acts as a signifier of weakness; those who wear it are expected to need help crossing the road and to be less able to perform tasks demanding strength. Stereotypes (fairly well founded in reality) that girls write more neatly and choose particular kinds of magazine stories are exposed, but perhaps one of the more controversial areas of Bill's education in what it means to be a girl is Fine's exploration of different attitudes towards competitiveness. Gilligan (1982) discusses research into how women seem to 'make a different kind of sense than men of situations of competitive achievement' (p. 14), and cites Sarsen (1980) to support the view that their anxiety about competition occurs 'only when . . . one person's success was at the expense of another's failure' (p. 15). The girls of Bill's class encourage 'her' to lose a race so that Paul, a boy who never succeeds, may have the experience of winning. Bill finds his male instincts prevent him from compliance, however much he may be prepared to do so in theory: 'He wanted to reach the line first, that was all. He didn't want to let Paul win. He wanted to win *himself.*' (p. 84) Fortunately, Paul is delighted and says, 'I've never come second in a race before. *Never!*' (p. 86).

While Fine does grapple with some of the psychological differences between males and females, this book, like *Tyke Tiler*, does relatively little to put forward a paradigm of the female as equal to but different from the male. Its overall message, reinforced by Bill Simpson's relief at reverting to masculinity at the end of the book, is that in our society, it's better to be a boy.

Anthony Browne's *Piggybook* (1986) similarly comes into the category of anti-sexism; it displays Mrs Piggott as a colourless and overworked wife on whom her husband and sons are dependent for food and care, until she walks out, leaving them to 'grub' for themselves. At this point they literally turn into pigs, only regaining human status when she returns and they take on some household duties. This book could be seen as a fairly savage attack on the male propensity for taking the woman for granted, so that it is perhaps as well from the female point of view that it is written and illustrated by a man! As in the other books considered, the end presents a problem; while Browne rejects the stereotype of the downtrodden female oppressed by housework, his portrayal of her finally finding her niche in mending the car raises the question as to whether she is going to be just as imposed upon in her new role. Are women really emancipated by taking on the same jobs as males? Perhaps we need to see as a consequence of this role change that she has a fuller position in society. At least Mrs Piggott seems to be enjoying her work this time.

The anti-sexist nature of Babette Cole's *Tarzanna* (1991) is signalled in the title, and certainly there is a liveliness and originality here which is more than a simple reversal of roles. Coming to England with Gerald, a boy she meets in her jungle home when he goes there to study spiders, Tarzanna liberates some animals from the zoo with Gerald's help, and later they go on to rescue the Prime Minister from some robbers who have tied him up, before returning to the jungle with Gerald's family. Other than her name, Tarzanna seems to have no specifically female characteristics, and her pattern of life can scarcely provide a role model for anyone to follow, but the extravagance and absurdity of the humour, supported by the caricature art, makes the book readily acceptable to both sexes and thus a small element in the process of making female characters visible.

In fact, what all the anti-sexist works considered have in common is the humour, a very effective tool with children. The way in which the normal is disrupted, the reversal of roles so that 'the world is turned upside down', seems to belong to the category of the 'carnivalesque' as put forward in the influential work of the early twentieth century Russian theorist, Mikhail Bakhtin (Morris, 1994), whose work has been discussed in Chapter 2.

It is not difficult to recognize elements of the 'carnivalesque', with its parodies, its suspension of hierarchical precedence, and its stress on bodily functions, in several of these books. The riddles in *Tyke Tiler*, like so many in this genre of children's humour, are lavish in such characteristics. They reveal what might (particularly at the date of publication, 1977) be regarded as daring:

'What did the crude oil say when it was coming out of the ground?' 'Knickers' (Kemp, 1977, ch. 7)

'Oh give me a home Where the buffalo roam And I'll show you a house with a very messy carpet' (ch. 10)

Other characteristics of carnival such as travesty and degrading of the human body can also be found in the remaining anti-sexist books discussed above, though *Tyke Tiler* probably is the most overt in carnivalesque qualities. It may, however, be salutary to reflect that Bakhtin claims that carnival in the long term often supports the status quo; once it has provided relief from the serious business of life, it becomes clear that the upside down form is not the direction of the future. At the end of the book Tyke is in bed recovering from the injury she has sustained in falling off the roof; she is on the point of going to the secondary school where we, unlike Tyke, know that life will be more serious and her friendship with Danny will be subject to more severe pressure as inevitably they will be in different groups, sets, or even streams. Her androgynous days will end with adolescence. This presages a return to normality and perhaps suggests that Kemp is putting the vision forward as an interlude which does not represent real change in society. This may of course reflect the author's own unconscious ideology.

Feminist and emancipatory fiction.

Adler (in Claire, 1983) defines a feminist book as 'A woman/girl -centred book . . . truthful about the reality of being female', and it is not difficult to find examples of children's books which fit this category. I would, however, prefer to make my focus slightly broader, and change the category to 'emancipatory', as I am aware that books which portray male characters without stereotyping them as 'macho' could be said to free male readers from the limitations placed on them by what they too often feel that maleness demands: maintenance of a stiff upper lip, thus expressing little emotion, happy or sad; restriction to certain occupations and hobbies; always being courageous; and thinking there is a particular place in society for females beyond which they should not transgress. I would claim in fact that most good 'feminist' fiction for young readers is likely also to be emancipatory to males. The problem, however, may be that if a book is too overtly 'feminist', it is less likely to be read by boys.

A number of recent books could be placed in the 'emancipatory' category: Monica Furlong's *Wise Child* (1987) and *Juniper* (1990), portraying the empowering of women in eighth century Mull; Malorie Blackman's *Hacker* (1992), about how a female computer wizard delivers her wrongly imprisoned father; Beverley

Naidoo's *Journey to Jo'burg* (1987) and *Chain of Fire*, (1989), in both of which the enterprising character of Naledi is shown within apartheid-ridden society; Berlie Doherty's sensitive exploration of the effect of pregnancy on both teenage parents in *Dear Nobody* (1991); Rosa Guy's analysis of dysfunctional families in her *The Friends* (1974) trilogy; Nina Bawden's equal valuation of both the male and the female young characters in their searches for identity in *The Outside Child* (1989) and *The Real Plato Jones* (1994); Rukshana Smith's sensitive explorations of intercultural tensions in *Sumitra's Story* (1982) and *Salt on the Snow* (1988); Jamila Gavin's broad canvas in *The Wheel of Surya* (1992) and *The Singing Bowls* (1989); and Mildred Taylor's books about a black community in the Southern United States in the 1930s.

The books I have mentioned here are not confined to a specifically feminist or anti-sexist message, but rather seek to consider the whole person in the whole community, and in doing so often provide an insight into female values and the strength provided by women's comradeship. Such books are likely to survive the vagaries of fashion and still be read even when the specific issues discussed are no longer relevant, and the battles for women's equality are finally won. They generally involve strong female characters, but not at the expense of undervaluing males simply because of their sex.

The fact that several writers in the list above are from ethnic minority backgrounds even though the subject I am considering here is gender rather than race, perhaps lends support to Thistlethwaite's contention (1990) that: 'black women's fiction contrasts with white women's fiction because it accents public perspectives as much as or more than private life' (p. 4). While I would not go quite so far as this, particularly in the light of the social emphasis in the work of Naidoo (who is not herself of ethnic minority racial origin, though she has been much involved with the situation in South Africa), there does seem some validity in it. In the anti-sexist books discussed above, Fine, Kemp and Cole seem to focus on the issue of gender alone, although it is only fair to mention Kemp's *Gowie Kirby Plays Chicken* (1979) where the agent for confidence-building in the personality of the socially deprived eponymous male character is an academically brilliant black American girl, who could be seen as paradigmatic in both sex and race. Those writers, black or white, who are looking at race or social issues, cannot and do not exclude the situation of women from their books, and perhaps as a result, make a more telling case for equality than does more specifically anti-sexist fiction.

The black American writer, Mildred Taylor, was inspired to write by her father's stories about his experiences as a boy in Mississippi in the 1930s. She chose, however, to transmute these by changing the narrator to Cassie Logan, the younger sister of Stacey, the character most closely modelled on her father's experiences. The earliest of the series, *Roll of Thunder, Hear my Cry* (1977), remains for me her most impressive work; it is a powerful novel embracing insights which might be best described by the term Alice Walker coined, 'womanist', since the strength of the female characters is intrinsically related to their racial identity and social position. The reader comes to learn of the racial intolerance through the dawning realizations of the narrator, whose strength grows throughout the novel. But a great impact is also made through the portrayal of Cassie's mother and grandmother. The latter, 'Big Ma', a widow, maintains the family cotton holding in the absence of her son, Cassie's father, who for economic reasons has to work on the railway. We recognize her dominant personality early in the novel, assisted by her physical description:

> Cassie, you better watch yourself, girl,' Big Ma cautioned, putting one rough, large hand against my back to make sure I didn't fall . . . . She was tall and strongly built. Her clear, smooth skin was the color of a pecan shell . . .
>
> (Taylor, 1977, p. 32)

The forceful descriptives, 'rough, large' and 'tall and strongly built' might almost suggest masculinity, yet 'clear' and 'smooth' balance these to provide the depiction of a woman who has needed to take on something of a male role but not lost her female attributes. She is characteristic of female strength in her society, which is of necessity matriarchal because the men have to seek employment elsewhere. Cassie's mother, a teacher at the local black school, is also a woman of considerable moral fortitude, who refuses to confine her history syllabus to that prescribed by the white establishment, preferring to lose her job and suffer economic consequences rather than forsake her principles. We come to understand that these women have the quality of being at the same time powerful and quintessentially female, and this is revealed by their maintenance of their integrity within an oppressive society; the private qualities are expressed through the public enactment.

It is perhaps no coincidence that a picture book which also manages to express the community of women over three generations, though in less difficult circumstances, is also concerned with issues of both gender and race. *Amazing Grace* (Figure 3) by Mary Hoffman (1991), illustrated by Caroline Binch, portrays a young girl, addicted to stories and drama, who is told by her classmates that she can't take the male white role of Peter Pan in the school play because she is a black girl. The question of femaleness is easily disposed of in the light of the play's stage history, but the contrasting reactions of the mother and grandmother to the question of race are illuminating; Grace's mother starts to get angry, but her grandmother takes Grace to a brilliant performance by a young black ballerina, to confirm Grace's conviction that, 'I can be anything I want.' Again, we see how it is impossible to separate the gender and race issues, since both are part of the identity of the characters concerned.

Both Taylor and Hoffman display in their work aspects which reflect some of the findings of writers who have concentrated on the differences between male and female psychology, reversing the exclusively male focus of Freud and his followers. Gilligan (1982) suggests that a characteristically female attitude towards the resolution of moral problems is to see 'a world which coheres through human relationships rather than through systems of rules' (p. 29). In *Amazing Grace*, the angry response of Grace's mother to the racist statement that Grace can't act Peter Pan because she is black, could be seen to reflect her assumption of the male mode of response; no doubt her reaction in a larger matter would be to seek recourse to the law. The grandmother, on the other hand, works through building up Grace's sense of self-esteem, to reassure her of her personal qualities, and this more relational mode could be seen as a specifically female response to the situation.

The same could be said of a situation in Taylor's book, when Cassie is deeply offended at having to make a formal apology to a white girl, 'Miz' Lillian Jean, for

Figure 3 Grace, her mother and her grandmother. From *Amazing Grace* by Mary Hoffman, illustrated by Caroline Binch. Copyright (c) 1991 by Mary Hoffman, text. Copyright (c) 1991 by Caroline Binch, illustrations. Used by permission of the publishers Frances Lincoln Ltd, 4 Torriano Mews, Torriano Avenue, London, NW5 2RZ and Dial Books for Young Readers, a division of Penguin Books USA Inc.

accidentally bumping into her (Taylor, 1977, pp. 95–97). Cassie's solution to the problem is neither open confrontation nor acceptance; she gives every appearance of acting as an inferior to the white girl but once she has learned all Lillian's secrets, subjects her in private to physical pain to force her to apologize in her turn. While this is hardly to be recommended on moral grounds, it does display what might be seen as a typically female desire to find a way round the situation rather than being bound by the rules; no doubt it also gives a salutary lesson to Lillian Jean.

Another feature of these books which reflects the findings of feminist psychologists is the fact that both the young girls grow in maturity through their connections with their mothers and grandmothers, rather than in the separation which psychologists focusing only on male development have seen as a necessary part of maturity. As Nancy Chodorow (quoted in Gilligan, 1982, p. 7) says: 'Female personality comes to define itself in relation and connection to other people more than masculine personality does.' Taylor's whole series about the Logan family reveals, in the distinctions made between the process of maturation of Cassie and her brother Stacey, an implicit understanding of this difference, and the two books about Grace by Hoffman and Binch show this younger girl to be well advanced on the same pathway.

Emancipatory fiction and male characters

It is difficult to separate fiction which seeks to establish women's access to areas of life not traditionally open to them from that which is equally emancipatory for males. Louise Fitzhugh's *Nobody's Family is Going to Change* (1976) presents Mr Sheridan as a barrister who is opposed to the desire of his daughter, Emma (short for 'Emancipation') to follow in his footsteps; his down to earth knowledge of the law convinces him that it is no place for a female. His son Willie wants to be a dancer, a profession which his father thinks is 'sissy'. Incidentally, this black American family is prosperous enough to employ a white servant, an aspect which could provoke fruitful classroom discussion. Although Willie is eventually allowed to take dancing classes, the title of the book indicates that no easy solution is to be found for Emma. It finishes with Emma's resolution to go ahead despite opposition; to her father's statement, 'I think any woman who tries to be a lawyer is a damned fool,' she replies, 'That is your problem, not mine.' Her resolve epitomizes the determination which is so often still necessary from any individual who wants to go even slightly outside the gender norm.

Boys who want to dance are also the subjects of two other books, Jean Ure's *A Proper Little Nooryeff* (1982), and *Jump* (1992) by Michelle Magorian, illustrated by Jan Ormerod. In the latter, Steven's mother says, 'Real boys don't go to dance classes,' a statement which, as we rightly predict, is proved wrong by the end of the book, when Steven is the star of the show in a 'basketball' dance which makes use of his jumping ability. The fact that the title and cover of the book highlight such a 'natural' masculine sport as jumping, rather than, for instance, 'Steven goes to dancing class', suggests that the publishers fear that the potential buyer, like Steven's mother, might not associate a 'real' boy with dancing!

One of the areas where emancipation in literature has followed that in real life, is in the caring side of male characters being valued. Anne Fine's *Flourbabies* (1992) examines how a group of boys, especially the semi-literate Simon Martin, whose father left home when he was very young, is made aware of what is involved in being a parent, through being given baby-shaped sacks of flour to tend. Simon comes to understand, and even forgive, his father, who left when he was a baby, as he appreciates in a small way the pressures of fatherhood.

Two picture books, Mary Hoffman's *Henry's Baby* (1993), illustrated by S. Winter, and Bob Graham's *Crusher is Coming* (1987), are also concerned with the attitude of males to young children. Both deal with the anxiety felt by a male who thinks that care for a young child is at variance with his 'macho' image. The latter book shows Peter clearing his room of stuffed animals and warning his mother to keep his young sister Claire out of the way, because the boy who is the epitome of maleness is coming to tea. Crusher, however, turns out to be far more interested in giving a piggyback to Claire than in seeing Peter's *Raiders of the Universe* video. There is a binary opposition between on the one hand such icons of maleness as Crusher's bandaged head, which signifies that he has just come from a rough football practice, or the skull and crossbones on Peter's door, and on the other images provided by the plethora of soft toys and the pink pig on Claire's wall. This forms a complex underpinning for Peter's change of heart: at the end we see him imitating Crusher and giving Claire a piggyback too. The message is clear: 'real' males have a caring side which in no way negates their masculinity.

Conclusion

My contention is that among the most effective ways to facilitate the progress towards a sense of identity for children of both sexes is through reading well-written and well-illustrated books, which avoid stereotyping characters into gender-roles. While this may sometimes be achieved by specifically anti-sexist books, it is often more effective if sexism is not the only subject. Books which represent the characters as individuals, with their own strengths and weaknesses, may help readers to realize that a person's qualities are unlikely to be determined solely by sex or gender identity.

References

Note that an extensive bibliography is also given at the end of this book. An asterisk indicates a picture book.

Non-traditional fairytales and associated material

Cole, B. (1987) *Prince Cinders**. London: Hamish Hamilton.
Cole, B. (1986) *Princess SmartyPants**. London: Hamish Hamilton.
Garner, J. F. (1994) *Politically Correct Bedtime Stories*. London: Souvenir Press.
Lurie, A. (1980) *Clever Gretchen*. London: Heinemann.
Mellor, B. (1984) *Changing Stories*. London: ILEA English Centre.
Munsch, R. (1982) *The Paper Bag Princess**. Leamington Spa: Scholastic.
Storr, C. (1955) *Clever Polly and the Stupid Wolf.* London: Faber.
Sczieska, J. and Smith, L. (1989) *The True Story of the Three Little Pigs**. Harmondsworth: Penguin.
Trivizas, E. (1993) *Three Little Wolves and the Big Bad Pig**. London: Heinemann.
Waddell, M. (1986)*The Tough Princess**. London: Walker.
Williams, J. (1978) *The Practical Princess and other liberating fairy tales* Leamington Spa: Scholastic.
Zipes, J. (1986) *Don't Bet on the Prince*. Aldershot: Gower.
Zipes, J. (1983, 1993) *The Trials and Tribulations of Little Red Riding Hood*. London: Routledge.

Non-sexist and anti-sexist fiction

Ahlberg, J. and Ahlberg, A. (1982) *The Baby's Catalogue**. London: Kestrel.
Browne, A. (1986) *Piggybook **. London: Julia MacRae.
Burningham, J. (1977) *Come Away from the Water, Shirley**. London: Cape.
Cole, B. (1991) *Tarzanna**. London: Hamish Hamilton.
Fine, A. (1989) *Bill's New Frock*. London: Methuen.
Hughes, S. (1988) *The Big Alfie and Annie Rose Story Book**. London: Bodley Head.
Kemp, G. (1977) *The Turbulent Term of Tyke Tiler*. London: Faber.
McMylor, P. (1996) *This Way Little Badger*. Loughborough: Ladybird.

Feminist and emancipatory fiction

Aardema, V. (1985, illustrated by S. Meddaugh) *Bimwili and the Zimri**. London: Hamish Hamilton.

Bawden, N. (1966) *The Witch's Daughter*. London: Gollancz.

Bawden, N. (1973) *Carrie's War*. London: Gollancz.

Bawden, N. (1989) *The Outside Child*. London: Gollancz.

Bawden, N. (1994) *The Real Plato Jones*. London: Hamish Hamilton.

Blackman, M. (1992) *Girl Wonder's Winter Adventures*. London: Gollancz.

Blackman, M. (1992) *Hacker*. London: Doubleday.

Blume, J. (1982)*Tiger Eyes*. London: Heinemann.

Browne, A. (1989) *The Tunnel**. London: Julia MacRae.

Chambers, A. (1982) *Dance on My Grave*. London: Bodley Head.

Cooper, S. (1983) *Seaward*. London: Bodley Head.

Creech, S. (1994) *Walk Two Moons*. Basingstoke: Macmillan.

Doherty, B. (1991) *Dear Nobody*. London: Hamish Hamilton.

Farmer, P. (1969) *Charlotte Sometimes*. London: Chatto.

Fine, A. (1992) *Flourbabies*. London: Hamish Hamilton.

Fitzhugh, L. (1976) *Nobody's Family is Going to Change*. London: Gollancz.

Furlong, M. (1987) *Wise Child*. London: Gollancz.

Furlong, M. (1990) *Juniper*. London: Gollancz.

Gavin, J. (1989) *The Singing Bowls*. London: Methuen.

Gavin, J. (1992) *Wheel of Surya*. London: Methuen.

Graham, B. (1987) *Crusher is Coming**. London: Collins.

Guy, R. (1974) *The Friends*. London: Gollancz.

Hoffman, M. and Binch, C. (1991) *Amazing Grace**. London: Frances Lincoln.

Hoffman, M. and Binch, C. (1995) *Grace and Family**. London: Frances Lincoln.

Hoffman, M. and Winter, S. (1993) *Henry's Baby**. London: Dorling Kindersley.

Hughes, S. (1979) *Up and Up**. London: Bodley Head.

Innocenti, R. (1985) *RoseBlanche*. London: Cape.

Kemp, G. (1979) *Gowie Kirby Plays Chicken*. London: Faber.

Magorian, M. and Ormerod, J. (1992) *Jump**. London: Walker.

Naidoo, B. (1987) *Journey to Jo'Burg*. Harlow: Longmans.

Naidoo, B. (1989) *Chain of Fire*. London: Collins.

Norton, M. (1952) *The Borrowers*. London: Dent.

Paterson, K. (1978) *Bridge to Terebithia*. London: Gollancz.

Pearce, P. (1983) *The Way to Sattin Shore*. London: Kestrel.

Smith, R. (1982) *Sumitra's Story*. London: Bodley Head.

Smith, R. (1988) *Salt on the Snow*. London: Bodley Head.

Speare, E. (1960) *The Witch of Blackbird Pond*. London: Gollancz.

Taylor, M. (1977) *Roll of Thunder, Hear My Cry*. London: Gollancz.

Taylor, M. (1992) *The Road to Memphis*. Harmondsworth: Penguin.

Tomlinson, J. (1968) *The Owl that was Afraid of the Dark*. London: Methuen.

Ure, J. (1982) *A Proper Little Nooryeff*. London: Bodley Head.

Voight, C. (1984) *Homecoming*. London: Collins.

Wells, R. (1988) *Shy Charles**. London: Collins.

Wilson, J. (1992) *The Suitcase Kid*. London: Doubleday.

Wilson, J. (1994) *The Bed and Breakfast Star*. London: Doubleday.

Wynne Jones, D. (1985) *Fire and Hemlock*. London: Methuen.

'Race' and Ethnic Identity

The little black Canny Cannibal children approached Pippi's throne. For some strange reason, they had got hold of the idea that a white skin is much better than a black one . . .

(Astrid Lindgren, *Pippi in the South Seas*, 1955–57, p. 51)

Writers and readers

It has already been noted (in Chapter 5) that many of the books which treat the subject of gender most effectively and with the least reliance on stereotypes are those which also present broader themes, such as social deprivation and, most notably, race, language and culture. Many of the writers of such books are people who for one reason or another have been politicized by their own or their group's experience of prejudice, and have come to realize that equality issues can seldom, if ever, be viewed in isolation from each other. The work of the distinguished black American writer, Alice Walker, has been pre-eminent in this field, for it is totally clear in *The Colour Purple* (1983), an adult book which has also become very popular among upper secondary readers, that the social and political oppression experienced by all the black population, is fundamental to the degree of oppression suffered by the women in particular. In focusing on the subject of race and culture in books for children, it also becomes apparent that much of the most impressive writing occurs in books which present powerful female characters; of these books a significant number are written by black women.

The category of race is of a slightly different nature from those of sex or gender; the sex of most humans is fairly clearly defined from birth, and for the majority of people their gender orientation is associated with their sex. The term 'race' however is far less definitive. Research shows that differences in so-called racial characteristics are far less prominent between different groups of humans than are the variations within most other animal species; over 99% of our genetic inheritance is apparently common to all of us. Although in the past, some distinctive physical traits may have resulted from the geographical isolation of groups of humans, or even from deliberate breeding among slaves, today there are few communities with any claim to be racially 'pure'; in modern society there has been a considerable amount of intermarriage which has blurred any such distinctions even further. Racial identity, for many people, especially those of mixed background, allows a higher degree of choice than does gender.

It would, however, be impossible to discard the category 'race' entirely; for one thing, any substitute term would demand many more words! In addition to this, even today, for a considerable number of people involved with books on the subject, especially the readers, the term 'race' has a much solider meaning than it has for geneticists.

I shall also, with some reservations, generally use the term 'black' to mean 'non-Caucasian', which means that a good many distinctions of culture, which in many cases provides a more significant difference than skin colour, are glossed over; culture will be given more specific attention in the next chapter.

Particularly notable among differences are those between people of Asian and African descent, and, within these two very broad spectra, those between for instance people of Ghanaian or Nigerian descent on the one hand, and those from families of Caribbean origin on the other. Nor are those of Asian stock any more monolithic; between Chinese, Bangla-Deshi and Indians, for instance there are again many differences of attitude, religion, culture, and social status. There have been many reports showing how very different both the attitudes towards school and the academic achievements of some of these groups have been (see *The Observer* 15 September 1996); differences of culture and of socio-economic status have been much more important than any so-called racial differences as a cause of such variations in achievement. Gender is also a far from negligible factor, and its effects are not entirely identical with the situation in the indigenous population. The blanket use of the word 'black' also tends to conceal any hostility between some of the different groups mentioned above; hostility and racism, even if an essential component of the latter is the power to put prejudices into action, are not confined to the 'white' or indigenous community.

It is inevitably difficult to determine how far the portrayal of race, a word which in my subsequent usage should always be regarded as having invisible quotation marks round it, has an effect on children who read books relating to it as an issue. If it is badly done, it may both give offence to 'black' readers and reinforce the prejudices of 'white' readers. Sensitivity on the subject has sometimes led to the opinion that black characters should only be portrayed by black authors and illustrators – something which would surely be impossible if a true picture of our ethnically very mixed society is to be conveyed by people of any race! Nevertheless, any depiction of race needs to be accurate, which also means that to produce a contemporary 'realist' text set in Britain or North America yet totally omitting black characters is unacceptable.

The Roehampton Survey of young people's reading (1996) shows that the majority of young readers say that whether or not the leading character in a children's book is of the same race as themselves makes little difference to their choice of a book; it seems to be less influential on choice than is the gender of such characters, and much less than their age or the period in which they live. Only 2.2% of girls between 14 and 16, for instance, say that a character in a book having the same colour skin is important to them, as against 22.2% who rate whether they 'live in the same time as you' as influential on their choice (p. 68). It should be noted that the survey was demographically representative in relation to ethnicity. However, this statistic relates to aspects of which the reader is conscious, and not to the effects of such portrayals on attitudes towards potential in society. There is in fact research, described extensively by Milner (1983; chapters 4–6) which shows that black children have often had a mental image of themselves as whiter than they really are.

'Political correctness' and anti-racism

People who are worried about the effects of 'political correctness' on children's literature since, say, the 1970s, are likely to present three main areas of concern:

1. the fear that existing literature for children will be adapted or even censored;
2. the effects of what they regard as the hypersensitivity of ethnic minority groups about well-meaning efforts to portray black characters, leading to the fear that only black writers or illustrators will be allowed to do this;
3. the effect on literature if authors try to write books conforming with a political agenda.

The first of these concerns has been considered earlier (Chapters 3 and 4); the second and third are difficult to separate and will form the substance of the present chapter, together with an evaluation of some of the books concerning ethnic minority children which have been produced in more recent years. My impression is that in the last 25 years there has been a noticeable swing from a reactive to a proactive approach, from trying to rid existing books of undesirable racist images and writing books which have attempted to combat racism, towards the creation of truly multi-ethnic and multi-cultural literature.

One of the first effects of the realization that children's literature was deficient in books which portrayed black characters in significant roles, were several books which set out to confront racism and at the time were largely acclaimed for this quality. Subsequently many of these books have been re-evaluated and greeted by some hostility because of their ambivalent effects.

Theodore Taylor's *The Cay* (1970) was given five major book awards, but is described by Albert Schwartz (in Stinton, 1979) as 'the story of the initiation of a white upper middle class boy . . . into his "proper" role in a colonialist, sexist, racist society' (p. 45). It depicts the white boy, Phillip, being shipwrecked on a very small island with another survivor, an old black man, Timothy. The racism of Phillip's mother, which he has inevitably imbibed, is made explicit at a number of points, and only implicitly condemned by its contrast with the tolerance shown by Timothy:

> Because it had been on my mind I told him that my mother didn't like black people and asked him why.
>
> He answered slowly, 'I don' like some white people my own self, but 'twould be outrageous if I didn' like any o' dem'. (p. 58)

At first Phillip despises Timothy, particularly when he discovers that the old man is illiterate, but in the blindness which results from an injury at the time of the shipwreck, Phillip becomes totally dependent on him, and at the same time learns much from Timothy's wisdom. This book has been welcomed by many people, but it has also sustained a good deal of criticism, particularly because so much depends on the reader's understanding of what the author is doing in portraying racist attitudes and trusting the reader to reject them. This recalls what Victor Watson (in Styles *et al.*, 1992) describes as 'irresponsibility' on the part of an author, who does not make explicit his condemnation of racism (cf. Chapter 2). Watson quotes Hollindale who says of *Huckleberry Finn*, 'You cannot experience the book as an anti-racist text unless you know *how to read a novel*' (Watson, p. 4; see also Chapter 2 above for more detail on Hollindale's work).

The first introduction of Timothy displays the danger of using an unreliable narrator; before Phillip loses his sight, he wakes up to find himself alone a raft with:

> a huge, very old Negro sitting on the raft near me. He was ugly. His nose was flat and his face was broad . . . The Negro said, 'You 'ad a mos' terrible crack on d'ead, bahss.' (p. 23)

Timothy is portrayed here and elsewhere as using a strongly marked dialect and having had no education, and his appearance is repulsive to the young boy. Throughout the book, by the use of first person narration, everything is mediated through the ignorant and prejudiced gaze of the young boy, who has been brought up as a racist but gradually learns the considerable qualities of Timothy. There is clearly the risk that the child reader may be oblivious to the message, and may in fact, from a racist perspective, take on Phillip's idea that black people are by birth less intelligent than white, without recognizing Phillip's growth in understanding by the end of the book, when the old man dies protecting him from a tidal wave, and is reverently buried. What is needed in a case like this is what Watson (1992) describes as 'responsible readers'; rather than banning the book because it doesn't make the process of condemning racism easy, the child reader needs to be educated to become aware of the more subtle shades of meaning involved in a mature reading of such a text.

Perhaps because of the way in which many people found it difficult to admit that children might be able to decode the racism shown in *The Cay* and put it into perspective, Taylor much more recently produced *Timothy of the Cay* (1993), which is far more explicit in its overt condemnation of racism, leaving less to be done by the reader. The narrative alternates between the first person narration of Phillip, who has an operation to correct his sight and returns to the Cay to find the grave of Timothy, and the third person narration describing Timothy's life preceding his encounter with Phillip, thus giving a more 'objective' perspective on black history. It also includes a more explicit condemnation of Phillip's mother's attitude. The newly enlightened boy questions his mother's reluctance to have black neighbours:

> 'Are you afraid of them?' I asked.
> 'Let's just say I'm uncomfortable around them.'
> 'Why? Did any black person ever do anything to you?'
> 'Phillip, don't question me,' she flared, the old tightness back in her voice.
> 'Timothy said that under the skin we're all the same.'
> 'I'm not interested in what Timothy had to say about this subject.' (p. 68)

Taylor's attempts realistically to convey Timothy's use of dialect and automatic acceptance of Phillip as his natural superior (explained in the later book as 'Just habit, a leftover from slave days.' (p. 54)) together with his portrayal of the old man's lack of education, could be seen as too challenging for some young readers. But at least no one could describe the portrayal of the character of Timothy as passive, another aspect frequently detected by critics within the well-intentioned books written by white writers. Armstrong's *Sounder* (1969) (discussed in Chapter 2 above) is another book later savaged by Schwartz (in Stinton, 1979, p. 49); the black family at the centre of the story are seen as suffering in silence, without any natural expressions of emotion.

What may be at work, here and elsewhere, is a conflict between the explicit ideology of writers such as Taylor and Armstrong, by which they would certainly defend the view of the equality of black characters, and some unexamined assumptions and even prejudices, which may still form part of their implicit cast of mind. This means that the books provide some very useful material for discussion for instance in the secondary school.

Another book from the 1970s which was highly acclaimed at the time but reviled later is Paula Fox's *The Slave Dancer* (1973). It won the Newbery medal, and Dixon (1978a) describes it as a novel of 'rare excellence . . . great horror and as great humanity. It seems to me it approaches perfection as a work of art' (p. 125). By contrast, four writers in Stinton's *Racism and Sexism in Children's Books* (1979) see it as racist because of the language and the passivity of the slaves.

The first person narrator, Jessie Bollier, is kidnapped and taken aboard a slave-trader, in order to play his pipe for the slaves' exercise on deck during their long voyage, so keeping them relatively fit and worth buying. Most of the time they are imprisoned below, and Jessie, angry and himself a prisoner, finds 'a dreadful thing in my mind. I hated the slaves! I hated their shuffling, their howling, their very suffering . . . I wished them all dead!' (p. 78). Despite his horror, he really craves their companionship and is fascinated by a young slave-boy, Ras. Ultimately, the only people who survive the wreck of the vessel are Jessie and Ras; when they land they are helped by an old black man, Daniel, who has presumably escaped from slavery, and Jessie voices at the end his own abhorrence for slavery. Jessie's hatred of the slaves is really an instant reaction rather than a considered opinion; it is clear that he isn't really against the slaves as such but rather against aspects of his own situation. His feelings presumably result from his own forced passivity, the fact that he did not and cannot rebel at his own captivity, and therefore feels as if the slaves should do so in his stead. Their failure to rebel is of course realistic, and it seems unreasonable for critics to criticize either this quality or the complex emotions felt by a character in an extreme situation. Again, we have use of the dangerous device of an unreliable narrator through whose reactions the evils of prejudice and slavery are displayed; it seems clear that this is a technique which is not easy even for some adult readers to appreciate, and it certainly demands explicit attention if books of this kind are used in the classroom.

Another book acclaimed at the time but subsequently accused of portraying black characters as passive is Bernard Ashley's *The Trouble with Donovan Croft* (1974), which won the Children's Rights Workshop Other Award in 1976. The title character is a black boy whose mother's departure to look after his grandmother in the Caribbean causes him to become an 'elective mute'. He is living with a white family as his father is unable to care for him (such interracial fostering has subsequently become uncommon) and is exposed to the racist hostility of the next door neighbour and of an unpleasant teacher. Here again, we have 'irresponsible' writing, as the reader is expected to judge the wrongness of the behaviour of these characters. Mr Henry is angry when Donovan will not answer to his name:

> As he raged, he slapped Donovan hard across the face with the palm of his hand. 'Tell me, you stupid black idiot!' (p. 56)

Again, the verbalization of abuse could be seen as dangerous to the inexperienced reader. Most of the criticisms of the book, however, have resulted from the passivity of Donovan and, in particular, his father, who seems unable to help his son, and contrasts with the competent and caring Chapmans. At least Donovan takes an active role at the end where he shouts to Keith and prevents him getting run over, but prior to that it is difficult for the reader not to see him as a victim deserving pity. Perhaps this reflects something of the ideology of well-meaning liberals at the time; we must do something for the blacks!

A more recent example of what could be described as 'irresponsible' writing is in Robert Westall's *Gulf* (1992); the psychiatrist, Dr Rashid, notes that however eminent he becomes, he'll always be thought of by some people as a 'Wog poofter' (pp. 73–74). How far this use of language can be judged to give ammunition to the racists, who surely are fairly well aware of it already, and the extent to which it could give offence in a mixed classroom, are aspects which need to be considered in the light of specific school circumstances, and I give some attention to this in my final chapter. In *Gulf*, Westall is also seeking to show that any point of view about an international conflict is conditioned by the effect of the media, and without either demonizing or deifying Saddam Hussein, to reveal the Iraqis as human beings too.

All the books discussed above have a claim to literary merit, but another facet of the debate concerning political correctness is the production of books which seem to have an issue like race as their sole agenda. Many such books are non-fiction, and some of these will be considered in Chapter 9, but two fictional examples may be worth mention here: Arvan Kumar's *The Heartstone Odyssey* (1988) and Judith Vigna's *Black Like Kyra, White Like Me* (1992). The first of these attracted a good deal of publicity when it was first published, particularly as it had been rejected by mainstream publishers; some of its supporters considered this to be on racist grounds. It would be churlish not to admit that good art and dance work was associated with the book, but the fact that its stylistic defects, which I have discussed at more length elsewhere (Pinsent, 1990), make it an unattractive read cannot do much good to the cause of anti-racism.

Black Like Kyra is a much slighter book which deals with the question of a black family moving into a white neighbourhood in the USA. The tone is heavily didactic; when the narrator Christy's friend Kyra and her family come to live next door, and are greeted with antagonism by the residents, Christy's father explains: 'Some people are scared of anyone who looks or acts different from them, especially if that person's skin is a different color.' No easy solution is put forward; Christy's previous best friends move away, though Kyra's family decide to stick it out. In its lack of easy solutions or evasions, this is to be welcomed, but it is difficult to imagine any child reading this book for entertainment. Its illustrations lack the polysemic qualities of most good picture books, where an added richness is supplied by aspects about characters or stories which would not have been apparent from the text alone; in this respect it contrasts with some of the books which I shall discuss below.

Emancipatory books

The subject matter of more recent writing for children related to race suggests that authors have found that it is more interesting to depict the positive qualities of a variety of ethnic backgrounds than to concentrate only on anti-racism. Negative aspects tend to be included in these only where they are relevant to a complete rounded picture.

Black characters in our multi-ethnic society

Many contemporary authors, both of illustrated and non-illustrated books, particularly those within the mode of realism, evidently feel that to limit themselves to child characters only of white European stock is unrealistic. *The Baby's Catalogue* (1982) by Janet and Allan Ahlberg depicts in non-narrative form the experience of a range of infants through the day, from morning to bedtime. Carpenter and Prichard (1984) give the information that the format of this book resulted from the discovery that their daughter's initial preferred reading matter was a mail-order catalogue. It portrays a black baby as one of the featured characters. A similar practice obtains in other work by the Ahlbergs, and in Shirley Hughes' picture books, sited in *Trotter Street* and elsewhere, which follow the everyday adventures of an ordinary group of children.

People who criticize this kind of inclusive treatment as 'political correctness' make much use of the pejorative term, 'tokenism'. The problem is, however, that British society today *does* include children from a diversity of ethnic backgrounds, and not to depict this in some way would also be open to criticism. It would be less satisfactory, however, if on the one hand this were the only mode of depiction of ethnic minority characters, which is far from being the case, or on the other, there were no books which only presented groups of children of the same ethnic group as each other. Books which present a mixture of children of different racial groups are not making race an issue, but simply portraying the realities of contemporary British life. The question of how much the child reader's attention is drawn to the diversity of the characters is one to be faced by the parent or the teacher of the very young children who are the implied audience of such texts.

The skin colour of the characters is of course more evident in picture books than those without illustrations, but many ethnic minority characters also occur in other contemporary children's books, especially those in a realist mode. These black characters, without being major protagonists, may be visible on the cover or their ethnic identity may be discussed in the text. In Nina Bawden's *Rebel on a Rock* (1978) the two adopted children of Carrie and Albert Sandwich (familiar to those who have read her *Carrie's War* (1973)) are black, and while this is not of great significance in the adventure described, it appears to be one of Bawden's ways of reflecting her belief in the equal status of all children; at the date of this novel, it was less unlikely that black children be adopted by white parents than it is today.

Bernard Ashley's *Running Scared* (1986) has a central character who is Asian, an aspect relevant to the plot in so far as it allows for the use of a Sikh temple, but perhaps more important in connection with identity; Narinder's feelings are indirectly voiced:

> all the frustrated, mixed-up emotion of being from an Asian family and born in London . . . Even in London – specially in London – talking your native cockney, wearing the latest gear, you could still be brought up short any time of the day by someone shouting 'Paki' . . . (p. 136)

Ruth Thomas follows a similarly inclusive policy; in *The Runaways* (1988), there is almost no mention that the boy is black, and in *Hideaway* (1994) the most apparent aspect of Leah's racial identity is her picture on the cover of the book; it has little to do with the plot though something perhaps to do with her characterization.

Perhaps the most significant aspect about the treatment of race in Michael Rosen's *This is our House* (1996), illustrated by Bob Graham, is the fact that it is not explicitly mentioned at all. The simple story is about a white child, George, having a game in which he takes possession of a cardboard box and denies any of his friends entrance, claiming, 'This house is all for me'. He says in turn that the house isn't for girls, it isn't for small people, it isn't for twins, it isn't for people with glasses and it isn't for people who like tunnels. Though three of the eight children who are denied entrance are black, no mention is made of their colour as a reason for their exclusion; this may be because race is a sensitive area, or because such a mention is best left to the teacher of the very young children who are the implied audience.

Alternatively, the implication may be that we are now so aware of race that it doesn't need an explicit mention, but I think it is one of those situations where the omission is more powerful than the inclusion would have been – the multi-ethnic nature of our society can be taken as a given. Naturally, the other children eventually take possession of George's house and at first exclude him, on the grounds that he has red hair, but he notices that this is also true of one of them and the concluding words of the book are: 'This house is for everyone!'

In Britain today, not only is society itself mixed, but many people come from a fairly mixed family background. This has always been the case, with the mingling of Anglo-Saxons and Normans, the Irish, the Jewish, and people from a variety of European inheritances, but it is now more evident. Cognisance is taken of this fact, and especially of marriages between people of different ethnic origins, in a number of children's books. Among a number of picture books which present this situation without drawing any explicit attention to it are three books by Eileen Browne and Tony Bradman (1986, 1988, 1990) about Jo, with a black mother and white father, a parental situation which is reversed for Billy and Belle in Sarah Garland's book by that name (1992). Verna Wilkins (1995) and Beverley Naidoo (1994) (see also Chapter 8) add the incidental depiction of mixed race parentage to their books featuring another equality issue, disability.

Race as an incidental aspect rather than the main focus is a characteristic of many books where a leading or otherwise significant character is black. *When I Grow Bigger* (1994), by Trish Cooke, illustrated by John Bendall-Brunello, features Thomas, a black infant whose father has been left in charge of him and three older children, two white and one black, while he would clearly prefer to concentrate on the gardening. Thomas's frustration at being small is eventually replaced by joy at being exalted to his father's shoulders from where he can look down on the other children. This is a very simple story in which the colour of the protagonist is in no way integral to the plot, yet where the art work makes the reader at the same time very aware of Thomas's ethnic identity and empathetic to his plight as the smallest.

Malorie Blackman's *Hacker* (1992) has a black protagonist who is considerably more in charge of her fate than Thomas is. A book like this, while doing relatively little to maintain any distinct racial identity, at least maintains visibility and gives an opportunity for black children to feel present in the text. Blackman is writing out of her own experience as a systems analyst, and some readers may feel a little uncertain what Vicky, the narrator, needs to do with the computer to prove that her father is innocent of stealing a million pounds, but we know it is something very clever of which no males, black or white, would be capable. Blackman would seem to be choosing to write about characters who are familiar to her and share her own British Afro-Caribbean background; her books mark the welcome arrival on the scene of reader-friendly writing by black women authors without going out of her way to feature race.

A more ambiguous example of a book with a leading black character without any explicit notice of her colour being taken in the text, is Gareth Owen's *Ruby and the Dragon* (1990), illustrated by Bob Wilson, and presented in a comic book format. Ruby, a black girl who is always late for school, wants a part in the school play; she is rejected for the role of the princess, as the dress does not fit her, and for the prince, because the helmet is too big, but is left playing the dragon. On the night of the performance, she loses her way to the stage and accidentally disturbs two burglars in the headmaster's office; they are somewhat improbably terrified of the dragon. Ruby at last makes her way to the performance, and the audience are surprised to witness crossing the stage in turn, the two fleeing burglars, a police-man who has swiftly been summoned, the school caretaker, and Ruby as the dragon. Against the play-script, Ruby defeats the prince, and finally is applauded, not only for saving the school valuables, but also for making the play more interesting.

My reactions to this text are ambivalent; on the one hand, it portrays a central black female character, who has a distinctive personality and triumphs at the end. On the other hand, however, it goes some way towards having Ruby fulfil some of the stereotypes attributed to black people by racists: she is always late, and she really isn't very bright, defeating the robbers and changing the play by accident rather than design. Yet a further reaction is to re-examine the situation; perhaps the portrayal of black characters has by now advanced to the stage that we can forget about trying to reverse passive, unheroic, roles, and instead, rejoice in the farcical comedy which is provided by a character who is only incidentally black.

There seems to be within this text the possibility of what has been termed 'nego-tiated' reading (cf. Cherland, 1994, p. 166); children (of any colour and either sex) who have been less successful in the educational process and feel that they will never triumph by cleverness might well empathize with Ruby's accident-prone and lively personality, whether or not this is the intention of the authors. The format of the book has probably been chosen to appeal to older children who may find read-ing conventional text difficult but are more confident with the different kinds of demands placed by a story being told in pictures, speech bubbles and occasional sub-picture narrative – demands which 'mainstream' readers often find taxing.

Political aspects of children's texts

Any imposition of categories on to fiction is bound to be arbitrary, and there is a fairly thin dividing line between some of the books considered above and those which could be described as having a more explicit political agenda. Such books often explore the relationship between the characters and the opposing or disempowering aspects of society. In some instances these books are set in the past, or within countries other than Britain – in places and periods where it is not so easy to regard the situation of the characters separately from society as a whole.

Even books for young children can display an awareness of the potential for clashes between people of different backgrounds. Without any of the explicit didacticism of *Black like Kyra* (see above), Mary Hoffman's *Amazing Grace* (1991) (discussed in Chapter 5) and Rosa Guy's *Billy the Great* (1991) (both illustrated by Caroline Binch) openly confront potential tensions. Billy's family live next door to a bigger boy, Rod, and his father. Billy's mother tells him: 'I don't want you to go to that boy's house again . . . He's too big for you to play with. Besides, his father has tattoos.' To the adult reader, the tattoo may serve as a signifier of possible racial hostility, but the tension only becomes overt when Billy's father accidentally kicks a football through the neighbour's window. 'Rod's father came out. He shouted at Dad. Rod's father was big and broad, and he had tattoos. "Don't shout at me," Dad said.' The dangerous situation is defused by the boys jointly playing at handstands and cartwheels.

This is an instance of a text which is likely to be read differently by adults and children, the former supplying so much of their experience of the kind of quarrel between neighbours which is rooted in both racism and mutual antipathy. The adult mediating the text to the child has the opportunity to supply as much or as little of this subtext as seems appropriate.

Jamila Gavin, herself of mixed British and Asian parentage, is adept at portraying contact, friendly and unfriendly, between people of different cultural background. In 'My name is Jasmine Grey', a story in her collection, *I want to be an Angel* (1990), the friendship between two young girls is threatened by the racist attitude of Rachel's grandmother, to the extent that Jasmine says, 'I wish I was white'. Rachel, however, reveals that her friendship transcends both this and the unpleasant behaviour of some other children. Finally the dog, Bramble, which has already been used by Gavin as a means of making this adopted character feel at home in her new family, becomes a sign of the restored friendship when Rachel finds the dog and restores him to Jasmine.

Nothing is quite so easy for the characters in Rukshana Smith's *Sumitra's Story* (1982) and *Salt on the Snow* (1988), books in which the tensions between British and Asian values and expectations are exposed in each case through the perceptions of a female character. Julie, in the later book, tries to befriend and teach English to an older Asian woman, Rashmi, who is virtually a prisoner in her brother's house. The prejudices and lack of comprehension on both sides are exposed; even if none of the Indian characters are as nasty as Julie's brother and his friends of the 'Pure Briton' party, Rashmi's brother is just as hostile to the friendship between his nephew, Vijay, and Julie. The style of the book is restrained, but the effect of the clusters of images associated with on the one hand blood (minor cuts, blood oozing from a frozen joint of meat) and on the other cold (lack of heating, wetness, snow) culminating in the violent scene where the injured Vijay is staggering through the snow, is powerful. It reinforces the sense of a lack of hope of understanding between the disparate cultures: blood associates with the myths of nationalism espoused by Julie's brother, and with the strong familial emphasis of Rashmi's people, while cold strengthens the sense that the Indian family have come to a hostile setting. There are no easy resolutions here, and though the outcome of the relationship between Julie and Vijay is left open, the final impression is a negative one.

Books which depict a setting overseas, in India, Africa, or the Caribbean, may run the risk of giving the impression to the indigenous reader that these countries are purely rural, without cities and the familiar elements of 'civilization'. On the other hand, to minimize the differences, and indeed the attractive qualities, of such environments may be equally falsifying. Eileen Browne's *Handa's Surprise* (1994), despite its artistic merits, might possibly be seen to sustain the stereotype that Africa is made up only of villages with thatched huts. This need not be a problem, provided it is discussed within a broader overall context. The story about the little girl, Handa, whose intended gift to her friend of a variety of fruits is changed, through the agency of a series of animals, to an abundance of Akeyo's favourite fruit, the tangerine, is both amusing and informative, and gives ample opportunity for prediction and playing with text and ideas. Despite the unfamiliar setting, it is easy for the child reader to empathize with the title character, and the colourful illustrations, based on a trip to Kenya by the author/ illustrator, are particularly attractive.

A number of recent books explore the effect on children brought up in England of the experience of going to the country of their parents' origin. The title story of Farroukh Dhondy's collection, *East End at your Feet* (1967) is about Kashyap, who has been uprooted from being a passionate supporter of West Ham, to Bombay, where he feels he does not belong. The eponymous character of Caroline Binch's *Gregory Cool* (1994) is equally unhappy with his initial impressions of his grandparents' home in Tobago; it is too hot, the food is too spicy, and unfamiliar insects bite him, so he consoles himself with a video game, until at last he begins to appreciate the advantages of the warm sea and the coconuts, and the friendship of his cousin.

The family situation in Mary Hoffman's *Grace and Family* (1995, illustrated by Caroline Binch) is more complex, and provides another instance of how a book may, without being didactic, help to make chldren aware of a number of difficult issues. Grace's mother and grandmother live in England, but her father, who has married again, invites her to holiday in The Gambia, so that the book examines Grace's unfamiliarity with Africa, her anxiety about her step-mother which results from her knowledge of so many fairytales with evil step-parents, and her search for her own identity within her divided family. Advised again by her wise grandmother, she concludes that families do not have to follow a specific pattern: '"Stories are just what you make them," said Nana. "Just like families," said Grace.'

A similar realization that she belongs in both places is the culmination of a longer and more complex book, *Comfort Herself* (1984) by Geraldine Kaye. The 11-year-old central character, Comfort, who has just lost her English mother, Margaret, goes to visit her father, Mante, in Ghana, but eventually returns to stay with her English grandparents, knowing that 'she was partly made of Mante and Margaret and Grandmother in Wanwangeri and Granny in Penfold, and partly of everything that had happened to her, but the rest was unique, *Comfort herself.*' (p. 159)

101

A desire to help children of African descent to be aware of their roots, and to inform all readers about differences in culture, seems to lie at the origin of Virginia Kroll's *Masai and I* (1992, illustrated by Nancy Carpenter); when she learns about East Africa, Linda thrills to the 'tingle of kinship flowing through my veins,' and throughout, the familiar rituals of western culture, like a birthday party and a car journey, are set against everyday life within a Masai village, culminating in her realization that she would look just the same and might even have the very similar name of Linde if she were indeed Masai.

Books like these, and the others named in the references to this chapter, are too complex to be crudely described as resulting from the impulse to be 'politically correct'. They show the child reader that societies all have different qualities, some of which might be difficult to cope with, others attractive, but that ultimately, people have to live within their own family and culture, while being aware of the many factors going towards the making of identity.

Relatively few books for young children could be termed truly 'political' in their engagement with society on a larger scale than the individual. One of those which could be so described is Reviva Schermbrucker's *Charlie's House* (1989, illustrated by Niki Daly) which without extraneous comment depicts the dreams of a small boy living in a crude and leaky shack in southern Africa. He uses clay and cardboard to construct a model of his dream house, which is furnished with objects such as a plastic bottle and a matchbox. In this house, there are marvellous things such as big rooms and he even has a bedroom to himself; at the end of the book he dreams himself driving a car past his very own house. The story is simple but revealing, in that Charlie's modelling activity is one which all children could empathize with, while the poverty of his real surroundings is worse than many of them would easily be able to imagine. No reasons are given for the extreme poverty, which gives scope for the adult to choose whether or not to explain it to the child.

Southern Africa is also the setting of Naidoo's two books about Naledi and her brother Tiro, *Journey to Jo'burg* (1985) and *Chain of Fire* (1989); the children live in a small village and are subject to the evils of apartheid, including forcible transportation to a 'homeland'. It could be argued that now this evil system has been abolished, there is no need for books about it, but apart from the desirable result of making children familiar with history and the still remaining effects of apartheid, the fact that totalitarian regimes still exist in many places means that children need to be educated about what people can do to each other. And this education is one which works best through the kind of identification which imaginative literature offers; as Naledi and Tiro make their 300 mile journey to seek their mother and tell her about the illness of their sister Duneo, we see through their innocent eyes the kind of servitude that their mother experiences. When she asks permission to go back home to attend to her sick daughter she is told, 'I hope you realize how inconvenient it will be for me. If you are not back in a week, I shall just have to look for another maid, you understand?' (p. 40). In both these books the reader is aware of strong female characters who take so much of the responsibility in a society where the men are often absent, in a way similar to Mildred Taylor's Southern America of the 1930s.

In Taylor's *Roll of Thunder, Hear my Cry* (1977; see also Chapters 2 and 5) the strongest agent against the falsification of history put out by the white establish-

102

ment is Cassie's mother, who loses her job as a teacher because she insists on teaching the true history of slavery. She is also responsible for encouraging other black residents to avoid the stores whose owners who exploit the blacks; instead they travel further for merchandise. In a way characteristic of black American writers, Taylor seems here to be uniting a feminist perspective with an anti-racist one, a stance which has been called 'womanist' in its refusal to separate the situation of women from the whole position of the group within society.

Rosa Guy also depicts strong women in her novels about Harlem, and through the education of her narrator, Phyllisia, in *The Friends* (1974) (see also Chapter 5) reveals how the deprivation imposed by society leads people like the narrator's father, Calvin, to a position where he cannot understand the situation of his own daughters or, indeed, be adequately responsive to the needs of his dying wife.

Fantasy and folk tale

In view of the power of fantasy for transcending boundaries and helping readers to experience situations which are otherwise totally unfamiliar, it is surprising how relatively little use is made of it as a means to showing the triviality of some of the apparent differences between people. A number of illustrators, however, manage effectively to convey in pictures what might be less easy to say only in words. Colin McNaughton's *Have You Seen Who's Just Moved in Next Door to Us?* (1993) touches in an anarchic way on the sensitive topic of unsatisfactory neighbours. We are shown, in verse and picture, some of the extraordinary characters who live in 'our street' ranging from pirates to King Kong and a dinosaur, and the reader's attention is held by the suspense – given how strange the inhabitants of the street already are, how can any new arrival be unacceptable? At last we discover that the people who have just moved in are a very ordinary looking family of parents, two children, a cat and a dog; these are the people that the narrator, who is finally disclosed to be a vampire, finds it impossible to have as neighbours. This is surely an extreme instance of the unreliable narrator!

The realization that what is ordinary to us may be very strange to someone else, also pervades one of the classics of this genre, June Counsell's *But Martin* (1984, illustrated by Carolyn Dinan). Four children are described in words but more vividly portrayed in pictures: 'Lee's face was smooth and golden. Lloyd's face was round and brown. Billy's face was square and red. And Angela's face was long and white but Martin's face was . . .'; we have to turn the page to find that he is green, a Martian with antennae, who is on holiday and whose appearance goes some way towards minimizing the antagonism which might be generated by any earthly ethnic diversity. As an entertaining experience this book needs no explicit teaching to bring out its message. Elaine Sturman, in a review in *Dragon's Teeth* (Summer, 1987, no. 27) however criticizes the book as simplistic, though well-meaning, as she feels it implies that 'physical characteristics are irrelevant', which can hardly be the case if Counsel makes them so apparent; she also claims that the school which the four human children attend is otherwise all-white, a conjecture for which the book seems to me to provide no foundation whatever. This is another unfortunate instance of critics being all too ready to fault material which, if not perfect, is at least very positive in its impact on most child readers.

Although less focused on the unity of the human race, the popular *Dr Xargle* series, by Jeanne Willis and Tony Ross, also makes clear how much human beings have in common. The series of lectures given by Dr Xargle to his multi-brained students show how he totally misinterprets human behaviour:

> To stop water getting into their one small brain they carry material on a pointed stick with sharp prongs. This is a dangerous weapon. Sometimes it attacks its owner. When many brollies get together they always go for the eyes. (Willis and Ross, 1992)

There is a good deal of intertextuality, some of which is likely only to be accessible to the adult, for instance, 'Mad earthhounds and earthlings go out in the mid-day sun'. This technique provides a range of levels of meanings for the adult and the child reader; what draws both together is the element of humour.

An area of fantasy which is also quite productive in helping children to appreciate that differences are often attractive is that involved with animals. David McKee is one of the most effective users of fantasy involving animals, frequently elephants; while his books can be read simply as beautifully illustrated stories, they have further meanings, amply supported by the extra readings demanded by the pictures. In *Tusk Tusk* (1978), the black and the white elephants hate and try to kill each other (Figure 4), but the peace-loving elephants retreat into the jungle, their grey descendants emerging after all the hostile elephants (a trunk makes an effective gun) are dead. There is no sentimental ending, however; after 'Since then the elephants have lived in peace' we have the potential shock of 'But recently the little ears and the big ears have been giving each other strange looks.'

Whether the idea that even those who seem attached to peace have the potential for hostility is understood by child readers will depend on their own maturity and experience. The final picture of elephants shaking trunks, however, defuses any totally negative final impression. Like any good fantasy, this book can be taken at any level appropriate to the reader; there is no explicit didacticism but it works at a deeper level, aided by the natural interest most children have in elephants.

Other books by McKee also feature elephants; *Elmer the Patchwork Elephant* (1989) shows how Elmer's difference from the ordinary grey animals, which embarrasses him so much that he wants to change it, is an asset rather than a liability. This conclusion has wider implications than simply ethnic difference.

I have found less use of this kind of fantasy in books for older children. George Goodwin's *There Ain't no Angels no More* (1978) presents an idyllic picture of the transformation of a street in which the inhabitants find it difficult to tolerate each other into a beautiful environment where everyone is at peace, but at the end it is disclosed that this is only a dream, a slightly dispiriting conclusion.

Folk tales from a variety of sources have been among a rich vein of material presenting unfamiliar places in an imaginative way. As long as children realize that stories like these are not presenting the reality of life as lived today, this legacy can be of considerable value to everyone. Verna Aardema's *Bimwili and the Zimwi* (1985, illustrated by Susan Meddaugh), a tale from Zanzibar, tells the story of the escape of an enterprising young girl from an evil old magician. Because of its distance from everyday reality, it also has the advantage of treating the potentially sensitive theme of 'stranger danger' safely and in a non-didactic way. Stories like

Figure 4 Elephants at war. Reproduced with permission from *Tusk Tusk* by David McKee, published by Anderson Press, London.

this are also very suitable for adaptation for acting (see Joan Anim-Addo's chapter on Drama in Pinsent, 1992).

As we have seen in looking at gender, new stories using traditional material can often provide a very attractive way of treating contemporary issues. Jacqui Farley's *Giant Hiccups* (1994, illustrated by Pamela Venus) has an unusual heroine, a friendly black female giant with indigestion; her troubles are ended by the provision of a meal by a multi-racial group of children. Here we have an example of the strength of the picture book in this area. The written text by itself would not reveal the multi-ethnic nature of this story, though the unusual gender of the giant is of course apparent. Part of the success of this story depends on the mixed feelings with which any young reader confronts the idea of a giant; enormous size could prove dangerous, yet fairytales also abound in friendly giants. This giant, Ayesha, enjoys making cups and plates, pots and pans, rainbow lollipops and pineapple jam – an interesting combination of objects which might be expected from a female with others which are less conventional. She is prepared to listen to the children's suggestions, and finally shares her meal with them. The reader is left with the expectation that her relationship with the villagers will be closer hereafter.

Conclusion

It is interesting to examine the ways in which the books which have been considered portray individuals in relation to their community. My impression is that the fiction which I have described as 'anti-racist' tends particularly to focus on one or two individuals who are at least for a time alienated from their community. Timothy and Phillip of *The Cay* have been shipwrecked, Jessie in *The Slave Dancer* abducted, and Donovan and Keith in *The Trouble with Donovan Croft* are isolated by the effect of the black boy's inability to speak. This alienation enables the authors to focus on racist attitudes in a way which a fully rounded portrayal of society would not allow. In some instances, the resolution of the book is achieved with the inclusion of the potentially marginalized individual into the community, as in *Elmer*, *Billy the Great*, and *Giant Hiccups*.

By contrast, the communities portrayed by Shirley Hughes, Michael Rosen, Eileen Browne and Tony Bradman and others are inclusive ones, leaving the impression that in this kind of group where colour seems merely incidental, there are no outsiders other than those, like George in *This is our House*, who temporarily cut themselves off from the community.

In those books which seek to put racism into a political context, however, the central characters tend to be very much part of *their* community but that group is often marginalized by society as a whole. This is particularly evident in Mildred Taylor's work. In Rukshana Smith's novels, there is a sense that the love between Vijay and Julie, in a kind of modern *Romeo and Juliet* story, separates them to some extent from their families, but that they are rather a focus for the consideration of society's attitudes rather than being individually marginalized.

One impression which comes over powerfully from examining this wide and varied range of books is that today there is an abundance of really good literature that represents all people as valuable, and carries the conviction that no one should be undervalued because of differences from the majority ethnic group. There needs no explicit didacticism to convey a meaning which has the potential to liberate its child readers. This happy situation is the result of the work particularly of a number of gifted authors and illustrators. These people include both white and black writers and artists, such as Mary Hoffman, Caroline Binch, Rosa Guy, Mildred Taylor, Trish Cooke, Jamila Gavin, Beverley Naidoo, Bernard Ashley, Malorie Blackman, Geraldine Kaye, Eileen Browne, Jennifer Northway, Verna Wilkins, Petra Rohr-Rouendaal and many more.

It has become apparent firstly that a number of people from ethnic minority groups have been attracted to this form of writing; and secondly, that there should be no exclusiveness. If there were, we might have lost the contributions of, for instance, Mary Hoffman, Eileen Browne and Helen Oxenbury. Political awareness, if it leads people to portray material which is important to them, can result in the production of first-rate books for children. These need not and should not be only crudely anti-racist. What is needed is an integrated attitude which respects the appearance and the traditions of all people; this means that anyone who shares these ideals, who makes the effort to become well informed, and has the ability to write or illustrate well, should not hesitate about making their contribution to this genre.

References

Note that an extensive bibliography is also given at the end of this book. Picture books are marked with an asterisk. In most cases, date and publisher are those of first British publication. In some instances, American publication may precede this.

1. Books including substantial elements explicitly countering racist attitudes

Armstrong, W. H. (1971) *Sounder*. London: Gollancz.

Ashley, B. (1974) *The Trouble with Donovan Croft*. Oxford: University Press.

Fox, P. (1973,1979) *The Slave Dancer*. Basingstoke: Macmillan.

Kumar, A. (1988) *The Heartstone Odyssey*. London: Allied Mouse.

Taylor, T. (1970) *The Cay*. London: Bodley Head.

Taylor, T. (1993) *Timothy of the Cay*. Harmondsworth: Penguin.

Vigna, J. (1992) *Black like Kyra, White like me**. Illinois: Whitman.

Westall, R. (1992) *Gulf*. London: Methuen

2. Books including black characters without giving their colour a particular focus

Ahlberg, A. and Ahlberg, J. (1982) *The Baby's Catalogue**. London: Kestrel.

Ashley, B. (1986) *Running Scared*. Harmondsworth: Penguin.

Bawden, N. (1978) *Rebel on a Rock*. London: Gollancz.

Blackman, M. (1992) *Girl Wonder's Winter Adventures*. London: Gollancz.

Blackman, M. (1992a) *Hacker*. London: Transworld.

Blackman, M. (1992b) *Betsey Biggalow is Here!* London: Piccadilly.

Browne, E. and Bradman, T. (1986) *Through my Window**. London: Methuen.

Browne, E. and Bradman, T. (1988) *Wait and See**. London: Methuen.

Browne, E. and Bradman, T. (1990) *In a Minute**. London: Methuen.

Cameron, A. (1989) *Julian, Secret Agent*. London: Gollancz.

Cooke, T. (1994) *When I grow Bigger**. London: Walker.

Cooper, S. (1983) *Seaward*. London: Bodley Head.

Dale, P. (1987) *Bet you Can't**. London: Walker.

Dharmi, N. (1990) *A Medal for Malina*. London: Hamish Hamilton.

Garland, S. (1992) *Billy and Belle**. London: Reinhardt.

Gavin, J. (1993) *Grandpa Chatterji*. London: Methuen.

Hughes, S. (1988) *The Big Alfie and Annie Rose Storybook**. London: Bodley Head.

Jarman, J. (1994) *The Jessame Stories*. London: Heinemann.

Joy, M. (1983) *Tales from Allotment Lane School*. London: Faber.

MacGibbon, J. (1974) *Hal*. London: Heinemann.

Naidoo, B. (1994) (Illustrated by Petra Rohr-Rouendaal) *Letang's New Friend**. *Trouble for Letang and Julie**, *Letang and Julie save the Day**. London: Longman.

Northway, J. (1991) *Lucy's Day Trip**. London: Deutsch.

Northway, J. (1993) *Get Lost Laura**. London: Scholastic.

Owen, (1990) *Ruby and the Dragon**. London: Collins.

Pirotta, S. (1989) *Solomon's Secret**. London: Methuen.

Rosen, M. (1996) (Illustrated by Bob Grahame) *This is our House**. London: Walker*.

Simeon, L. (1992) (Illustrated by Petra Rohr-Rouendaal) *Marcellus' Birthday Cake**. London: Mantra.

Thomas, I. (1990) *Princess Janine**. London: Deutsch.

Thomas, R. (1988) *The Runaways*. London: Beaver.

Thomas, R. (1994) *Hideaway*. London: Random House.

Wilkins, V. (1995) *Boots for a Bridesmaid*. Tamarind.

Wills, J. (1992) *The Pop Concert*. London: Andersen.

3. Wider aspects

Binch, C. (1994) *Gregory Cool**. London: Frances Lincoln.

Browne, E. (1994)*Handa's Surprise**. London: Walker.

Cooke, T. (1994) (Illustrated by Helen Oxenbury) *So Much**. London: Walker.

Desai, A. (1982) *The Village by the Sea*. London: Heinemann.

Dhondy, F. (1976) *East End at Your Feet*. Basingstoke: Macmillan.

Gavin, J. (1990) *I Want to be an Angel*. London: Methuen.

Gavin, J. (1983) *Kamla and Kate*. London: Methuen.

Guy, R. (1991)(illustrated by Caroline Binch) *Billy the Great**. London: Gollancz.

Guy, R. (1974) *The Friends*. London: Gollancz.

Guy, R. (1984) *Paris, Pee-wee and Big Dog*. London: Gollancz.

Hoffman, M. (1991) (Illustrated by Caroline Binch) *Amazing Grace**. London: Frances Lincoln.

Hoffman, M. (1995) (Illustrated by Caroline Binch) *Grace and Family**. London: Frances Lincoln.

Kaye, G. (1984) *Comfort Herself*. London: Deutsch.

Kroll, V. (1993) *Masai and I**. London: Hamish Hamilton.

Naidoo, B. (1985) *Journey to Jo'Burg*. London: Longmans.

Naidoo, B. (1989) *Chain of Fire*. London: HarperCollins.

Paulsen, G. (1994) *Nightjohn*. Basingstoke: Macmillan.

Schermbrucker, R. (1991) *Charlie's House**. London: Walker.

Smith, N. (1990) *Imran's Secret*. London: Julia MacRae.

Smith, R. (1982) *Sumitra's Story*. Basingstoke: Macmillan.

Smith, R. (1988) *Salt on the Snow*. London: Bodley Head.

Taylor, M. (1977) *Roll of Thunder, Hear my Cry*. London: Gollancz.

Walker, A. (1983) *The Color Purple*. London: The Women's Press.

4. Fantasy and animal stories, etc

Aardema, V. (1985) *Bimwili and the Zimri**. Basingstoke: Macmillan.

Burningham, J. (1970) *Mr Gumpy's Outing**. London: Cape.

Cannon, J. (1995) *Stellaluna**. St. Albans: David Bennett.

Counsell, J. (1984) (Illustrated by C. Dinan) *But Martin**. London: Faber.

Farley, J. (1994) *Giant Hiccups**. London: Tamarind.

Goodwin, G. (1978) *There Ain't no Angels no More*. London: Collins.

Lacy, S. (1990) *Bubblegum Magic*. London: Methuen.

McKee, D. (1978) *Tusk Tusk**. London: Andersen.

McKee, D. (1989) *Elmer**. London: Andersen.

McKissack, P. (1987) *Flossie and the Fox**. Harmondsworth: Penguin.

McNaughton, C. (1993) *Have you Seen who's just Moved in Next Door to Us?** London: Walker.

Rutnett, M. (1994) *Jessica Harriet's New Neighbours**. London: Hutchinson.

Willis, J.and Ross, T. (1992) *Dr Xargle's Book of Earth Weather**. London: Andersen.

Literature, Language and Culture

No child should be expected to cast off the language and culture of the home as he crosses the school threshold, nor to live and act as though school and home represent two totally separate and different cultures which have to be kept firmly apart. (Bullock, *A Language for Life*, HMSO, 1975, p. 286)

'Foreign' languages and cultures

The books discussed in the preceding chapter have in common a focus on racial differences; some of them seem to have as their implicit ideology the belief that 'we're all the same under the skin', while others, taking a more overtly political stance, are concerned primarily with rights, taking equality as a given. While such books cannot and do not ignore language and culture, these factors do not in general receive the same degree of attention as is given to them in the books discussed in this chapter. Unlike most of the literature which has been considered so far, many of these deal with the experience of children who have not been born in the country in which the book is set; sometimes they have come as refugees or economic immigrants. These books therefore inevitably raise the question of the 'alien' – a person or group who possesses a culture felt by the 'mainstream' to be 'foreign', or who speaks a language which is literally foreign to them. Inevitably many of the books considered here also have 'black' characters, but that aspect is not the main focus of my discussion.

Language and culture are almost impossible to separate, since the values of any group are inevitably strongly associated with the way they speak about these values. In practice it is often more difficult for the indigenous population to accept divergences in these areas, since there appears to be a greater element of choice; aliens can, after all, adopt the culture of the indigenous group and learn the language, so that if they have chosen not to do one or other of these things, it can seem like rejection, not doing 'when in Rome as the Romans do!' The fact that culture is very often associated with religion can also seem threatening; Muslims, Hindus, Sikhs and others, even if born in a Western country, have a different set of beliefs which may lead to different values and practices. What is often even more disturbing for the 'mainstream' population is the situation of minority groups which have lived in the country for many years yet still possess values which challenge its social mores, as in the case of Travellers and Gypsies, and, in the USA, those Native or First Americans who are particularly attached to their traditional customs.

'Official' attitudes on the subject of language and culture, as far as they exist, may be defined as:

1. People are free to adhere to their own religious and cultural values, as long as these do not infringe the rights of anyone else.
2. People should have the freedom to speak their own language; children with a different mother tongue from English should not lose the opportunity to become competent in it. All languages are of value.

Such 'enlightened' attitudes are sometimes regarded as 'politically correct' and greeted with antagonism or scepticism by some sections of the population. But even those who would on the whole pay lip-service to them may sometimes find themselves ill at ease when clashes occur, as for instance when sentiments about animals are brought into conflict with Kosher or Halal ritual slaughter practices. Many people, at a level where they are scarcely conscious of the fact, probably have a feeling that it would be better if 'good, sound, English (or American) middle-class values' were possessed by everyone.

Linguistic orthodoxy about young children being encouraged or allowed to speak their first language is also difficult for many English-speaking people to accept. Many non-English speaking parents, who want their children to grow up fluent in English, also find this policy unattractive; as a result, quite often the parents prefer to speak imperfect English at home rather than, for instance, good Urdu or Turkish. (See Pinsent, 1992, for a discussion of some of the factors concerned.)

Learning our language and culture

The school is one of the main agents of enculturation for children from abroad; it is also the place where they are going to need to acquire English both to learn there and in due course to function actively in society. Inevitably it is a place where conflicts are going to arise. In recent years there have been a number of books which have represented the encounter between the expectations of the educational system and the experiences of children who have come into it speaking little or no English. Such books, while they are probably in the first instance written because the author is interested in and concerned about the children, have often been published, and bought and used by schools, to help first language English readers understand the problems facing the child whose parents are refugees from war or poverty. As such children become more competent in English, they too may find these books helpful, as they assist the children to come to terms with their own situation.

It seems certain that the authors of the books I shall go on to consider are very well intentioned, and have an explicit ideology of wanting to represent the children described as equal in value with any others in the schools. In analysing these and other books, however, it seems that they often fall into the trap of representing not only our language but also our culture as what everyone needs to acquire. This kind of view may well be held subconsciously by some of the authors, but in any case ideas of the superiority of the English language are so much bound up in our culture that it is difficult for even the best intentioned writer to avoid them.

In chronological order, the books to be considered here are: *Tough Luck* (1987) by Berlie Doherty; *Kiss the Dust* (1991) by Elizabeth Laird; a short story, 'Deadly

Letter' by Mary Hoffman, in her collection, *Ip Dip Sky Blue* (1992); *Lost for Words* (1993) by Elizabeth Lutzeier and *Jazeera's Journey* (1993) by Lisa Bruce. A fuller account of issues concerned with these books is given in my paper, 'We Speak English in this School' (1994). All of these books have in common the fact that the young girls who are the central characters need both to learn to speak English and also to become part of a group from which they are isolated by both their language and their unfamiliarity with their schoolmates' customs.

The language aspect is of course particularly important; several of these authors show their awareness of the pain caused to an articulate young person by being unable to communicate. In *Kiss the Dust*, Tara, a Kurdish girl, has already had 3 months of intensive English, but is still terrified the day before she is due to start at an English school:

> She hadn't slept a wink all night. She'd had terrible dreams of stern teachers demanding crossly why she couldn't understand, why her English was so full of mistakes, why she seemed to have forgotten all the Maths and Science she'd ever been taught. (p. 265)

In fact, once she arrives in school, she has more difficulties with the informal atmosphere in the classroom than with the language.

The plight of a child in this kind of situation is perhaps most effectively evoked in *Lost for Words*; Aysha, an intelligent, very articulate girl from Bangla Desh, is labelled in two schools with the words, 'No Language' on her form, and is frustrated because she would like to talk to schoolmates:

> All the words she had ever known, all the jokes she had ever told, had been taken away from her. In Jamdher, everyone had talked of how clever she was and how she was bound to bring honour to her family by doing well at school. In London, they treated her with pity, as if she could neither hear nor speak. (p. 54)

One of the first things the girls concerned do is to look for friends; Tara is anxious to discover whether the girl she is sitting next to is a Moslem, and Aysha, who has been placed in too low a class because her ability has not been recognized, is assisted by the concern of a less able girl from this class. Despite the reader's realization that the immigrant girls are clever, it is difficult not to see them as victims. Although Tara and Aysha are shown to possess a high degree of resolution, the message that is conveyed is one of weakness rather than strength; the books seem to be directed mostly towards first language English speakers to help them to recognize the plight of such children.

In *Tough Luck*, based on Doherty's experience as a resident writer in a Yorkshire comprehensive school, the sense of the 13-year-old Pakistani girl, Nasim, being a victim, is even greater. There is a vivid picture of her sense of isolation as the rest of the class ridicule her attempts to speak English:

> 'In school I must only have vegables.'
> 'Vegables!' Susan snorted. 'Vebbagles. Vlebbiges!'
> 'Quiet!' snapped Miss Peters. 'Vegetables, Nasim.'
> 'Yes, Miss. Vebbles. Vebbles.' Bubbles of laughter broke out again. Nasim smiled round at them. (p. 69)

The effect of this kind of parodic interchange is much greater than the brief moment of admiration which is allowed when Nasim admits that she knows three languages as well as English (p. 109). Her displacement and powerlessness are emotively conveyed; scarcely has she begun to settle down in the unfamiliar surroundings of the school than she is summoned back home to get married.

It is clear that all these writers are strongly advocating tolerance from both pupils and teachers for those who do not speak English nor understand the customs. One of the most memorable scenes in *Lost for Words* is near the end (pp. 141–44) when an inexperienced teacher, the ironically named Miss Power, reacts against a few words in Bengali spoken by Aysha, although by this time the girl actually speaks English well:

> 'We speak English in this school.' The new teacher's voice cracked and splintered, like a ruler breaking as it hits the desk. She tried again, speaking more quietly this time because the class was quiet. 'We speak English or we shut up . . .' (p. 142)

When, later, Miss Power speaks directly to Aysha, she speaks more loudly, and 'cut a space round each word as if she were using a fine pair of scissors to cut out a very delicate paper chain.' The description of this incident displays the anxiety of the teacher; we are told that: 'She had just finished her training course and no one had told her what to say to a pupil who couldn't speak English' (p. 142). Even more effectively, the images evoke a sense of both sharpness and fragmentation, and provide insight into the states of mind of both pupil and teacher, the latter both feeling and generating a sense of hostility. The result of the incident is to inspire Aysha to declare before the class her intentions for her future: 'I'm going to be a doctor' (p. 144), but although this could be seen as a triumph for the girl, it is secondary to Lutzeier's determination to display the inadequacy of some teachers' responses to non-English speaking children. It is, however, unlikely that such a situation would in fact happen today in English schools; although funds for support for non-English speaking children may be diminishing, few or no newly qualified teachers would be left to flounder in Miss Power's position.

While it is indeed desirable that the indigenous population be made aware of the needs of immigrant and refugee children, it is surely also important that books which refer to their plight should make obvious their strengths. One book which attempts to do this is *Jazeera's Journey*, the story of an Indian girl who comes to England with her parents; it is partly told in letters written to her grandmother in India, and partly in a third person narrative. The author's desires to remove certain misapprehensions (for instance, that all Indians are poor) and to counter racism, are apparent; the explicit ideology behind the book seems to be that children from other countries are as intelligent and even as middle class as those from England, that there is more in common between people of different races than divides them, and that old people have wisdom and often communicate better with the young than their own parents do.

But the central incident which allows Jazeera's classmates to appreciate her quality also suggests that Bruce's criteria are very Eurocentric. When a pianist is needed for the school concert, Jazeera, who has had piano lessons in India, comes forward and convinces her teacher and classmates of her ability by playing Beethoven's 'Für Elise', a piece which she has been taught by her grandmother:

For a moment there was silence in the classroom as the last note faded away. Then Jazeera was jolted back to the present by thunderous applause. 'My word,' said Mr Foster grinning from ear to ear. 'We have a musical genius in Class 4.' (pp. 70–71)

There is nothing instrinsically improbable about an Indian girl being a competent pianist of Western music; Beethoven is the heritage of the whole world. I think, however, that the point would be better made if Jazeera were to convince everyone of her worth by something more culturally distinctive, and, perhaps, slightly less dependent on adults' values. Her classmates might have found a performance of Indian popular music more convincing! (An interesting account of this, by Punitha Perinparaja, occurs in *Dragon's Teeth*, Summer 1988, Issue 30, p. 8.)

In 'Deadly Letter', the corresponding 'acceptance ritual' is indeed at the level of the children rather than the adults, but it remains something from English culture rather than brought by the child from her home country. Prity, an Indian girl, is taught by Nosher, an older Asian boy, how to play a game enjoyed by all the children in her first English school. The confidence she gains from this helps her to settle into the school, but she soon has to move elsewhere. At her new school she is invited to play:

> 'Do you know any Indian games?' asked Lauren, trying to be friendly.
> 'Not really,' said Prity, grinning, 'but I learnt a good English one in Tottenham!'
> And soon all the first and second years in Canning Street's playground were playing Deadly Letter. (p. 21)

The implicit message seems to be that the way out of the trap is through sport; interestingly this seems to be a theme in several of these books and others on a similar theme. In both *Lost for Words* and *Tough Luck* the girls are anxious to have tracksuit trousers so that they can compete in school games, with some success in Aysha's case; and in another book treating linguistic isolation, Ian Strachan's *The Second Step* (1991), about a family of Vietnamese boat people in England, the central character Lee, frustrated at his difficulties in communication, seems to be due for brilliant success once it is discovered that he is a potential tennis star. It is clearly difficult to convey to young readers the concept of acceptance by the group, while retaining both credibility and something of the qualities of the characters' own culture.

In all these books the sense of lack of welcome is conveyed quite powerfully through the depiction of the physical surroundings. Rain and grey weather are often mentioned:

> November in London was colder and greyer than anything Aysha had ever known. (*Lost for Words*, p. 41)

> At half-term the sides of the street were still piled with grey snow. (*Tough Luck*, p. 91)

> If freezing winds and damp drizzle counted as 'mild', how was she going to bear the winter in this terrible country? ('Deadly Letter', p. 7)

> It is cold and miserable here. It always seems to be raining and we can't go outside. (*Jazeera's Journey*, p. 25)

Fortunately, as the characters become more settled in this country, the weather tends to improve!

Food is another aspect which is used metonymically to signify lack of welcome. Jazeera suffers from 'a white gooey sauce over a few lumps of tasteless chicken with lumpy mashed potatoes and boiled carrots' (pp. 38–39). Prity hopes that dinner will warm her up but can't eat much:

> There were things they called samosas but she couldn't recognize the shape or the taste of them; they were dry too, and the dinner lady served them with a dollop of mashed potato and some bright orange beans. ('Deadly Letter', p. 7)

These children at least fare better than Aysha in *Lost for Words* and Nasim in *Tough Luck* who don't even discover school dinners for several days. Once Nasim arrives at the school dining room, she isn't much better off:

> The room stank of cabbage and gravy . . . Nasim looked down at the plate of meat in front of her.
> 'Is it halal meat, please?' she asked.
> 'Never heard of that, love,' the dinner lady laughed. 'It's good mutton, that.'
> 'If not halal meat I can't eat.'
> 'Suit yourself . . .' (p. 52)

It is at least heartening to observe that in *Ip Dip Sky Blue*, published in 1992, some attempt, albeit not very appetizing, is being made to present non-English food, as against the situation depicted in the earlier book!

It would therefore appear that many of the authors who are making a real attempt to depict the experience of children newly arriving in English schools, fear that such children are not receiving a warm welcome from the schools, and that the attempt of the educational establishment to cater for them is not particularly well informed. In a way similar to that seen in the area of race, where authors often presume a white readership who need to accept guilt and responsibility, it seems here that the audience envisaged is the host community. This is fair, for as indicated earlier, many of the immigrant children are unlikely to be able to read these books until they have been in the country some time, and there is a need to educate other pupils into appropriate actions. It would seem equally important, however, to convey a sense that these children have something to give to the school culture – all too often what they are portrayed as offering is a version of Western culture rather than something distinctive which they bring with them.

It may be significant that two books which seem to create a rather fuller picture of the situation of immigrants lacking the language of the countries they are forced to live in are by writers who have a close involvement with the culture they are depicting. Joan Lingard's *Between Two Worlds* (1991) is based on the experiences of the family of her Latvian–Canadian husband during the second world war, and Gaye Hiçyilmaz's *The Frozen Waterfall* (1993) about the experience of a Turkish family in Switzerland, is supported by her own Turkish and Swiss experience. As a result, although the isolation of young people unable to speak the language is no less intensely conveyed, family values make at least as much impression, and a richer effect seems to be created than in the narrower focus of the books discussed above. Selda, the chief character of *The Frozen Waterfall*, expresses vehemently her feelings about being isolated from communication:

She felt so shut off from everybody else, so useless and helpless. It was like being struck dumb and then being praised for croaking. (p. 176)

This book also touches on the issue of barriers between cultures, particularly on matters of female dress, but the story gains an added depth by bringing in the theme of illegal immigration, and, perhaps because the setting is a small Swiss town rather than a large city, it is easier to become aware of the situation of the whole Turkish community and individual relationships within the family than in the books set in English cities.

Lingard's book is the sequel to *Tug of War* (1989), which describes the flight of the Peterson family from Latvia, and finally, their arrival in Canada. The later book, like Hiçyılmaz's, describes the struggle of all the family: at school, in work, and in particular in their relationships with the people around them. On his first day in school, Tomas embarrasses himself by saying, 'I am the new teacher', instead of 'pupil', but by the end of the book he is being trusted to help a new pupil who lacks English, and the whole family go out to see the plot of land they have bought on which they plan to build their new house. The symbolism of having settled into their new country is inescapable, and without implying that they have sacrificed any of their existing culture – the house will be in a forest like those back in Latvia – it suggests integration into their new society. The greater degree of conviction conveyed to the reader in the books by Lingard and Hiçyılmaz perhaps results from the fact that the problems faced by the immigrant families are ones which the authors, in their own family circles, must have talked about many times.

Cultures on the fringes of society

Most immigrant groups are usually only too anxious to fit into the pattern of education and work pursued by their neighbours. Problems about cultural differences are, however, often more acute with groups whose values are alien from mainstream society. The divergent standards of Gypsies and Travellers often reach the news, as their house dwelling neighbours find it difficult to understand non-mainstream attitudes to work and school. To do justice to both communities is not easy, especially as most writers have a natural sympathy with the settled group. All too often, writers of the past have shown a patronising approach; in *The Castle of Adventure* (1946) Enid Blyton (quoted by Dixon, 1986) depicts a little Gypsy girl, Tassie, as unwashed, and being 'more like a very intelligent animal than a little girl' (pp. 65–66). In the revised edition (1988), however, she has been transmuted to a 'wild girl' (p. 23) and lost the demeaning comparisons, though she is as dirty as ever.

More recent writers have tried with some success to be more tolerant, in accord with efforts which have been made by a number of councils (cf. Fran Duncan, in Pinsent, 1992). Geraldine Kaye's *Winter in Small Street* (1990) shows in a simple way for young children the difference between the attitudes to school of a little Gypsy girl, Minty, and her family, and those of the more settled community. Although she has no idea what it entails and her family cannot see the need, Minty goes to school, and is given the part of Mary in the Nativity Play; to the dismay of her classmates she is absent from rehearsals as her family leave the neighbourhood for a short period:

The last Friday of term was the Christmas play. Minty knew that quite well and she knew her words, too. So she was quite surprised when she got to school after dinner on Friday and everybody started shouting out, 'Minty's back, Minty's back.' They had been off getting holly for a week but the caravan was back on the empty space now and Ma and Reuben were busy selling bunches of holly with plenty of red berries up and down Small Street. (p. 31)

In this book, the divergent standards of the different groups are presented fairly, without any explicit authorial comment, nor, indeed, any indication of judgement from any authority figure such as the teacher. What has been termed by Bakhtin a polyphonic effect (cf. Chapter 2, and Lodge, 1990, p. 86) is attained; the reader is forced to admit that there are divergent discourses, both of which have good and bad aspects, and is left to make a judgement about the situation.

Much the same is also true of a short story, 'The Caravan People', in Nadya Smith's *Imran's Secret*, which depicts the awkward relationships between some members of a multi-ethnic class of children and the Travellers on a site near the school. A Sikh girl, Jaswinder, makes the connection between the racial abuse she has experienced from a neighbour, Mrs Green, and the way the same neighbour says unkind things about the children from the site. Without any over-explicit propaganda, Smith succeeds in showing that even if different standards obtain between people who live in houses and those who travel in caravans, there is much commonality. There is no sentimentality here; before any kind of friendly relationship is formed between the children and the Travellers, the latter have moved on, something very likely to happen in real life.

Another recent book which tries to do justice to such a different way of looking at life is Elizabeth Arnold's *The Parsley Parcel* (1995), which, through the reactions of a Romany child, Freya, shows some of the freedom of life which may be absent in our more organized world. As Arnold says in a postscript to her novel:

It would be a great loss to society if a culture that has existed so successfully, for so long, should be destroyed. (p. 199)

Books like these, which present material in a fair and interesting way, can go far to supporting such a wish.

The portrayal of the people variously termed 'Red Indian', 'Amerindian' or 'Native' or 'First' American has also in the past been subject to negative stereotyping, abhorrent to many writers today. The whole question of nomenclature is touched on several times in Sharon Creech's *Walk Two Moons* (1994), the main subject of which is a girl coming to terms with her mother's death. Sal recalls:

My mother especially liked Native American (she said 'Indian') stories. She knew legends from many tribes: Navaho, Sioux, Seneca, Nez Perce, Maidu, Blackfoot Huron. She knew about thunder gods, earth makers, wise crows, sly coyotes, and shadow souls . . . (p. 101)

It is apparent that Creech's refusal, here and elsewhere in this book, to use any of the 'politically correct' terms, does not arise from a lack of knowledge or sympathy. The generic use of 'Indian' could however cause confusion, particularly in England, and maybe the best way to avoid the kind of stereotyping which its overuse in a 'Cowboys and Indians' context has caused, is a knowledgeable employment of the names of the different groups.

This would of course demand much more information about groups and customs than is possessed by most British readers; a book which supplies this in attractive visual form is Susan Jeffer's *Brother Eagle, Sister Sky* (1992). Another way of dispelling prejudice is in Martin Waddell's and Philippe Dupasquier's *Going West* (1983). Through the eyes of a child, and using a cinematograph technique which depends as much on the pictures as on the text for details of the story, this book shows both the hardships of the settlers and the reasons the Indians had for disliking them. Again we have a polyphonic or dialogic narration, for although the child's voice is the only one heard as such in the text, she faithfully recounts what the adults say:

> Friendly Indians came to our camp. They told us that bad Indians are trailing Mr Crowe's wagons . . . We saw a dead Indian. Big Chokey says we stole the Indians' land. They don't like us. That is why they killed Mr Crowe . . .

Terms like 'friendly' and 'bad' in this passage are relativized to the child's consciousness, and though the situation is too complex to be fully explained in an ostensibly simple book with little written text, it is in no way either polarized into unshakable hostility between the factions, nor made so overtly political as to make the book over-didactic.

Andre Norton, a very prolific American science fiction writer for young people, has in her many books about the exploration of other planets consistently made use of her knowledge of Native American history and culture. Norton's family background includes Wyandot Indian, which may partly account for her desire to show how the closeness to nature of these native American people has a message for people today. Her tales of the exploration of other planets and the problems brought about by colonization also recall the early history of the 'West'. *Beastmaster* (Norton, 1959) portrays Hosteen Storm, one of the few Terran survivors from our planet, now destroyed, who is of Navajo stock. The reader inevitably empathizes with him, as his earthly origins make him the closest to us, and as a result, we are drawn to identification with his values such as closeness to nature, particularly animals, and his concern for the natives of the planet being colonized. These are the Norbies, humanoid in appearance apart from having horns on their heads. Norton's engagement with the issues of colonisation is remarked on by Margery Fisher (1967) who writes:

> the relationship with the 'good' range-riders reflects present-day thinking, not the attitudes of a century ago. It is as though our classic African stories had been re-written about an idealized Ghana or Tanzania.
>
> (*The School Librarian*, **15**(2), p. 40)

Similar values are propounded in *Fur Magic* (1968), where Norton uses Indian folktales to signify how a young boy, Cory, grows stronger and loses his fears as a result of being temporarily metamorphosed into a beaver.

Works such as these indicate that the important quality in writing about minority cultures is not so much the avoidance of 'incorrect' nomenclature as a high degree of knowledge and sympathy with the individuals portrayed.

The representation of dialect

One of the many sensitive aspects related to language is the representation of non-standard English. On the one hand, accuracy to the speech of the characters not only conveys a greater degree of credibility, but it also shows that their language is worth putting into written form, giving it a kind of accolade comparable to that of the standard language. On the other hand, it needs to be done accurately if it is not going to appear ludicrous, it creates more problems for the reader, especially the less competent child reader, and it could be argued that it merely supports the 'incorrect' use of English.

Such problems are not of course confined to 'black' speech, for another factor is that of status. In Britain, Scots has generally been seen as high status, but Birmingham and Geordie dialects, as well as British Black Vernacular, have been less highly thought of. A similar situation in America is reflected in readers' reactions to the use of language by the illiterate old black man, Timothy, in Theodore Taylor's *The Cay* (1970), which was one of the reasons for the unpopularity of this book with some critics. When asked by Phillip if he comes from Africa, he replies, 'I 'ave no recollection o' anythin' 'cept dese islan's. 'Tis pure outrageous, but I do not remember anythin' 'bout a place called Afre-ca' (p. 31). This combination of ignorance and non-standard language intensifies the possibility that the child reader will join Phillip, before he recognizes Timothy's worth, in despising the old man.

Taylor is relying on the reader finishing the story and perhaps sharing Phillip's remorse at the inadequate opinion he has held of Timothy. This is clearly a risky policy, or one which in school demands the teacher's co-operation in emphasizing what Taylor leaves unsaid; whether it is enough to render the book unsuitable for the young reader remains more difficult to determine. It is clear that Taylor took the criticisms to heart, as in *Timothy of the Cay* (1993), the reader learns much more about the reasons for the title character's lack of education, and about the fact that having become a relatively prosperous man, he has come back from retirement to aid the war effort, out of a sense of duty. While his accent is still rendered phonologically, his use of syntax and vocabulary seem to have become less distinctive, and his addressing Phillip as 'bahss' is less marked.

Even in recent and acclaimed British children's books, there are some uses of non-standard English, often confined to an older generation. In Hoffman and Binch's *Amazing Grace* (1991), Grace's grandmother doesn't always use Standard English verb forms: 'It seems that Natalie is another one who don't know nothing'; 'If Grace put her mind to it – she can do anything she want.' This may cause anxiety to some readers, especially as the second of these quotations is the final line of the book, but I would consider them to be overriden by the grandmother's sympathetic portrayal. Those who are worried about so-called 'political correctness' might say that this kind of usage legitimizes non-standard forms, but since it is more than likely that children will already be accustomed to these both at home and on the television, it could be claimed that it gives more place within the school culture for dialect forms which may well be spoken by children's parents or especially as here, grandparents. Grandpa in Caroline Binch's (1994) *Gregory Cool* uses regular Caribbean syntax: 'You a fool, Gregory. You not cool.' Gregory's own acceptance of his relations' culture is signalled by his adoption, at the end of the book, of their dialect: 'Cool Greg an' the Mighty Lennox, we comin'.'

There is no easy answer to the question of how much dialect should be used in books, but it should be noted that including it is no new occurrence; a number of books by, for instance, Sir Walter Scott, Thomas Hardy and D. H. Lawrence could be cited and this does not seem to have deterred teachers from using them in the classroom. One difference is that such books have been read by older children than are likely to encounter the books mentioned above. What seems crucial is that such uses of dialect should not be seen as patronizing, and they certainly should be accurate, as was generally the case in the work of the major novelists mentioned.

A book where the use of language associated with Afro-Caribbean speech rhythms is most noticeable is Trish Cooke's *So Much* (1994, illustrated by Helen Oxenbury). Its depiction of characteristically British black culture and language patterns marks a stage of development which publishers would scarcely have dared to display some years previously. The simple story involves the reactions to a young baby expressed by a series of his relations who arrive for a party:

> . . . It was . . . Nannie
> Nannie and Gran-Gran
> Nannie and Gran-Gran came inside
> with their handbags cock up
> to one side and their brolly hook up
> on their sleeve. 'Yoooooo hoooooo!
> Yoooooo hoooooo!' they said
> 'I want to eat him, I want to eat the baby,
> SO MUCH!'
> And they hug him
> and they love him
> and they make him
> feel so cosy,
> singing songs and dancing
> till it was time for sleeping.
> 'Zzzzzzz . . .'

The rhythms of this and similar passages are not those of Standard English, and there are a number of departures from conventional syntax ('cock up', 'hook up'), while the behaviour of the two grandmothers in 'singing songs and dancing' is not that which might be expected from their indigenous counterparts. The pictures strongly reinforce the message of a culture which for many readers will be both unfamiliar and appealing. Here we have a clear recognition that ethnic minorities have a pattern of behaviour which is neither identical nor inferior to that of the majority, and this is presented without any extraneous matter justifying it.

The very way this is set out immediately makes it look like poetry – especially its use of repetition, recalling the strong Caribbean tradition of folk poetry. The form of this no doubt metamophosed from the African language origins and relied heavily on chant-like qualities, as seen on the one hand the negro spirituals. Shirley Brice Heath (1983) gives a comparable example from the Afro-American community she named Trackton; a two and a half year old boy responds to hearing a bell with:

Way
Far
Now
It a church bell
Ringin'
Dey singin'
Ringin'
You hear it?
I hear it
Far
Now. (p. 170)

There is something which is both appealing to children and liberating about verse using language which probably ultimately derives from African languages. John Agard and Grace Nichols, both of Caribbean origins, have written and collected a good deal of verse which encapsulates a non-British English language and culture. The following poem by Agard (in Agard and Nichols, 1990) has some attractive humour:

Call alligator long-mouth
call alligator saw-mouth
call alligator pushy-mouth
call alligator scissors-mouth
call alligator raggedy-mouth
call alligator bumpy-bum
call alligator all dem rude word
but better wait
till you cross river. (p. 59)

There is little here that could cause concern about non-standard English, other than the slightly 'daring', from a child's point of view, use of 'bum'. It is easy to see how this poem could lead to some fun with language. The following poem by Grace Nichols (in Agard and Nichols, 1991) also includes some non-standard uses, again, interestingly enough, associated with a grandparent:

It so nice to have a Granny
when you've had it from yuh Mammy
and you feeling down and dammy
It so nice to have a Granny
when she brings you bread and jammy
and says, 'Tell it all to Granny.' (p. 69)

Agard (Agard and Nichols, 1991) perhaps should have the final word on this issue in a poem which presents a perspective using material sanctified by age:

Tom Tom the piper's son
stole a pig
A-SO DEM SAY
and away he run
A-SO DEM SAY
the pig was eat
A-SO DEM SAY

and Tom was beat
A-SO DEM SAY
but my teacher say
A-SO SHE SAY
it ought to be
the pig was eaten
and Tom was beaten
A-SO SHE SAY
and my teacher does talk sweet
and my teacher does write neat
and my teacher don't eat pig meat
A-SO SHE SAY (p. 56)

This rhyme shows how much less critical the reader is likely to be of non-standard syntax in traditional verse ('away he *run*' for instance); it also provides some interesting material for discussion. We have the emphatic refrain, itself with a non-standard format, we have strong use of rhythm and rhyme, a happy combination of the Caribbean and the traditional. Also the stress on the authority figure of the teacher lends it the feel of the child's voice. It shows how time can make readers blind to such departures from standard forms, and also quiets fears that children will 'catch' them from poetry like that of Agard and Nichols. Children have a keen ear for dialect, and a clear understanding of the differences between *Neighbours* and *Coronation Street*; if the language of rhyme and the playground (cf. Opie, 1959) has not led to children 'catching' 'bad' English, some use of it in rhymes is unlikely to do so either. Instead, as well as fun, it can validate for the child some of the language of home.

Conclusion

What children need is an awareness of the different kinds of cultures; accepting the value of other people's in no way means that we denigrate the qualities of our own. This very fact should make us appreciate that people who possess a language or culture very different from our own may be equally happy with their own. Both children and adults will probably be more successful in learning new languages and understanding new cultures if they already possess a strong grounding in their own language and culture. Books which portray other languages and cultures as they are, without preaching or being patronizing, are likely to be effective in creating respect on both sides.

References

Note an extensive bibliography is also given at the end of this book. An asterisk indicates a picture book.

Learning our language and culture

Akinyemi, R. (1991) *Hamster Weekend*. London: Hamish Hamilton.
Ashley, B. (1990) *Boat Girl*. London: Walker Books.
Bruce, L. (1993) *Jazeera's Journey*. London: Methuen.

Dhami, N. (1990) *A Medal For Malina*. London: Hamish Hamilton.
Doherty, B. (1987) *Tough Luck*. London: Hamish Hamilton.
Gavin, J. (1992) *The Wheel of Surya*. London: Methuen.
Hicyilmaz, G. (1993) *The Frozen Waterfall*. London: Faber.
Hoffman, M. ed. (1992) *Ip Dip Sky Blue*. London: HarperCollins.
Kidd, D. (1992) *Onion Tears*. London: Viking.
Laird, E. (1991) *Kiss the Dust*. London: Heinemann.
Lingard, J. (1991) *Between Two Worlds*. London: Hamish Hamilton.
Lutzeier, E. (1993) *Lost for Words*. Oxford: University Press.
Smith, N. (1990) *Imran's Secret*. London: Julia MacRae.
Smith, R. (1982) *Sumitra's Story*. Basingstoke: Macmillan.
Strachan, I. (1991) *The Second Step*. London: Methuen.

Other minority cultures

Arnold, E. (1995) *The Parsley Parcel*. London: Heinemann.
Creech, S. (1994) *Walk Two Moons*. Basingstoke: Macmillan.
Doherty, D. (1992) *Snowy**. London: HarperCollins.
Godden, R. (1972) *The Diddakoi*. Basingstoke: Macmillan.
Jeffers, S. (1992) *Brother Eagle, Sister Sky**. London: Hamish Hamilton.
Kaye, G. (1990) *Winter in Small Street**. London: Methuen.
Norton, A. (1966, first American edition 1959) *Beastmaster*. London: Gollancz.
Norton, A. (1968) *Fur Magic*. London: Hamish Hamilton.
Smith, N. (1990) *Imran's Secret*. London: Julia MacRae.
Waddell, M. (1983) (Illustrated by P. Dupasquier) *Going West**. London: Andersen

Language and poetry

Agard, J. and Nichols, G. (1991) *No Hickory, No Dickory, No Dock*. London: Viking.
Binch, C. (1994) *Gregory Cool**. London: Frances Lincoln.
Cooke, T. and Oxenbury, H. (1994) *So Much**. London: Walker.
Hoffman, M.& Binch, C. (1991) *Amazing Grace**. London: Frances Lincoln.
Nichols, G. (1990) *Poetry Jump Up*. Harmondsworth: Penguin (first published by Blackie
   in 1988 as *Black Poetry*).
Samuels, V. (1990) *Beams*. London: Methuen.
Taylor, T. (1970) *The Cay*. London: Bodley Head.
Taylor, T. (1993) *Timothy of the Cay*. Harmondsworth: Penguin.

There are many other volumes by Agard and Nichols and the work of James Berry should also be seen.

CHAPTER 8

Literature and Society:
Age and Disability

> The best story and picture books are those which include the child with special needs as a matter of course, not those where the situation is contrived to include such a child. (Beverley Mathias, 1993)

As is the case with most 'equality issues', that of disability involves two distinct aspects, both of which are relevant to children's literature. The first of these is nomenclature. The names used in the past to describe people suffering from a range of different conditions are often regarded today as at the very least imprecise, and in some cases offensive to the people concerned. This may apply not only to terms with a pejorative ring, such as 'thick', 'mad' or 'mental', but also to words not originally intended to be emotive, such as 'blind', 'deaf' or 'crippled', which are not really accurate enough to refer properly to the variety of conditions covered. These terms are also inevitably redolent of outmoded attitudes, when people with sight or hearing difficulties were seldom thought of as individuals in their own right but rather as objects for pity, examples of heroic virtue, or, in some cases, stereotyped villains. (See Chapter 3 for a critique of the way in which disabled people are portrayed in some of the 'classics' of the past).

The descriptions which replace such terms, like 'Visually Impaired' or 'With Mobility Problems' are often more awkward, and are therefore ridiculed or parodied – to the extent that some people probably think the parodies are serious, 'politically correct', alternatives. The dust jacket of *Politically Correct Bedtime Stories* (Garner, 1994) which jokes: 'Anyone who is in tune with the times knows that Snow White took refuge with seven vertically challenged men . . .' is likely to draw a rueful smile from anyone who has tried to write about disability! The requirements of the Warnock Report (1978) that mainstream schools should cater for children with disabilities has brought to the attention of teachers and pupils the needs of such children, and recent literature has generally handled such subjects with more sensitivity. There has also been a much greater sense of self-worth among the communities of those who experience certain kinds of sensory impairment. This is probably most apparent in the non-hearing community's valuing of Sign, an alternative language which is more accessible to many of them than spoken English, and is a rule-governed language in itself rather than an inferior form of spoken language (cf. Oliver Sacks, *Seeing Voices*, 1989).

Whatever the desired policy today, there is no doubt that a great many published books use terms such as 'blind' and 'deaf'. The words 'dumb' and 'cripple', however, are less common, as they are rightly thought to be imprecise; of the few children who are completely unable to speak, most are profoundly deaf and probably excellent communicators by other means, though some may be suffering from emotional problems (like Donovan Croft in Ashley's book of that name).

The second aspect mentioned above, the *mode* of depiction of disabled characters, is obviously of greater significance than the terms used to describe them. It is interesting that Rachel Anderson, whose books about mentally disabled children I will be considering later, and whose son is mentally handicapped, seems to have little hesitation about using non 'politically correct' terms in *The Bus People* (1989), a collection of stories for older readers which could also interest adults. The 'bus' takes the children to a school for those with learning difficulties and Bertram, the bus driver, a character who is portrayed sympathetically, not only smokes, but also describes his young passengers as 'nutty as fruit-cakes' (p. 2). It would appear that Anderson's own experience has led her not only to write in a way which creates empathy with the children and the parents concerned, but also means that she disregards matters which she considers less significant.

Disabled people have the right to be accepted for themselves as individuals, and to be autonomous. In recognizing them as equals in society, we need to give them the opportunity to encounter in literature people like themselves performing active roles. This does not however presuppose the assumption that only disabled people will identify with any disabled characters in the books; nor should we think that readers who have any form of specific difficulty will either only or automatically identify with characters who have similar problems to themselves. As Jack Ashley states in the Foreword to *The Spell Singer* (Mathias, 1989), a collection of stories by well-known authors:

> In any discussion of disability, one of the most common expressions is 'the disabled'. This implies a non-existent homogeneity and obscures the individuality of disabled people.

A drawback of some well-meaning books, which is however less common today, has been to suggest that whether by a miraculous operation or because of their edifying patience, the character portrayed will recover from their loss. This is particularly the case when the disability has been used to point a lesson – like Katy's accident in *What Katy Did* (1872) or Phillip's blindness in Theodore Taylor's *The Cay* (1970). It is not doing a service to readers (able-bodied or otherwise) if they are allowed to form the impression that disability results from wrong-doing or that it can always be cured. Obviously it may sometimes be helpful to portray problems which *are* temporary, as in Judy Blume's *Deenie* (1980) where the title character suffers from adolescent idiopathic scoliosis and for 4 years will have to wear a back brace which she thinks makes her unattractive. The descriptions of hospital procedures, the greater tolerance which Deenie feels towards a girl with eczema, and even Blume's characteristic inclusion of other issues, in this case masturbation, could certainly be of value to many readers with no knowledge of this specific problem.

Sensory and mobility difficulties

There are several different ways in which disablement is treated in children's fiction today and these may be summarized as incidental, realism, and distancing by means of an historical or a fantasy approach. These will be dealt with in turn.

The incidental approach

Disabled characters are increasingly included in books about a variety of subjects; they are thus seen as a normal part of a mixed society, without any specific comment being made. This is often easiest to do in picture-book format, where little or nothing need be said explicitly, because the situation is made clear by the illustration. Equally understandable is the fact that this is generally done with characters in wheelchairs or on crutches, as this is much easier to portray visually than is hearing or seeing impairment.

A few recent books for young children have attempted to educate their readers in this way, though sometimes the very inclusive aspect seems a little contrived. Nan Bodsworth's *A Nice Walk in the Jungle* (1989) shows a multi-racial class which includes a child in a wheelchair; their teacher leads them, somewhat improbably, into the jungle, where she fails to observe nearly all of them being eaten (wheelchair and all) by a boa-constrictor. Needless to say, once she turns against the snake, all the children are liberated.

Beverley Naidoo's three books about an African girl, Letang, coming to an English school and making friends with the physically handicapped Julie (1994), all show both children as active members of the class. When one of the children calls Julie by 'a nasty name', the explicit moralizing by the teacher is perhaps over-didactic: 'I am upset that some of you are calling names to hurt someone. When I was little I was called "deafie" and it still hurts me now.' This is, however, the only place in the books where the message is not almost entirely left to the pictures to reinforce.

Verna Wilkins' books for the Spinal Injuries Association, *Boots for a Brides-maid* and *Are We There Yet?* (1995) (see Figure 5) do not put any direct emphasis on the fact that the mother in the first book and the father in the second are in wheelchairs; scrutiny of a picture makes intelligible the child's remark, 'I can see our parking place' but the message is not obtrusive. Books like these are well on the way to normalizing the situation of the physically disabled: it is perhaps indicative of the extent to which disabled people have not yet been fully integrated within our society that generally, if readers or television viewers come across characters in a wheelchair or on crutches, they can be almost certain that this fact will have some significance in the story.

The realistic mode

One of the most common ways of depicting disablement is portraying such characters as central within a realistic story set in contemporary Western society. In such books, certain themes may be highlighted, such as the isolation often experienced by those who do not fit into society's expectations, their difficulties about sexual relationships and about taking charge of their own lives, and sometimes, the fact that with some medical conditions they may only have a limited life span. Although the emphasis in a particular book may be upon a certain disability, if the book is well written, it can apply more generally. Such books, as well as helping a disabled reader to develop a sense of self-esteem, may also be educative for the rest of society, and in many instances, passages are included which show that many well-meaning people have an inadequate understanding of both the sensibilities and the abilities of these individuals.

Figure 5 Nicky and her mother, from Verna Wilkins and Pamela Venus, *Boots for a Bridesmaid* (1995), reproduced with permission of the publishers, Tamarind Books.

There is a danger that the disabled person, adult or child, may become isolated from the rest of society. Meindert de Jong's near-classic, *The Wheel on the School* (1956) is set in a Friesian village associated with the author's early twentieth century childhood. Janus, a fisherman who lost his legs because of blood poisoning resulting from a mosquito bite, is portrayed as isolated and embittered. The children of the village are sent out by their teacher to try to find an old wheel to put on the school roof to attract the storks to nest there. Two boys, Pier and Dirk, look in Janus' yard but he thinks they are thieves with an eye on his cherry-tree. As he comes to believe their story and to become active in the project to bring back the storks, he is also drawn back into the village community, finally becoming the agent for rescuing two storks battered by a storm. The power of this simple but far from simplistic story lies partly in its evocative symbolism; the return of the storks to nest on the school building is an image of rebirth. Janus' story is perhaps the most powerful of the group of tales linked by the quest.

It is often claimed that lack of hearing is the most isolating of disabilities, and Jean Ure's *Cool Simon* (1990) shows how very difficult it is for a boy who can only understand what people say by lip-reading, and whose speech is consequently very unclear, to integrate into a new school community unless someone there has an understanding of both his situation and, if possible, his language. Fortunately for Simon (who incidentally is portrayed on the cover of the book as black though there is no reference to this in the text), he is befriended by Sam, an unpopular and isolated girl who gains just as much from the friendship as he does. This book, in addition to having some unpleasant characters from another school, shows that well-meaning teachers and pupils may be inadequate in a situation they have not experienced before; Simon is initially put into the care of the cleverest boy in the class, Badar, who is however not very good with people and doesn't understand Simon's needs. Simon's speech is well reproduced; for 'I'd like to do that' he says, 'I like do dat,' and when introduced to Catherine and Soozie, he says, 'Caddin and Doody . . . I goo [cool] Dimon' (p. 38).

Many young readers might find Ure's rendering of Simon's speech difficult to understand, but it is nearly always immediately interpreted, and its very incompre hensibility brings to the fore the issue of the need to subdue the natural impatience which may be felt by the listeners in a situation like this. A central theme is the question of playing football; Simon is not allowed to play in his best position, midfield, and, as a girl, Sam has been excluded from the team. She comments: 'They're not only sexist, they're deafist and all! Sticking you in goal just 'cause you've got a hearing aid' (p. 45). While the incident which brings about the integration of Simon into the class, and allows him to demand that Sam be allowed to play football with the boys, may be felt to be a little melodramatic, the book is effective and in no way sentimental, and could prove illuminating to many young readers.

A similar lack of sentimentality, and use of contemporary idiom, are to be found in Susan Sallis' *Sweet Frannie* (1981), a first-person narrative about a teenager paralysed from the waist down. She has just come to a residential home where she can at last have her own room and express her very extrovert personality and her enthusiasm for practical jokes; one of her first actions is to carry away the false teeth of an elderly resident who, surprisingly, is ready to join in the fun. One of the main themes of the book is the question of the possibility of a sexual relationship for someone in her situation; after a slightly turbulent start to their acquaintance, she and a double amputee, Luke Hawkins, fall in love, and naturally feel the need for physical expression of this love, something not easy in their circumstances. A down to earth note is supplied by Frannie's anxiety that no one would be likely to find her attractive because her condition often causes her to wet her knickers.

An additional strength of this book is the way in which it subjects to scrutiny the attitudes of those who 'befriend' the disabled. Frannie 'inherits' from a previous inmate who has just died, a couple, Aunt Nell and Uncle Roger, who are initially shocked at Frannie's irreverent attitudes and lack of conformity to the 'good', passive, invalid stereotype. Rather than them simply being portrayed negatively, however, their motivations, basic kindness, and the stresses their marriage is subject to, are seen as part of a learning process for everyone.

The inadequate attitudes of other people are also displayed in Jean Ure's *See You Thursday* (1981), the story of a young blind music teacher, Abe. In the house where he lodges, there is a girl 8 years younger, Marianne, who gradually develops a strong feeling for him; his reciprocal affection is perhaps fostered by the fact that he is in a tutor–student relationship with her, having discovered that she has an excellent alto voice. As their relationship gets closer, Marianne's mother becomes concerned, and Marianne speculates as to why her mother had let the room to him in the first place. Abe answers:

> 'I imagine because she thought that being blind, I would be safe to have around . . . like some kind of pet eunuch.'
> 'That's obscene!'
> 'Shattering to my ego, certainly. I wouldn't exactly call it obscene.'
> 'Well it is! It's like saying that just because you can't see, you can't –'
> 'Yes,' said Abe. 'Well, people do, don't they?' (p. 136)

The adult reader may note with some amusement the way in which Abe's speedy rejoinder prevents Marianne's remark from being over-explicit, which might render the book 'unsuitable' for a teenage readership! Exposure of faulty attitudes could be seen as being a little intrusive at times, for instance when Abe talks of a landlady who rejected him from her lodgings:

> 'but unfortunately *I* wasn't suitable for *it* . . . the minute we turned up they took one look at me and said no.'
> 'What do you mean, they said no?'
> 'No. N-O. No blacks, no babies, no blind.' (p. 149)

The didactic quality here may reflect the fact that the book was written in the early 1980s, but it does not detract from its effectiveness in dealing with the important issues not only of society's attitude to visually impaired people, but also of relationships between people of different ages.

Two books of Australian origin, Alan Marshall's *I Can Jump Puddles* (1955) and Ivan Southall's *Let the Balloon Go* (1968), both deal with the topic of the degree of autonomy possible to boys with mobility problems. Marshall's autobiographical novel portrays the onset of his illness and its effects, and his struggle to demonstrate to himself and others that he is equal, in the male-dominated society of early twentieth century Australia. By the end of the book, he has succeeded in showing his father that he can ride a horse, but probably the most significant part of his achievement is to resist the possible effect on his self-concept of expressions of pity, such as 'A kid crippled up like you should be home resting in bed' (p. 159).

The achievement of John, the disabled hero of Southall's book, is both to climb a tree *and* to get down again, despite the tactless remark of the policeman who is trying to help him: 'Anybody can climb a tree. It's the getting down that's tough' (p. 104).

A still more limiting influence on the activity of some disabled people is one not imposed by society but by their own condition: physical weakness and the likelihood of an early death. Writers who seek to show that disabled people have equal rights to autonomy and individuality may sometimes need also to display an awareness of such situations which, despite only affecting a minority of people, are particularly emotionally involving. The challenge of avoiding morbidity in writing about death is one which a number of recent children's authors have taken on; while the subject pervaded Victorian children's books, it is only in the last third of this century that it has found much place in writing for young people. (See the reference section at the end of the chapter for some titles.)

In *Sweet Frannie* (Sallis, 1981) the reader gradually learns, well before Luke does, that Frannie has a weak heart and may die at any time. Her death only occurs after the end of her narrative and after a brief period of happiness with Luke, whose voice supplies an epilogue to the book, tying up any details the reader still needs to know. David Hill's *See Ya Simon* (1992) focuses much more directly on the weakness and impending death from muscular dystrophy of the title character. In spite of this theme, Hill is clearly trying to create a positive impression, particularly by a means of a relentless use of jokes and the contemporary idiom supplied by the voice of Nathan, the teenage narrator. The plot is more episodic than those of some of the other books described; incidents at school and at home showing Simon's sense of humour are more important than the fulfilment of Nathan's aspirations towards the most attractive girl in the class, Brady. Simon's very refusal ever to complain may perhaps limit the effect of this book; as Nathan says:

> It would be so easy to spend all your time feeling sorry for yourself if you were him, and he hardly ever does that. More often he gets ratty because people at school are too soft on him. (p. 19)

It is a matter for debate as to whether books like this should ignore the dark side of the disabled character. It is easy to understand why authors want to portray the characters positively, and this book, which is written in memory of 'N. J. B. 1975–1990', may well reflect Hill's actual experience of a boy who was as cheerful and outgoing in the face of weakness and death as Simon is. It could therefore be of considerable value in informing young people who are in normal health, but I wonder if it could be depressing for a disabled teenager to read a book which presents a character who is facing up to his situation in an almost superhuman way.

By contrast, Ian Strachan's *The Boy in the Bubble* (1993), while nearly as prone to joking as *See Ya, Simon*, shows Adam, who has SCID (severe combined immunodeficiency) and has to live in a completely sterile environment, to experience many of the problems which might be anticipated from a person isolated from his contemporaries and lacking any normal tactile contact. He is often bitter about his condition and his lack of experience of life, especially the sexual aspect; his brief opportunity for a normal relationship just before his death recalls the situation of Sallis's Frannie; although the book has some didactic elements, and is clearly intended to help the reader to understand, among other things, how devastating is the effect of a situation like this on all family members, it avoids mawkishness.

In Chapter 2, reference was made to the way in which literature concerned with death and disablement fairly often seems to include 'carnivalesque' elements, such as the use of expletives, the mention of bodily functions, and some reversal of hierarchical roles. In many of the books mentioned here, carnivalesque aspects go well beyond simply the provision of jokes to relieve tension and make difficult subjects accessible to young readers. For one thing, the jokes themselves often include a morbid readiness to dismember the body concerned, in a way that recalls Bakhtin's seeing this as a characteristic carnival trait. Early in *The Boy in the Bubble*, Adam asks the narrator, Anne, 'Why couldn't the skeleton go to the ball?', and supplies the answer, 'Because he had no body to go with' (p. 44). These words are spoken by a boy whose condition means that death could happen any time and this means that the many riddles like this have the function of helping to prepare the reader for the inevitable.

Another characteristic element is explicit language, though there are of course problems for authors who want their books not only to appeal to young readers but also to be bought and recommended by adults! Near the end of this book and just before his death, Adam is freed from the bubble and says:

> 'There's only one other thing, now that we're properly together, which I could have possibly wished for . . .'
>
> Adam was about to put his wish into words, not that he really needed to, when Mr Jackman returned. (p. 150)

The rather contrived reticence here recalls the similar situation in Ure's *See You Thursday*, described above. Perhaps because terms concerning excretion are less challenging than those concerned with sex, less caution is met in Hill's *See Ya Simon*, where the Third form in the school are called the Turds, and the Fourth, the Stale Turds. It may not be fanciful to suggest that one of the reasons for the abundance of such elements in books dealing with death and disablement is the desire of the authors concerned to depart from the kinds of stereotypes of people suffering from such conditions as saintly victims; if they, or those around them, are seen to share some of the down to earth needs and weaknesses of ordinary humanity, they become more like the rest of us, and less likely to be set on a pedestal. It is difficult to imagine some of the saintly 'cripples' of classic texts, like Cousin Helen in *What Katy Did*, having physical needs, still less sexual desires!

Fantasy fiction, historical fiction, and picture books

Some authors have combined the portrayal of disability with the use of fantasy, perhaps to avoid the difficulties consequent upon a contemporary setting. The problem with this approach is that if a specific disability like lack of sight or hearing is the subject, then some degree of realism is needed, which can conflict with the mode in which the fantasy situation is made credible to the reader. If, however, the way in which an individual differs from other children is made less specific, even to the extent of not explicitly mentioning disability at all, the use of fantasy may be far more successful, and I propose to go on to consider this after discussing some books which are more specific.

Madeleine L'Engle's *The Young Unicorns* (1969) for instance, has a blind girl with spectacular musical ability who succeeds in leading other children out of a maze of tunnels because of her ability to find her way in the dark. The credibility of scenes involving Emily seems to make the science fiction element, about the Alphabats who are seeking to control the world, all the less credible, making the success of the book a little uneven.

Both Joyce Dunbar's *Mundo and the Weather Child* (1985) and Berlie Doherty's *Spellhorn* (1989) use fantasy to treat the difficult subject of children coming to terms with their disability. Dunbar, who herself is partially deaf, takes the subject of total loss of hearing – a theme less common in literature than either lack of sight or of mobility. After his illness, 7-year-old Edmund is somewhat consoled by seeing in the garden of their old house a perpetually 7-year-old 'weather child', who addresses him as Mundo and whose often apparently illogical behaviour nevertheless prepares Edmund for friendship with the little girl who lives opposite.

130

The book is likely, however, to appeal to an adult reader rather than a child, as Edmund's perceptions seem too mature for his ostensible age; when his mother is cross with him for the first time since his illness, he muses:

> Dimly I perceived that ordinary anger meant ordinary love which meant that I could be an ordinary boy. That was what I wanted now . . . my mother turned and I saw that she was weeping; then she said she was sorry. All the good that had been done was spoiled. (p. 127)

Doherty's book also presents stylistic problems, some of which may be the result of its unusual genesis, as the by-product of a project to write a radio play with the aid of some children from a school for the partially sighted. The central character, Laura, possesses inner sight of another world, where she becomes the 'Mighty High' of a group of 'Wild Ones'. These seem to have certain qualities of earlier people as their language has a kind of pseudo-Anglo-Saxon quality; the Old Woman who precedes Laura as their leader says in her 'wordspeak':

> We're nosy to see what manfolk has got up to. It makes us heartsad, too, sometimes . . . we see the nice world going dumpy. Bad smells all over the air. Loud noises scraping our earholes. Manfolk makes things rusty, and scratched, and uglydumps. (p. 45)

The plot is very complex, but would seem to suggest that a form of 'splitting' took place in Laura when she lost her sight, and that she is tempted to revert to the dark side of her personality where in some kind of way she can see, an aspect which recalls how Edmund in the previous book is able to *hear* the Weather Child's voice. What is puzzling is that Laura's 'Wild Ones' have a 'real' effect in 'today's' world; their first incursion on the scene is when they burn down the houses of the local villagers, something which is unlikely to endear them to the reader.

Both these books seem to me to be over-ambitious in seeking to present within children's books the psychological processes which the child faced by disability may be experiencing in coming to terms with the situation. Nevertheless, if the more difficult sections are mediated by an adult, children may well respond to the power which many scenes possess.

An alternative, and often more successful, mode of distancing is by setting the story in the distant past. This can also enable the reader to generalize to a greater extent than if the particular disability is set in an everyday twentieth-century context, and removes pressure which may be felt if a book is read to a class including children with a similar condition. Rosemary Sutcliff, who suffered from Still's disease, a form of arthritis which inhibited her movement, constantly focuses on characters with an impaired ability to function in the harsher societies of the past. While in no sense their disability is minimized, we can also see how it has made them what they are – more human, more compassionate, more mature people. *The Eagle of the Ninth* (1954) and *Warrior Scarlet* (1958) are notable for the way they respectively place the wounded Marcus, and Drem, who has a useless shield arm, at the centre of heroic yet multi-faceted tales set within societies with no tolerance for people like them. One of the most effective of her stories, however, and more accessible to younger children than these, is *The Witch's Brat* (1970), about Lovel, who is 'built crooked, with a hunched shoulder and a twisted leg that made him walk lop-sided like a bird with a broken wing' (p. 1).

Lovel becomes a colleague of Rahere, the founder of St. Bartholomew's Hospital, and is able to help others, partly because of his inherited ability to understand herbs and set bones, but also because those he helps recognize that he too has suffered from similar problems to theirs. There is clearly a danger here of the over-idealized disabled person, but the story gains from seeing into his thought processes, rather than putting him on a pedestal.

The danger of over-idealization is also present in Lucy Boston's use of the icon of the blind girl in *The Chimneys of Green Knowe* (1958). The danger that the eighteenth century Susan, who is both brave and clever, might become as irritating in her perfection as for instance Mary in Laura Ingalls Wilder's *By the Shores of Silver Lake* (1961, see Chapter 3), is avoided by the way in which Susan's adventures are mediated to the reader through the stories told to a young boy, Tolly, by his great-grandmother. Susan is also at times oppressed by unpleasant adults, and is friendly with Jacob, a black servant boy who is also positively presented to the reader. Unfortunately Jacob suffers from the traditional depiction of the black child as unable to speak idiomatic English and there are some indications of stereotyping (see Chapter 1 above) but I think the book overcomes these by Boston's portrayal of the warmth of the relationship between the children. Susan is active, at times naughty, climbing trees to the dismay of her mother but the admiration of her seafarer father.

Books about disability which are set in the past can be very liberating, especially in the case of Sutcliff, probably because of the empathy created by her own mobility difficulties. Nevertheless, I think that often the most effective means of showing that society should have a place for everyone, whatever their limitations, is through fantasy books, which may often not explicitly deal with disability at all. Such books can be universally relevant, because fantasy facilitates the exclusion of the details of contemporary society and allows more focus on the psychological than the sociological aspects.

A book which does this simply but very effectively is *Ruby* (1992) by Maggie Glen. This is a picture book about a teddy bear who is made out of the wrong material and therefore has the letter 'S' stamped on her paw. She interprets this as meaning 'Special' though she is told it means 'second-rate'. After escaping from the factory, she arrives at a toyshop where she is bought by a little girl, Susie, who resembles Ruby in wearing the initial, 'S', in her case on a chain round her neck. Although she is told that Ruby is inferior, Susie refuses to buy any of the 'first-rate' toys. Because of its lack of direct reference to any disability, and its clear message about Ruby's worth, this book could be quite helpful in building the esteem of children who know they have been labelled as having 'Special Needs' and feel that something inferior is implied by this description.

A similarly undirected ego-boost could be derived from Bernard Ashley's *Cleversticks* (1992), illustrated by Derek Bragell, where Ling Sung on his first day at school feels inferior because he cannot do things which some of the other children find easy, like buttoning his coat. They are all fascinated, however, by his adeptness with chopsticks; 'all of us have special abilities', seems to be implied. There are many other picture books which have no direct connection with the subject of disability but which may nevertheless convey a message about being special or accepting people who are different, sometimes more effectively than books which are too specific. (See references at the end of this chapter for some suggestions.)

For slightly older children, E. B. White's *Stuart Little* (1946) might be appealing. It begins:

> When Mrs Frederick C. Little's second son was born, everybody noticed that he was not much bigger than a mouse. The truth of the matter was, the baby looked very much like a mouse in every way. He was only about two inches high; and he had a mouse's sharp nose, a mouse's tail, a mouse's whiskers, and the pleasant shy manner of a mouse. Before he was many days old he was not only looking like a mouse but acting like one, too – wearing a grey hat and carrying a small cane. Mr and Mrs Little named him Stuart, and Mr Little made him a tiny bed out of four clothespins and a cigarette box. (p. 7)

There is never any suggestion that Stuart is other than human, and this book provides an effective combination of absurdity and the strength and vulnerability of the central character, whose exploits prove that size and 'normality' are not everything.

Language and learning disabilities

Enabling children with learning difficulties to take a place in society is a complex matter, and literature can only help in a small part of this, particularly since the kind of books which portray people in their situation may often be too difficult for the children themselves to understand. What is probably more important is to ensure that 'normal' girls and boys become aware that such people, whether children or adults, deserve acknowledgement that they are human beings with full human rights.

In literature of the past there have been all too many portrayals of 'idiots' who are treated cruelly and whose image is often used as a negative comparison. For instance, in George Eliot's *The Mill on the Floss* (1860), when Maggie has cut her hair, her brother Tom says:

> Oh Maggie . . . oh, my buttons, what a queer thing you look! Look at yourself in the glass – you look like the idiot we throw our nutshells to at school.
>
> (Chapter 7)

Even today, many people's attitudes may have been conditioned by this kind of portrayal and need adjustment. This is particularly important for children, because in their endeavour to make sure that they conform with what they come to see as the 'normal' expectations of society, they find it all too easy to judge that the way to do so is to compare themselves favourably with others who are less able. For helping children to recognize the rights and worth of everyone, the fantasy books mentioned in the previous section may be particularly useful, in that the situations are not specific, though in some instances a word or two from the teacher may be necessary to help children to detect the connection.

Most books relevant to the situation of chldren with learning disabilities are, however, likely to be within the genre of realism, though the subject is less often portrayed than that of physical disability. Most of the books produced in this somewhat sensitive area seem to be addressed rather to those not directly experiencing the effects of disability. The experience of a child with a very limited understanding of the world is not easy for the 'normal' person to appreciate; it is easier to show the effect of having a disabled sibling, as in Betsy Byars' *The Summer of the Swans* (1970) or Elizabeth Laird's *Red Sky in the Morning* (1988). Rachel Anderson however, in *The Bus People* (1989), makes a very convincing attempt to enter the world of the handicapped child. In the story of Rebecca, a Down's syndrome girl whose happiness about being her sister's bridesmaid is taken away by aunts with 'brittle' voices, who say, in Rebecca's hearing:

'And now she's getting positively gross.'
'They ought to have had her put away somewhere right from the start.'

(pp. 12–13)

Rebecca tries not to understand, but the next day when she overhears:

'We don't want any embarrassments. You know it wouldn't be fair on poor Graham's family. Coming all this way. Now maybe if, despite the brain, she was something to look at, had a bit of grace about her . . .'
. . . Rebecca could no longer pretend to herself she did not understand the meaning of yesterday's brittle stream of words. (pp. 14–15)

Unfortunately the mother and the sister let the unpleasant aunts get away with their prejudice, and Rebecca is stuck behind a pillar in church, having realized that she will never wear the pretty pink dress.

In Anderson's comparable story for younger readers, however, *Jessy and the Bridesmaid's Dress* (1993, with Shelagh McNicholas) there is a less harsh ending; though the dog maltreats the dress, the little Down's syndrome girl is able to wear it to her teacher's wedding because her mother repairs it. In the first of these books, Anderson shows her ability to respond to the more mature reader's need to have some appreciation of the world view of the disabled child; for the younger reader, or possibly the reader or listener with learning problems, her emphasis seems to be on the portrayal of such children as a totally accepted part of society.

There are a number of books about children with less severe problems, and, possibly because of the verbal nature of the medium, speech difficulties (as distinct from those associated with hearing loss) are among the most frequently depicted in literature for children. Often in such cases, the cause is emotional, and by the end of the book, the child, through another emotional experience, is beginning to talk normally again, as in Bernard Ashley's *The Trouble with Donovan Croft* (1974) and Monica Furlong's *Robin's Country* (1995). The temporary nature of the problem in these cases may slightly limit its value, for children need to appreciate that in most instances disability is something which people need to live with all their lives, but the presentation of the isolation which such characters suffer is of wider relevance.

Rowena, the heroine of Morris Gleitzman's *Blabbermouth* (1992) and *Sticky Beak* (1993) (discussed in Chapter 2 above), is unable to speak as a result of a physiological problem; the subject is treated with a great deal of humour, though there is no shirking of the difficulties in communication involved. *Blabbermouth* begins, 'I am dumb', something which the reader may take metaphorically until we see the letter which she has written to explain her situation to classmates at her new school:

'G'day', the letter said, 'my name's Rowena Batts and, as you've probably noticed by now, I can't speak. Don't worry, but, we can still be friends cause I can write, draw, point, nod, shake my head, screw up my nose and do sign language. I used to go to a special school but the government closed it down. The reason I can't speak is I was born with some bits missing from my throat. (It's OK, I don't leak.) . . .' (pp. 2–3)

The relentless tone of humour continues; when a class jokester tries to make capital from Rowena's plight, he is losing the sympathy of the class until Rowena gets angry, and as she says, 'I'm not just mute, I'm dumb' as she forces an unfortunate frog into his mouth and then, symbolically, seals his lips with sticky tape (p. 5). It is easy to see the attraction of Gleitzman's books to the young reader, and they succeed in being both informative and fun to read.

Dyslexia has also received some attention in books for children; Quicke (1985) expresses some reservations about T. Kennemore's *Wall of Words*(1983) in which Kerry, aged 9, feels immensely relieved when she discovers she is dyslexic, rather than 'backward'; Quicke suggests that this situation downgrades those children who are really slow learners. Several more recent books, such as Pippa Goodhart's *Flow* (1995) and Theresa Breslin's *Whispers in the Graveward* (1995) have featured dyslexic boys as central characters, without giving undue attention to the debatable subject of labels. Anne Fine's *How to Write Really Badly* (1996) focuses on the lack of self-esteem of Joe, and the way the new boy, Chester Howard, who is the narrator, manages to draw to everyone's attention the fact that Joe has a very considerable talent for model-making. It is apparent too that Fine is trying, in an indirect and frequently humorous and subversive way, to help children who might be drawn to the book because they feel that they too 'write really badly', and to give them some practical ideas, for instance about how to find specific letters in the dictionary. Certainly Joe in this book is revealed as able, despite being poor at writing and arithmetic; it is, however, possible that some readers might not so easily discern where their own talents lay.

The intention of all the authors discussed above seems to be on the one hand to empower children with difficulties to take their proper place in society and to have self-esteem, and on the other, to help other people to appreciate their qualities. To be well meaning, however, is not enough, and teachers and librarians need to scrutinize with great care any books in which the theme of disablement is explicit – they may be very useful in certain circumstances, but the authors inevitably vary in their abilities to handle sensitive topics.

The elderly in recent fiction for children

In literature of the past there was often a tendency to portray the older people as either sweet or senile or both. Red Riding Hood's Granny sets the scene, as an easy victim; it must be remembered, however, that Red Riding Hood herself was not always portrayed in pre-Perrault versions of the tale as quite so naive and stupid (cf. Chapter 5 above) and it is more than likely that Granny has also suffered from depictions which have stripped her of the power of being a source of wisdom to the tribe. Some rewritings of the tale have, however, transformed her role:

Red Riding Hood flung open the door into the kitchen and there was her great-grandmother pulling a blazing branch from the stove. With this branch she advanced on the growling wolf, old and bent though she was. (Liverpool women, 1972; in Mellor, *Changing Stories*, 1984, p. 44)

A good deal of literature of the past has taken a sentimental view of the old, and it is only today that we are beginning to see grandparents portrayed as they are, fully involved in their community. This may be because with people living into a more active old age, there are more children's writers who are grandparents themselves. There are of course quite reasonably a number of books which deal with the fact that grandparents are likely to be the first (other than pets) to give children the experience of encountering death (see references at end of chapter for some titles), but there are also an increasing number which seem to defy the stereotypes of infirm and foolish old age. I want to focus here on books which present the elderly as equal and significant members of society.

It has already been noted (in Chapters 5 and 6) how the grandmother is the source of wisdom in Mary Hoffman and Caroline Binch's *Grace* books, and other books for young children also concentrate on presenting a positive image. Jill Paton Walsh's *When Grandma Came* (1992, illustrated by Sophy Williams) shows Madeleine's grandmother as a much travelled and by no means retiring person. The scenes are paired, the first double spread of each pair showing the grandmother on her travels, the second showing the granddaughter. With the text, 'I have been to the jungles of India, far away, and heard the tiger roar in the stripy shadows . . . but I have never, no never, heard anything as rowdy as you!' we see a small grandmother figure, with her binoculars, at a not very safe distance from a group of three tigers amid trees and long grass, followed on the next page by a picture of the little girl banging a drum while the grandmother in an armchair is covering her ears, and a stripy cat leaves the room in a hurry.

The granddaughter increases in age as the book goes on, from a baby at the beginning to a confident little girl, wearing her grandmother's hat and carrying her binoculars, who seems ready to start on her own travels, at the end. This book has only two human characters, and is a quiet, beautiful and effective feminist and anti-ageist statement.

Some grandparents are much more subversive. The grandmothers in Babette Cole's *The Trouble with Gran* (1987) and Alison Dexter's *Grandma* (1992) are by no means as elegant as Walsh's, but they are just as active and far from the stereotype. Grandfathers too cannot be written off as nice old men on the fringes of society. Jamila Gavin's *Grandpa Chatterji* (1993) contrasts the two grandfathers of Neetu and Sanjay; Granpa Leicester is a stickler for neatness, while their grandfather from India is more of a visionary and affords the children something of an introduction into Indian culture. That grandfathers can however be embarrassing at times is evident in Leon Rosselson's *Rosa's Grandfather Sings Again* (1991), where the old man insists on singing at the school concert despite the granddaughter's reservations about his voice. In Jean Wills' *The Pop Concert* (1992), Alicia dislikes the false teeth which she sees next to her grandfather's bed, but she has a pride in his saxophone playing.

One of the most stereotype-defying grandparents is to be found in Nina Bawden's *Granny the Pag* (1995), where the title character smokes and rides a

Harley Davidson. Natasha regards her grandmother as a much better guardian than her parents; though these are not unpleasant in themselves they are much too absorbed in their theatrical careers to be interested in her. Natasha's invented name 'Pag' for her grandmother is later defined: 'It's come to mean someone who's special in some way. Sort of famous or powerful. Someone who can make things happen. Like a judge, or a policeman . . .' (p. 98). Natasha's choice of guardian is later ratified by a court.

In a primary school 'news' period, Natasha is reluctant to talk about her grandmother, and her teacher, Hilda, misunderstands her silence:

> On Sunday, the Pag and I had been out on the bike for what she called a *real old zoom* on the motorway. It was the most exciting thing in the world . . . but it wasn't the sort of thing the others had told about and I didn't want to be different. Hilda said in a kind voice, 'I know your mum and your dad are famous people . . . . But your granny is a wonderful person in a way you will understand better when you are older.' She thought I was ashamed because I didn't live with my mother and father. But it didn't matter. She had said the Pag was 'wonderful'. And I could tell by the way she said 'famous' that she didn't think so much of my mother and father. (p. 10)

In this book, Bawden portrays the complexity of a child's feelings about the quality of an old person. When Rosie, a friend of Natasha's, suggests to a lawyer that the grandmother is 'not just an *old lady*' but a famous person, Natasha replies, 'Don't be snobbish, Rosie. If she wasn't a Pag, just an ordinary old person, she'd be just as important.' This book defies the reader's expectations of how a grandmother should behave, showing her as a unique individual, who is also vulnerable; at the end, Natasha rescues her from drowning and the Pag says: '"If I'm to hang around till you're grown," – cough, puff and sob – "I'll have to stop smoking." And she did.' (p. 153). This kind of portrayal can help the young reader to recognize that the old are equally important as the young and not to be dismissed as has-beens!

'Political' issues

Some critics of contemporary children's literature seem to be under the impression that authors dare not talk about certain subjects, for fear of using 'politically incorrect' language, and that, instead, they spend all their time depicting 'gritty realism' where children are presented with 'correct' political attitudes. While this seems to me to be a caricature, it is true that the obverse of the process of trying to ensure that books about disability or age provide a reasonable kind of depiction of everybody, or indeed that race and gender are also fairly portrayed, is the fact that a number of popular children's authors have written books about other contemporary situations. Such books have been seen, generally by rather traditional critics, as being too politically committed and as trying too hard to indoctrinate their young readers in 'correct' attitudes on matters like ecology, poverty and social deprivation. Authors sometimes also tackle subjects such as broken families and bullying, instead of the 'safe' topics which some adults may like to think should be the province of children's books.

People who complain of such books that they are too political often have the illusion that the term 'ideology' only applies to material with a 'left-wing' stance. It is, however, just as ideologically motivated to pursue a policy of non-involvement in matters like housing or hardship as it is to attempt to intervene. It is equally a political decision to judge that young people should *not* have books which deal with contemporary issues as it is to write them. To regard fiction, whether for children or for adults, as merely escapist, is as ideological an attitude as it is to treat fiction as a means of disseminating political points of view. Neither position does justice to the value of literature in itself.

Another criticism sometimes made is that politically committed writing is not generally good writing. Clearly any decision about the quality of a book can only apply to that specific text, and if a work is not a good book, it probably won't be read. Suffice it to say that some of the most powerful literature of the past has also taken a political or a committed stance; several works of Dickens, George Eliot and Elizabeth Gaskell come immediately to mind. In these cases, however, the issues involved, such as basic human rights for factory workers in *Hard Times*, seem very clear to readers today, and it is not so easy to recognize how controversial they seemed then.

The other criticism which might be made about children's books which portray contemporary issues is that young people may not be ready to consider some of these subjects, such as divorce, single-parent families, teenage pregnancy, relationships with step-parents, violence, sexual harassment, and problems about sexual orientation. That this is manifestly not the case, a glance both at the news and at the magazines so popular with teenagers will easily prove. Some people think it wrong to expose children to knowledge about explicit sex or about death, and want children to keep their innocence while they can, but this doesn't do justice to children's experience in today's society. Nor does it allow for the fact that children's literature, with the exception of most books of the early part of the twentieth century, has always been concerned with such issues, especially death.

Some of the authors who are most often mentioned in this context have also been considered above because of their realistic portrayal of disability, or in connection with gender, race and culture. They include Bernard Ashley, Judy Blume, Paula Danziger, Berlie Doherty, Anne Fine, Rosa Guy, Janni Howker, Jean Ure and Jacqueline Wilson, all of whom write a high proportion of their fiction in a realist mode. Since it is clearly impossible to do justice here to all these writers, and a number of others, there is more information in the references to this chapter.

All the authors named above are popular with young readers, perhaps because they give the impression of living in the same world as the young. It is noteworthy too how often this very use of a contemporary idiom means that the serious subjects presented are treated with humour, while at the same time an insight is given into the mind of a child or adolescent who is often enduring extremely painful emotions.

That difficult issues can be presented in a way which is accessible to young children is apparent from many picture books; a notable example is the treatment of the subject of the effect on a child of a divorced parent entering into a new relationship, something experienced by many young people in today's society, in Annalena McAffee and Anthony Browne's *The Visitors who Came to Stay* (1987). This depicts Katy, a little girl who lives with her father after the break-up of her parents' marriage, whose quiet routine is threatened when he enters Mary, who 'had the widest smile Katy had ever seen', and her son Sean, who loves practical jokes, come to stay. Despite her father's apparent happiness:

> Katy was fed up. She didn't like sharing her house, her garden, her toys, her walks and her meals. She didn't like sharing her Dad, and one day she told him so.' (p. 22).

When as a consequence he breaks with Mary, it is impossible for him and Katy to return to the previous tranquillity, and the house seems empty, so they go to visit Mary. As they go down the garden path to the house, Katy is ready with a joke 'camera' to squirt water into Sean's face. To summarize the story like this, however, omits the very important feature of Anthony Browne's surrealistic illustrations, which allow the young reader to appreciate in a much fuller way than could be effected by the text alone, the disruption caused by the visitors' presence; they provide a kind of counterpoint to the emotions which the words describe quite sparingly.

Sharon Walsh (in Pinsent, 1993) investigated the responses to this text of several groups of children, aged 5, 7, 11 and 14, she found:

> For the youngest pair of pupils, aged 5, the disruption in Katy's life was symbolised by the expression of alarm on her teddy bear's face when the visitors first enter her home. A reading of the text by the 7-year-old pupils suggested that the surrealistic images scattered throughout the book were an indication that Katy was dreaming about her future and that once she returned to reality, harmony would be restored. (p. 21)

The sophistication of these and the other responses she recorded make clear that children of all ages are capable of a high degree of sensitivity to the content; in fact some of the younger children appreciated features which were often unremarked by the older readers. After all, young children are by no means exempt from the emotions involved, though they may lack the vocabulary to describe them. Pictures may sometimes therefore be a more appropriate mode of access to exploring these emotions.

While treatment of the painful emotions involved in family relationships is likely to be acknowledged as relevant by many people, and forms the subject of numerous books today, notably by Anne Fine, Judy Blume and Jacqueline Wilson, there would be much less universal agreement about the desirability of portraying the rather different situation of the dawning realization of homosexuality. The controversy concerning Suzanne Bosche's *Jenny Lives with Eric and Martin* (1983) was based on the desire to protect young children from an awareness of same-sex relationships. Surprisingly, Aidan Chambers *Dance on My Grave*, published a year earlier, seems to have attracted no particular attention, although it is far more explicit in its depiction of a physical relationship between two male characters. The lack of concern about it could be the result of the book demanding a much more competent reader, one who could cope with the post-modern technique of using differing modes of narration, such as a social worker's notebook, a school essay, as well as the journal of the 16-year-old Hal, who gradually comes to realize that his love of the slightly older Barry is more than fraternal. In fact the main point of interest about the relationship is Hal's need to understand human differences;

while his love has been too possessive, Barry's character is such that he cannot cope with a permanent relationship.

It is more likely, however, that the reason why no controversy erupted about this book is because it was never perceived as being associated with a particular political group. In the case of the smaller and slighter book, *Jenny*, the link with the old Inner London Education Authority, which put it on reading lists, caused it to become identified with what was described by right-wing politicians as the 'loony left'. Thus this somewhat innocuous, not very distinguished, book became a victim of political ideology, where Chambers' much more considerable achievement, like several later books for young people about homosexuality, such as Janet McDermott's *Yasmin* (1994), about lesbianism, remains little known.

Paula Danziger's *The Cat Ate my Gym Suit* (1974; British edition 1986) also impinges on political issues. While its focus of interest is Marcy Lewis, aged 13, whose first person narrative begins: 'I hate my father. I hate school. I hate being fat. I hate the principal because he wanted to fire Ms Finney, my English teacher.' (p. 1), its theme is different kinds of loyalty to America. As a teacher new to the school, Ms Finney gives the pupils the chance to write about what bothers them by saying: 'I remember that when I was a kid, I used to be so embarrassed because I wore braces on my teeth and everyone used to call me "Tinsel Tooth"' (p. 9). This helps Marcy to come to terms with her own feelings and in spite of her lack of confidence about her appearance, to make friends with a boy, Joel.

Ms Finney, however, is disliked by the more traditional members of the Board of Education for the school, especially when it is observed that every day she refuses to recite the 'Pledge of Allegiance' to the American flag which is seen by many people as 'symbolic of patriotic pride and commitment to country. For others, not reciting the Pledge is also symbolic' (author's introduction). The conflict in local society brought about by the teacher's dismissal, which is later reversed, also drags into the open issues such as a disagreement about roles between Marcy's parents. Ms Finney's views are that she is teaching children 'to love and respect the English language . . . in ways that will interest and excite students', but she does not believe that 'this country offers liberty and justice for all . . . until I see it happening, I will not say the Pledge' (pp. 105–6).

At the end, Marcy learns that 'Ms Finney was going to graduate school to get a doctorate in something called bibliotherapy. That's counselling using books and writing. That sounds good' (p. 113).

The use of first person narrative is likely to induce the young reader to share the politically committed views which Marcy either expresses directly or relates with approval. This book might prove unacceptable to adults who feel that the author is unduly influencing her teenage readers to her own point of view. My opinion, however, is that books like this provide an excellent means of airing controversial questions, so that adolescent readers can be empowered to weigh up for themselves the methods the author is using to convey her point of view, and to get more information before making any decision for themselves.

One of the things which readers may well want to know more about at the end of Danziger's book is the subject of bibliotherapy. This has been defined as simply 'helping with books', or, more fully:

> use of books to influence total development, a process of interaction between

140

the reader and literature which is used for personality assessment, adjustment, growth, clinical and mental hygiene purposes; a concept that ideas inherent in selected reading material can have a therapeutic effect upon the mental or physical ills of the reader. (Good, 1966, quoted in Pardeck and Pardeck, 1987)

There are some aspects of this process, as defined here, which I endorse and which could be related to the kind of books which I have been discussing in this chapter, but I remain somewhat unhappy about the concept of bibliotheraphy, since it seems to have rather too much of an automaticity about it – apply this book to this situation and it will work in a similar way to using an antibiotic against an infection. I think that books which touch on the kind of issues considered above can be of immense value to both the individuals affected by the problem, and to others who need to find out more information about it. But I am unhappy about the books being *used* in this way – still less do I like the kind of book which seems to have been written only with this kind of function in mind.

A good deal of work has been done on the choice of texts for bibliotherapy by Jean and John Pardeck (1984) but unfortunately its value for the British reader is diminished by the fact that nearly all the books they discuss seem to lack any British editions, which makes it difficult to judge their quality as literature. There are undoubtedly many books which have a good deal to say to children with various difficulties, and the really important thing is for teachers and librarians to know about them as well as knowing their pupils, and then to try to make a match.

Fewer complaints seem to be voiced about involving children with issues concerning the environment, though again this could be seen as an aspect of 'political correctness'. Children in fact often have a natural interest in the environment which is, after all, their future. A series popular with pre-teenage children is *Animal Ark*, which is about a veterinary practice, and it seems to assume a range of attitudes which some adults might not find entirely acceptable. In Lucy Daniels' *Cub in the Cupboard* (1994), for instance, there is a strong assumption that fox-hunting is evil, a position reinforced by the unpleasantness of the characters in the book who are in favour of it. Michael Foreman's *Dinosaurs and all That Rubbish* (1972) and John Burningham's *Oi! Get off our Train* (1989) are picture books which are both concerned with the state of the planet and the resultant danger of species vanishing, a subject which few adults will object to being presented to children.

A more challenging book on the same theme is Peter Dickinson's *Eva* (1988), which depicts a future world where there are very few green spaces left, and, consequently, there are very few animals at large. The few chimpanzees which still exist are in a colony kept for laboratory experiments, a situation which is condemned (as, indeed, by analogy, are similar situations today) by the unusual means of the consciousness of a human character, Eva, being implanted within a young female chimp, Kelly. Through Eva's experiences we come to understand the immorality of treating animals as if they were merely reservoirs of human parts. Since this is a powerfully written book, it certainly raises questions about how literature may persuade. As elsewhere, what is needed is for young readers to be aware of how their emotions are being influenced by means such as using the consciousness of the focal character, and the powerful pictures generated of the commercial use of the animals. On a television programme, Eva comes to realize that her expression of anguish about the situation:

> spoke for Kelly, and the other chimps, and all the children of earth, the orangs
> and giraffes and whales and moths and eagles, which over the past few cen-
> turies had turned their backs on humankind and crawled or glided or sunk
> away into the dark. (p. 146)

The elegiac power of the language used here depends on the almost rhetorical
repetition of the word 'and', building up a sense of an endless procession, the
extended and intertextual metaphor of the animals moving in their own specific
ways 'into the dark' as a figure for their extinction. Young people are very likely to
share sentiments like these, as an interest in preservation of the planet is a consistently popular subject, but they should be helped to recognize that Dickinson's
mode of evoking it is far from ideologically neutral.

Many people might find problematic some of the books which familiarize children with the worst episodes of the second world war. R. Innocenti's *Rose Blanche*
(1985), Margaret Wild's *Let the Celebration Begin* (1991) and Jane Yolen's *Briar
Rose* (1994), all take on the difficult topic of concentration camps. Even David
McKee's *Tusk Tusk* (1978), which is, among other things, an anti-war document,
might be regarded by some as unsuitable for the young children who seem to be its
first audience. It is, however, important that those concerned with children's
education should familiarize themselves with this kind of material to make up their
minds as to whether, and if so, at what age, it might be presented to their pupils.

Conclusion

The books considered in this chapter have been of many kinds. Most people would
perhaps have no problems about the need for books to depict disabled people as real
people, with the right to as much dignity as anyone else. The danger here is of
sympathy becoming patronizing, and of the resultant production of inferior books.
Books about more obviously political issues can be more problematic, but to try to
prevent children from encountering them would be a mistake.

The fact is that children live in a real world and need to have quality books on all
issues. We cannot just allow them to consider uncontroversial subjects, and there
are very few totally 'safe' books. What teachers, librarians and parents need is a
good knowledge of the books that exist, and the use of tact in handling them. We
need to help children appreciate the fictional nature of literature, so that they don't
believe everything which is presented to them. They need to be aware that an
author, with a full range of normal human prejudices, has written the book, that a
publisher has decided it is economically worth publishing and a bookseller that it is
worth selling. They need to understand that nothing is value-free, not the books,
nor the TV programmes, nor the magazines and that no one is without prejudices,
not their teachers, nor their parents, nor even themselves!

References

Note that an extensive bibliography is also given at the end of this book. In general, the details are those of the first British edition. Paperbacks are marked with an asterisk. †Indicates the book also deals with death.

1. Physical disabilities

Blume, J. (1980) *Deenie.* London: Heinemann.

Bodsworth, N. (1989) *A Nice Walk in the Jungle**. London: Viking.

De Jong, M. (1956) *The Wheel on the School.* London: Lutterworth.

Hearn, E. (1990, illustrated by M. Thurman) *Franny and the Music Girl**. London: Magi.

Hill, D. (1992) *See Ya, Simon.* London: Viking.

Marshall, A. (1974) *I Can Jump Puddles.* Harmondsworth: Penguin.

Mathias, B. (ed.)(1989) *The Spell Singer.* London: Blackie (includes a variety of disabilities).

Naidoo, B. (1994, illustrated by P. Rohr-Rouendaal) *Letang's New Friend**, *Letang and Julie Save the Day**, *Trouble for Letang and Julie**. Harlow: Longmans.

Sallis, S. (1981) *Sweet Frannie.*† London: Heinemann.

Southall, I. (1968) *Let the Balloon Go.* London: Methuen.

Speare, E. (1960) *The Witch of Blackbird Pond.* London: Gollancz.

Strachan, I. (1993) *The Boy in the Bubble.*† London: Methuen.

Sutcliff, R. (1954) *The Eagle of the Ninth.* Oxford: Oxford University Press.

Sutcliff, R. (1958) *Warrior Scarlet.* Oxford: University Press.

Sutcliff, R. (1970) *The Witch's Brat.* Oxford: University Press.

Wilkins, V. (1995, illustrated by G. McLeod & L. Willey) *Are We There Yet?**. Camberley: Tamarind.

Wilkins, V. (1995, illustrated by P. Venus) *Boots for a Bridesmaid**. Camberley: Tamarind.

2. Loss of sight

Boston, L. (1958) *The Chimneys of Green Knowe.* London: Faber.

Doherty, B. (1989) *Spellhorn.* London: Hamish Hamilton.

Garfield, L. (1967) *Smith.* London: Constable.

L'Engle, M. (1969) *The Young Unicorns.* London: Gollancz.

Moon, L. (1994, illustrated by A. Aycliffe) *Lucy's Picture**. London: Orchard.

Taylor, T. (1970) *The Cay.* London: Bodley Head.

Ure, J. (1981) *See You Thursday.* Harmondsworth: Penguin.

Wilder, L. I. (1961) *By the Shores of Silver Lake.* London: Lutterworth.

3. Loss of hearing

Dunbar, J. (1985) *Mundo and the Weather Child*, London: Heinemann.

Ure, J. (1990) *Cool Simon*, London: Orchard Books.

4. Learning difficulties

Anderson, R. (1989) *The Bus People.* Oxford: University Press.

Anderson, R. and McNicholas, S. (1991) *Best Friends**. London: A.& C. Black.

Anderson, R. and McNicholas, S. (1993) *Jessy and the Bridesmaid's Dress** (originally published as *Jessy and the Long-Short Dress*). London: A.& C. Black.

Byars, B. (1970) *Summer of the Swans.* London: Viking.

Laird, E. (1988) *Red Sky in the Morning.* London: Heinemann.

Masters, A. (1993) *Spinner.* London: Blackie [Autism].

Shyer, M. (1987) *Welcome Home Jellybean*. London: Collins.
Wrightson, P. (1968) *I Own the Racecourse*. London: Hutchinson.

5. Speech and language difficulties

Ashley, B. (1974) *The Trouble with Donovan Croft*. Oxford: University Press.
Furlong, M. (1995) *Robin's Country*. New York: Knopf.
Gleitzman, M. (1992) *Blabbermouth*. London: Pan.
Gleitzman, M. (1993) *Sticky Beak*. London: Pan.
Kemp, G. (1977) *The Turbulent Term of Tyke Tiler*. London: Faber.
Wells, R. (1988) *Shy Charles*. London: Collins

6. Dyslexia

Breslin, T. (1995)*Whispers in the Graveyard*. London: Methuen.
Fine, A. (1996) *How to Write Really Badly*. London: Methuen.
Goodhart, P. (1995) *Flow*. London: Methuen.

7. Fantasy and picture books relevant to disability

Ashley, B. (1992, illustrated by D. Bragell) *Cleversticks**. London: Collins.
Browne, A. (1989) *The Tunnel**. London: Julia MacRae.
Browne, A. and Strauss, G. (1991) *The Night Shimmy**. London: Julia MacRae.
Cannon, J. (1995) *Stellaluna* *. St. Albans: David Bennett.
Glen, M. (1992) *Ruby* *. London: Gollancz.
LeGuin, U. (1972) *The Tombs of Atuan*. London: Gollancz.
McKee, D. (1980) *Not Now, Bernard**. London: Andersen.
McKee, D. (1989) *Elmer, the Patchwork Elephant**. London: Andersen.
Norton, M. (1952) *The Borrowers*. London: Dent.
O'Brien, R. (1972) *Mrs Frisby and the Rats of NIMH*. London: Gollancz.
Ridley, P. (1991) *Krindlekrax*. London: Cape.
Pearce, P. (1962) *A Dog so Small*. London: Constable.
Sendak, M. (1967) *Where the Wild Things Are**. London: Bodley Head.
Smythe, G. and James, A. (1989) *A Pet for Mrs Arbuckle**. Harmondsworth: Penguin.
Tolkien, J. R. R. (1937) *The Hobbit*. London: Allen & Unwin.
White, E. B. (1946) *Stuart Little*. London: Hamish Hamilton.

8. Positive portrayal of age

Bawden, N. (1995) *Granny the Pag*. London: Hamish Hamilton.
Bruce, L. (1993) *Jazeera's Journey*. London: Methuen.
Cole, B. (1987) *The Trouble with Gran**. London: Heinemann.
Dexter, A. (1992) *Grandma**. London: ABC.
Ernest, K. (1993) *Hope Leaves Jamaica*. London: Methuen.
Gavin, J. (1993) *Grandpa Chatterji*. London: Methuen.
Gavin, J. (1995) *Grandpa's Indian Summer*. London: Methuen.
Hedderwick, M. (1985) *Katie Morag and the Two Grandmothers**. London: Bodley Head.
Igus, T. (1992, illustrated by H. Bond) *When I was Little**. Orange, New Jersey: Just Us Books.
Hoffman, M. (1991, illustrated by C. Binch) *Amazing Grace**. London: Frances Lincoln.
Hoffman, M. (1995, illustrated by C. Binch) *Grace and Family**. London: Frances Lincoln.
Kaye, G. (1984) *Comfort Herself*. London: Deutsch.
Rosselson, L. (1991) *Rosa's Grandfather Sings Again*. London: Viking.
Voight, C. (1984) *Dicey's Song*. London: Collins.

Walsh, J. P. (1992, illustrated by S. Williams) *When Grandma Came**. London: Viking.
Wills, J. (1992, illustrated by S. Harris) *The Pop Concert*. London: Andersen.

9. Death

Blume, J. (1982) *Tiger Eyes*. London: Heinemann.
Buchanan Smith, D. (1989) *A Taste of Blackberries*. Basingstoke: Macmillan.
Burningham, J. (1984) *Granpa**. London: Cape.
Fine, A. (1983) *The Granny Project*. London: Methuen.
Fox, P. (1994) *Western Wind*. London: Orion.
Isherwood, S. (1994, illustrated by K. Isherwood) *My Grandad**. Oxford: Oxford University Press.
Lowry, L. (1990) *A Summer to Die*. London: Collins.
Lowry, L. (1987) *The Woods at the End of Autumn Street*. London: Dent.
Magorian (1981) *Goodnight Mr Tom*. London: Kestrel.
Paterson, K. (1978) *Bridge to Terebithia*. London: Gollancz.
Piumini, R. (1993) *Mattie and Grandpa**. Harmondsworth: Penguin.
Varley, S. (1984) *Badger's Parting Gifts**. London: Andersen.
Zindel, P. (1969) *The Pigman*. London: Bodley Head.

10. Ecological issues

Burningham, J. (1991) *Oi! Get Off Our Train**. London: Random House.
Daniels, L. (1994) *Cub in the Cupboard*. London: Hodder.
Dickinson, P. (1988) *Eva.†* London: Gollancz.
Foreman, M. (1972) *Dinosaurs and all That Rubbish*. London: Hamish Hamilton.

11. Bullying

Blume, J. (1980) *Blubber*. London: Heinemann.
Coppard, Y. (1991) *Bully*. London: Red Fox.
Gibbons, A. (1993) *Chicken*. London: Dent.
Guy, R. (1984) *Paris, Pee Wee and Big Dog*. London: Gollancz.
Guy, R. (1974)*The Friends*. London: Gollancz.
Kemp, G. (1990) *Ferret*. London: Faber.

12. Family issues: divorce, single parents, teenage sex and pregnancy, sexual orientation, etc.

Ashley, B. (1980) *Break in the Sun*. Oxford: Oxford University Press.
Blume, J. (1979) *It's Not the End of the World*. London: Pan.
Blume, J. (1976) *Forever*, London: Gollancz.
Chambers, A. (1982) *Dance on My Grave*. London: Bodley Head.
Cleary, B. (1956) *Fifteen*. Harmondsworth: Penguin.
Cross, G. (1990)*Wolf*. Oxford: University Press.
Danziger, P. (1986) *The Divorce Express*. London: Heinemann.
Doherty, B. (1991) *Dear Nobody*. London: Hamish Hamilton.
Fine, A. (1989) *Goggle Eyes*. London: Hamish Hamilton.
Fine, A. (1992) *Flour Babies*. London: Hamish Hamilton.
Gleitzman, M. (1990) *Two Weeks with the Queen*. Basingstoke: Macmillan.
Guy, R. (1974) *The Friends*. London: Gollancz.
Guy, R. (1989) *The Ups and Downs of Carl Davis the Third*. London: Gollancz.
Howker, J. (1985) *The Nature of the Beast*. London: Julia MacRae.
Impey, R. and Galvain, M. (1990) *My Mum and Our Dad**. London: Viking.

McAfree, A. and Browne, A. (1984) *The Visitors who Came to Stay**. London: Hamish Hamilton.

McDermott, J. (1994) *Yasmin*. London: Mantra.

Westall, R. (1981) *The Scarecrows*. London: Chatto.

Wilson, J. (1991) *The Story of Tracy Beaker*. London: Doubleday.

Wilson, J. (1992) *The Suitcase Kid*. London: Doubleday.

Wilson, J. (1994) *The Bed and Breakfast Star*. London: Doubleday.

War

Bawden, N. (1973) *Carrie's War*. London: Gollancz.

Foreman, M. (1993) *War Game**. London: Pavilion.

Innocenti, R. (1985, text by I. McEwan) *Rose Blanche*. London: Cape.

McKee, D. (1978) *Tusk Tusk*. London: Andersen.

Swindells, R. (1984) *Brother in the Land*. Oxford: Oxford University Press.

Walsh, J. P. (1969) *Fireweed*. Basingstoke: Macmillan.

Westall, R. (1975) *The Machine Gunners*. Basingstoke: Macmillan.

Westall, R. (1990) *The Kingdom by the Sea*. London: Methuen.

Wild, M. (1991) *Let the Celebrations Begin!**. London: Bodley Head.

Yolen, J. (1994) *Briar Rose*. London: Pan.

Equality and Information Books

'Now what I want is, Facts.' (Dickens, *Hard Times*, ch. 1)

In this chapter I propose to look briefly at some of the varied range of material with which children are confronted, usually but not exclusively in school, which purports to prepare them for a 'real' world; among this very amorphous collection are reading schemes, textbooks, dictionaries, encyclopedias, atlases, and such factual books as they might choose in to follow up their own interests. While it is true that most of this kind of material might not be included in some strict definitions of 'literature', to ignore the fact that children are exposed to many books which are not fictional would be to take too limited a view of their experiences with written text.

Authors of non-fiction are frequently rather more blatant than fiction writers in their endeavours to influence young readers; because they are explicitly seeking to teach subject matter, without the veil which fictional devices may cast over particular ways of seeing the world, they sometimes seem to feel themselves free to express more overtly the points of view which they want the young to imbibe. Equally, the expectations which children have of this kind of material means that they are more inclined to accept without question what school textbooks say.

Another significant aspect is that it is less easy for a writer of 'factual' material for the young to be out of step with society and still expect to be published. Publishers may not notice, or may hope that parents and teachers do not notice, radical or non-conforming attitudes in fiction – they are less likely to be so obliging when dealing with non-fiction.

It is clearly impossible to do justice to the treatment of equality issues within all these books, nor can any one person have the expertise to deal adequately with the breadth of the school curriculum. What I hope to do in this chapter is to show some of the ways in which ideology has been displayed in the past in 'factual' material and to consider the extent to which good intentions and informed attitudes today are not always met with unqualified success. I shall also make use of some of the findings of the Roehampton Survey (1996) concerning the differing preferences of boys and girls about the non-fiction which they choose to read.

Reading schemes and alphabet books

In the past, the world of the reading scheme was white and middle class, with the male characters performing all the interesting or prestigious activities; the cover of the original Ladybird 9a, *Games We Like* (1964), for instance, displays two girls dressed up as nurses, with a boy, wearing a top hat and a stethoscope, taking the doctor's role. It has always been a subject for argument as to whether this kind of imbalance, which as we shall see still continues, though to a less marked extent, is likely to affect the expectations of vulnerable initial readers. Since it is generally recognized that girls outperform boys in the Primary school, it does not appear that they have been significantly disadvantaged in educational achievement by the roles in which they have been depicted.

Whether or not the fact that these formative books have constantly relegated girls to a second place, while until more recently, black or Asian characters, or even white working class, tended to be absent altogether, has had any effect on the readers' expectations is difficult to prove. But they have certainly given a picture of society which during the seventies became increasingly outdated. More recent compilers of reading programmes have clearly taken race and gender issues on board, though one of the answers to the question of ethnicity and class, the use of animal characters, has not necessarily solved the question of gender imbalance, as can be seen in the *Open Door* programme, produced in the early 1980s. More recent reading schemes, such as the very popular *Oxford Reading Tree*, certainly involve black or Asian characters, but females are still sometimes subordinate to or present in smaller proportions than males, even though the girls do perhaps have slightly more active roles today than in the past.

I have looked in more detail at two fairly recent reading schemes, *Wellington Square* (1989) and *Flying Boot* (1994), to see what kind of picture they create. *Wellington Square* has certainly shed the middle-class ethos, and perhaps because its compilers were hoping to create interest from parents, and encourage them to read with their children, it has certain parallels with the popular TV 'soap', *East Enders*, being set in a London square. There are some ethnic minority characters, the Asian 'corner shop' proprietors and a black family; obviously the books could be open to the charge of tokenism in this respect, but I would rather say that they are providing evidence of awareness of a multi-ethnic society.

The scheme is designed particularly 'to meet the needs of many children from around seven to 11 years old and above, who . . . are "slow to get off the ground in reading"' (*Teachers' Resource Pack*, I, p. 9). I am not concerned here with the merits or demerits of the eclectic approach to the teaching of reading which the scheme embraces, though by its nature it facilitates the provision of an effective and varied range of material. The stories are aimed at an older age range than most initial reading schemes (compare the one below) and are likely to be attractive to many children.

A factor which may well have influenced the choice of subjects and characters in these stories is the intended audience of children who have not been making the expected degree of progress in learning to read; it may therefore be assumed that a higher proportion than usual of the readers are likely to be boys, since it is generally agreed that there are more boys with reading problems than girls.

Snowling (1987) says, 'The sex ratio of 3.3 males to every female with specific reading retardation is similar to that reported for other developmental language difficulties' (p. 7). This expected readership may account for the disproportion in the material. Of the characters introduced in Level One, there are nine adult women, of whom four appear to have no other occupation than being 'mothers', at least at this stage of the series, and two are single, probably elderly, women; other female characters are the music shop owner, head teacher and police constable. There are 14 adult men: four shopkeepers, one gardener, one policeman, one fireman, one expert on animals, two garage workers, two teachers; only two men have at this stage have no identifiable occupation other than being fathers. There are four boys and two girls, and four pets, of which three are male and one is of un-identifiable sex. At Level Two, five more male characters are introduced, including the Duke of Wellington (in a dream) and a gunman who attempts to rob a local factory. The same kind of imbalance occurs in the 12 stories, which constantly feature boys' interests, especially football; about seven have without question a dominance of boys, and the remaining five could be said at best to provide an equal balance. The focal character, who has just moved into the neighbourhood, is a boy, Rick, and we see through his eyes most of the time, observing how well he is settling down and making friends.

Perhaps because of the intended audience of slightly older children, there is more awareness of a less cosy world than many reading schemes create, and at some points the subject of bullying is hinted at. The assumption seems to be made (cf. Chapter 5) that while girls are prepared to read about boys, boys are reluctant to read about girls. It could also be suggested that the imbalance reflects the world as it is, rather than as it should be. The compilers presumably think it likely that more men will be shopkeepers and that women who keep shops may represent the more frivolous and aesthetic side, as in Mrs Chant's music shop. More men will own factories, or even tote a gun! Interestingly, the school which the children in the series attend departs from this male hegemony and has a female head; the existence of two male primary school teachers is also surely a positive step.

How far is the fact that many of the readers will be boys a justification for the marginalization of the female characters? Would it be risking the alienation of these boys if more females were included in books which are compulsory reading?

Like those of *Wellington Square*, the compilers of a more recent reading scheme, *Flying Boot* (1994) also seem to have given some attention to the questions of the representation of ethnic minority and non-middle class characters. The oldest of the child characters in this scheme, Selma, is of Asian origin, and while this appears to have no effect on her clothing or behaviour, we do see her with her family, and her grandmother in particular is portrayed in appropriate garb. The depiction both of families and of society in general takes full account of the contemporary situation.

Although there is some imbalance in the sexes of the human characters (three boys to two girls) this is compensated for by Selma being the oldest and clearly the most knowledgeable child, in particular by being able to read to the other children (Stage 2, Book 6). The adventures seem well balanced, and only in one instance do we see a boy taking a role which could be enviable to all, piloting the 'Flying Boot' of the title (Stage 3, Book 10).

Nevertheless, the balance of the series is strongly influenced by the fact that the central non-human character, Max, who performs all the magic, can travel any-where or become invisible, and is generally calculated to appeal to the child reader, is male; he is described in the general account of the scheme as 'rather like a green gonk'; 'he spends his time making letters of all shapes, sizes and materials. He travels in his amazing Big Boot to deliver the words that he has made.' He is accompanied by one male, Gobbler, and one female, Magpie, who also have a word-changing function. Max's creation is very much in the mould of the stereo-typical male, powerful and knowledgeable, and affects the gender-balance of the reading programme. It may well be that its main progenitor, Ted Wragg, either consciously or subconsciously felt that a central male character would be more effective than a female, more appropriate to his intention of such a character not being bound by the limitations of space and time, but providing 'humour [and] occasional anarchy, the unexpected'; after all, the stereotype of women does not portray them as unconventional or comic. I find it difficult to resist the idea that Max in his word-making capacity is a figure of the creator of the scheme himself!

Another important early source of images which can affect the way young readers see themselves is in alphabet books. Like the rest of non-fiction writing, these have always reflected a good deal about society's perceptions of the young (cf. my chapter in Hancock, 1997), so it is interesting to note those books which do take account of both the aspirations of females and the multi-ethnic nature of society.

Verna Wilkins' *ABC: I can be* (1993) presents among other female roles, 'Pamela is a plumber', 'Qin Fen is a quarry worker' and 'Sakina is a surgeon'. This kind of policy may be criticized as giving a distorted view, since as yet few women are plumbers or surgeons, or indeed engineers and firefighters, who are also featured, but it can be defended on the grounds of current trends. If, as here, a realist view of society seems to be the chosen genre, it might be inappropriate to go too far beyond the contemporary situation; only a humorous picture book would be likely at the moment to claim for instance, that 'Polly is the Pope'! It can also be helpful for boys to see men depicted in less usual roles, as 'Nick is a nurse,' 'Liam is a lampmaker' and 'Ivor is an illustrator'. Books aimed at the very young can help girls to see themselves in situations which they may not otherwise have thought of. They can also let boys play with the idea of both males and females doing different kinds of jobs. A particular feature of Verna Wilkins' book is the way in which she uses characters from a wide range of different ethnic backgrounds, indicated by their names as well as by their appearance, such as 'Kui Hua is a kitemaker'. The slight imbalance in the female favour (there are 15 female and 11 male characters) is surely amply justified by the aeons of preponderance of males.

A different but equally constructive approach is taken by Ifeoma Onyefulu, whose photographs and descriptions in *A is for Africa* (1993) of objects and places associated with traditional African life clearly reveal her consciousness of both race and gender issues. Well over half the pictures relate to both sexes, and the numbers which are illustrated specifically by females (including the almost inevitable 'Q for Queen') or by males are about equal. What is still more significant about this book, however, is the way in which the author puts into a positive light the aspects of African tribal life which have remained somewhat questionable in other books. Unlike those books which have always represented African villages as merely primitive (see below concerning *My First Atlas*), the positive side of this life is depicted:

> Hh is for mud Houses, just right for a hot climate. Most places in Africa are hot during the day and cool at night. In the daytime, the mud walls keep out the hot sunshine. At night, the mud bricks release the heat they have absorbed during the day and warm the inside of the house.

It makes a real change to see aspects of life like this being celebrated rather than apologized for!

Reference books

The Guidelines discussed in Chapter 1 give some attention to the danger of using outdated reference books, and scrutiny of some of these very soon bears out the need for caution. It is in fact quite illuminating for adult readers today to look with a critical eye at books which they themselves may once have used, in school or at home. The kind of awareness this generates can be useful in evaluating more contemporary material.

Critical discussion of out-of-date material can also provide something of a revelation for school pupils, and help dispel the illusion that because it is in print, it must be true. Ideology is much easier to detect in material published 50 years ago than it is in today's products, but once recognized, it helps account for the attitudes of some of the adults who were educated using these materials; it also helps raise awareness of the limitations and blind spots in contemporary material. After all, it is only in fairly recent years that some of the principles we now regard as absolutes, such as the equal right of both sexes and people of all ethnic origins to both education and employment, have been taken for granted; indeed, they are still very open to question in some cultures today. It is possible that in the future, people will be greeting with amazed horror customs which we take for granted today.

An instance of how assumptions concerning gender can influence material which might at first seem relatively objective, is in the contextualization given by *The Children's Picture Dictionary* (1951) for various senses of the word 'cry':

> Jack gave a cry when he fell off his bicycle. He gave a shout. Jill began to cry. Tears fell from her eyes. She was crying. She cried.

The difference between boys who shout and girls who weep is vividly displayed!

As might be expected, encyclopaedias and atlases are fertile sources of the unquestioned assumptions of their compilers. Their pride in empire is often displayed in a way which presumably was natural at the time but now seems jingoistic; *My First Atlas* (1952) appears to be a pleasant, innocent, child-centred little book, featuring on the cover Sam and Susan, who provide a human focus. The first picture inside the book is of the children outside their school, Sam naturally in front, and from then on we gradually arrive at maps of the British Isles, mediated to the child through the idea that these two child characters have spent holidays in the mountains and by the sea. The child's natural curiosity about different parts of the world is utilized by portraying our child leaders at the docks, watching the ships from other places. The map of the world on the next double page spread is made more attractive by little pictures displaying 'lumberjacks' from Canada, mounted 'Australians' with vast flocks of sheep, 'Arabs' in the desert sands with a camel, 'Indians' with a palanquin and an elephant, and three nearly naked 'negroes' sitting on the ground in front of their straw hut.

The crudeness of this last picture, and the fact that it is inappropriate for a sizeable proportion of the people to whom it refers, such as black Americans, means that it provides an over-simplistic stereotype to the young children for whom this atlas is intended. Unfortunately, stereotypes like these, which were probably quite formative for many people who imbibed them with their early school lessons, are not easy to eradicate. Even in the 1950s, this kind of picture must have been fairly unrepresentative of the majority of the 'negro' race, being more typical of 100 years previously, but at that stage, most of the people responsible for the production of atlases for children would have seen no reason to question its assumptions about the barbarousness and lack of education of the people depicted.

By contrast, a recent publication, specially designed for pre-school children, Philip Steele's *First Atlas* (1993), has clearly taken equality issues on board and makes a real attempt to avoid offensive language or stereotypes, while remaining informative and attractive to the young child. The nearest it comes to Anglo-centrism is to begin with North-West Europe; in other respects the continents are treated with balance, and the original inhabitants of different parts of the world are given due credit. It is reassuring to find evidence that authors and publishers are reflecting a consciousness of equality issues and finding an attractive way to convey this to a child audience, without any sense of preaching.

Eurocentrism is, however, perhaps inevitably to be found in the very influential *Children's Encyclopedia*, edited by Arthur Mee from its beginning as a serial publication in 1908 to its production in ten volumes in 1925. The two initial colour plates are very indicative of Mee's cognitive framework. The first shows Anne Hathaway with her elbow on the window-sill looking soulfully out into the eyes of Shakespeare, balding but still young, standing in the garden and reading from a sheaf of papers; the picture is headed: 'Shakespeare fancies a new rhyme.' The second colour plate, headed 'Brothers and Sisters are we all', portrays about 50 children in national dress (an invaluable transparent covering sheet indicates their identities), of whom a few tiny pygmies, negroes and Hottentots in the far corner are the only representatives of a large section of the human race. Far more promi-nent, separated from the black children by a few others of rather suspect groups like Arabs and Turks, are some much larger children from France, Holland and the rest of Europe. Though the Editor's dedication is to 'Boys and Girls Everywhere', he clearly has no inkling that a high proportion of the population of the world could feel marginalized.

Interestingly, the picture omits any children in national costume from the British Isles, to whom Mee is probably addressing himself more than any others. I suspect that at a subconscious level this omission is related to the preceding picture of Shakespeare; instead of images presumably already familiar to the British child reader, we have the hero figure of one of the great Englishmen, to be put forward for emulation by all English boys (the girls don't count, at least in much of the androcentric style of the text).

Mee's work was immensely influential on subsequent encyclopedias for chil-dren, and ran into many editions in England and elsewhere, being translated into many languages (I wonder if they all retained the illustrations!) and continuing in print until the 1950s (cf. Carpenter and Prichard, 1984, p. 112). Again, it is clear that many adults have grown up without questioning the influence of this and simi-lar Anglocentric views about the world; many copies of it must still be in print in attics and second-hand bookshops. It displays how important it is for children to be educated to query what they read.

This need for education to assist readers in the process of discrimination about texts is nowhere more vital than in scrutinizing the perspectives supplied about other parts of the world, especially those which, when the books were printed, were dominated by some of the European colonial powers. Sections on Africa in both of two later encyclopedias for children, *The Wonderland of Knowledge* (Ogan, 1933) and *The New Encyclopedia for the Younger Generation* (Guillot, 1958) are equally inadequate and patronizing, despite their different dates, and it is not until the 1970s that we start to find any real attempt to redress the balance. In today's classroom, the role of the printed encyclopedia is often taken over by the CD-Rom, where it is important for teachers to facilitate the full participation by girls, who are often somewhat marginalized in the use of computer technology (see below).

It would, however, be unwise to assume that because more recent books on factual subjects are generally careful, at least on the surface, to avoid offence, they necessarily present a more accurate picture. D. Bailey's *Families* (1989), a colourfully illustrated book which is part of the *First Facts* series, which the publishers Macmillan, claim is 'ideal for children who are ready to read and enjoy information books', is explicitly intended to communicate an optimistic message about the human race: 'We are like one big family' (p. 44). Unfortunately the book seems to convey a different implicit message from this; much of it seems to assume that, with a few exceptions, people from Africa, India, South America, all still have a peasant economy. Nor is all the information totally reliable:

> The Muslim religion allows men to have more than one wife. Our picture shows a man in northern Nigeria with five wives and their children . . . . Most Muslims now choose to have only one wife. (p. 11)

In fact, the limit is four, and the last sentence scarcely does justice to the large Muslim communities in Britain and other Western countries which have no vestiges of polygamy.

Books like these are, however, trying to fulfil the useful function of giving information to their readers about people in the rest of the world without, at least at surface level, doing anything to assume that one section of the population is better than another. In this process, they may sometimes come up against the charge of 'political correctness', where the book concerned possesses so little interest in its own right that it is impossible to think of children wanting to read it for any other purpose than to satisfy their teachers or as part of a project. It is easy to see how the latter function may be fulfilled by books which set out to describe, in a straightforward way, the situation of for instance a real family (as in the Crossfield Family's *Seven of Us* (1978)); but less easy to understand the purpose of those pseudonarrative books which are dependent on rather unreal characters. J. Jones' *To the Temple for Arti* (1987) is an example of this genre, where the stilted dialogue and the illustrations, which are a cross between photographs and truly imaginative pictures, tend to detract from any kind of verisimilitude:

> 'We were talking to the teacher about our lovely Diwali. Where are we going?' Meena asks.
> 'Dadi Maa is ill. We are going to the temple for arti. We must say prayers for her.' Sunil and Meena are sad that their granny is ill.

Books like this seem to me to be unlikely to achieve their presumed intended aim, of showing that minority ethnic groups and the religions they practise are very much like the rest of us (the temple has been converted from a church), because the picture of Hinduism it conveys seems to be expressed from the outside, and gives the impression that it is all concerned with flowers and fruit and 'tinsel to make everything pretty and bright', so that in a kind of way it is perceived as not quite so adult and serious as Western Christianity. (More detail is given in my forthcoming article in *Paradigm*, 1997) A recent date may not, then, guarantee the accuracy or truth to life of the contents of reference books.

Children's preferences concerning information books

The choices which children make about non-fictional material seem to be more strongly influenced by their gender than are their choices of most fictional books, and gender frequently ranks as a more important factor than most of the others, including age, which determine their choice of such books. The major issue which is generally raised is whether girls are really less likely to read factual books than boys are. How far, if at all, are either boys or girls disadvantaged in school-work as a result of the kind of choices concerning information books that they make, by the kind of book they prefer, or by the ways in which they read them? How far can or should teachers try to influence such choices?

The Roehampton Survey (1996) reveals some interesting facts about young people's reading in the area of information books, and dispels a few illusions. Although it appears to be true that at most ages, boys do read more non-fiction than girls do, this is not the case at Key Stage 1 (5–7 years), nor is the difference as marked as some people might have expected. What is interesting is the fact that girls consistently read these books for homework more than boys do, though boys equally consistently read more of them for pleasure; again the differences are not very marked.

The Survey questions referred to are:

Q.1 'Do you read information books?' (For children over 7, the answers for 'sometimes', 'often' or 'very often' have been combined; younger children had a simple Yes/No choice; this was question 47 of the Survey.)

Q.2 'Do you read information books for pleasure?' (For children over 11, the answers for 'sometimes', 'often' or 'very often' have been combined; younger children had a simple Yes/No choice. Children under 7 were not asked this question or the next. This was question 51a of the Survey.)

Q.3 'Do you read information books to help with your homework?' (Conditions as for Q.2; this was question 51b of the Survey.)

The responses to these questions are shown in Figure 6. There are many interesting things which could be said about these figures (see Survey, pp. 214–19 for further discussion), but many of these are connected with aspects such as the varying emphases for different age groups, and the demands at different stages of the National Curriculum for England and Wales. It certainly appears that gender differences in relation to reading information books are less than many people have believed.

The subjects preferred by boys and girls reveal more differences, some of which might be anticipated. Boys of all ages like reading about machines much more than girls do; the fairly respectable 33.9% of 5-year-old girls (as against 43.6% of the

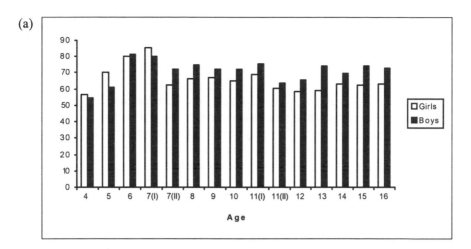

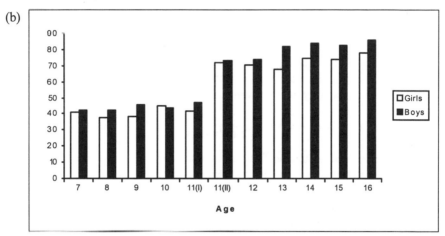

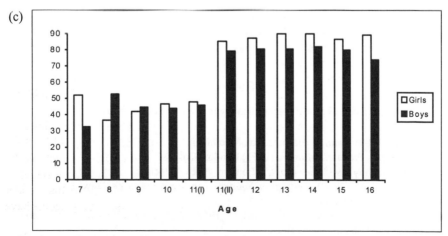

Figure 6 (a) Young people reading information books. (b) Young people reading information books for pleasure. (c) Young people reading information books for homework. These three figures are taken from the Roehampton Survey (1996).

boys) who admit to this choice reduce to 7.3% at 16, against 46.1% of their male contemporaries. Neither the dominance of boys' choice of sport nor that of girls' choices of animals and plants reach to anything like these proportions. More noticeable is the preference that girls consistently have for biographies, rising to 71.8% of 16-year old girls against 37% of boys. This suggests that teachers might well make use of this interest to encourage girls to read the lives of scientists and engineers, especially females, to encourage their interest in machines; if they consistently ignore this side of their environment, they may well lose the opportunity to follow careers which they may regard as unfeminine, like engineering. Encouragingly, little difference was observable, however, in areas such as the stars and space, or other parts of the world, or even, for most agegroups, how the human body works.

The other area of predictable difference was preferences about the way such facts are presented. Consistently, boys liked lists of facts and record breakers more than girls did, with a difference of about 15% in their choices, and CD-Roms were much more popular with boys than with girls in all age groups over 8 years, the margin in the secondary school being in the region of 17–20%. The disparity in attitudes to CD-Roms raises some questions about the extent to which girls are being given access to computer technology, for it would seem apparent that the varied and interesting material available is certainly not of appeal only to boys, though they are taking the most advantage of this technology. Teachers perhaps need to give more attention to equality of opportunity in this area.

Conclusion

This brief examination of non-fictional material reveals that there are some inadequacies, both in the way in which ethnic minorities and females are represented in all kinds of books from reading schemes to encyclopedias, and in the access to all parts of the curriculum to which this relates. Publishers are certainly trying to improve the situation, but teachers nevertheless need to cast a critical eye over even recent publications. They also should take account of the attitudes of their pupils to different kinds of material, ensuring that they don't make too many assumptions about what is likely to be attractive to boys or to girls, while also ensuring equality of access to newer computer technology.

References

Note that an extensive bibliography is also given at the end of this book.

Bailey, D. (1989) *Families*. Basingstoke: Macmillan.
The Children's Picture Dictionary (1951) London: Collins.
Crossfield Family (1978) *Seven of Us*. London: A.& C. Black.
Gaines, K. *et al.* (1989) *Wellington Square: Teacher's Resource Pack*. Levels 1 & 2, Basingstoke: Macmillan.
Guillot, R. (1956) (translated by Michael, M.,1958) *The New Encyclopedia for the Younger Generation*. London: Spring Books.
Jones, J. (1987) *To the Temple for Arti*. London: Blackie.
Mee, A. (n.d.[1925])*The Children's Encyclopedia* (10 vols.). London: Educational Book Company.

Murray, W. (1964)*Games We like*. (Ladybird Key Words Reading Scheme, Book 9a) Lough-borough: Wills and Hepworth.

My First Atlas (n.d.[1952])Edinburgh: W. & A. Johnston.

Ogan, E. (n.d.[1933]) *The Wonderland of Knowledge* (12 volumes). London: Odhams.

Onyefulu, I. (1993) *A is for Africa*. London: Frances Lincoln.

Steele, P. (1993, illustrated by C. Henley and C. Russell) *First Atlas*. Godalming: Ted Smart.

Wilkins, V. A. (1993) *abc I can be*. Camberley: Tamarind.

Wragg, T. (1994) *Flying Boot* (Stages 1, 2 & 3, and Descriptive Material). Walton-on-Thames: Nelson.

Literature, Equality, and the Classroom

'Kneeling ne're spoil'd silk stocking: quit thy state;
All equall are within the churches gate.'
(George Herbert, 'The Church Porch', lines 407–8, from *The Temple*, 1633)

'All men are created equal' (Abraham Lincoln, Gettysburg address)

The belief which underpins all that I have written in this book, a belief which is shared today with people of many creeds and none, is in the equal value of all human beings, whatever their sex, ethnic identity, physical abilities, intelligence or even moral qualities. A glance in a Dictionary of Quotations speedily makes apparent that this is a characteristically modern belief. There seem to be more authors talking about the *inequality* of human beings than about their equality, and even the two I have selected as epigraphs for this chapter have their limitations. Did Herbert consider the equality he talks about to be confined only to the church building? Despite the fact that as a seventeenth-century man of noble birth he would inevitably have accepted the external trappings of inequality, I would suspect that the fact that the word 'Church' is for him a signifier of far more than either the building or the institution means that he had a wider view; although this would suggest that his understanding of human value may have been ahead of his times, it would, however, inevitably have been linked to his faith and is unlikely to have included those outside the Christian Church.

Abraham Lincoln's much quoted words have also come to seem too limited because of his use of 'men'; it is difficult for the modern reader to know whether by this word he is excluding women from the concept, as well as from the practice, of equality, or simply using 'men' to 'embrace' women. Like Herbert, though from a less specifically Christian point of view, he is assuming that belief in God is the foundation for a belief in equality. By contrast, the conviction that some sections of the human race are of less value than others and can even be seen as not fully human, has underpinned some of the most unpleasant actions of this and other centuries.

If our adherence to a *belief* in equality is not held at depth, but is merely a part of a whole package of ideas we have accepted without question, it is possible that a scarcely recognized underlying *feeling* that all human beings are *not* truly of equal value may affect our actions and judgements. It is unfortunately all too easy to pay lip-service to ideals without realizing that underneath, as the result of our own experiences of life, and primitive aspects of the human sub-conscious, all is not sweetness and light.

The roots of people's attitudes towards equality

In order to confront equality issues in society, we need also to confront our own attitudes, and to be prepared to admit that we ourselves may be inclined towards the Orwellian modification: 'all animals are equal, but some are more equal than others' (*Animal Farm*, ch. 10). Each of us has been brought up in a specific place at a specific level of society, in a family that, at least as young children, we were likely to think was better than other families ('my mum is prettier than yours', etc.); in our own education we have read books which expressed a range of biases and we have been taught by teachers with a variety of prejudices; as a result of our experiences every one of us has a host of unexamined assumptions, many of which we may never recognize until they are challenged in some way. To act effectively, particularly in relation to children, it is desirable that we should be prepared to identify our own prejudices where we can, and be alert for their existence where they are not immediately apparent; we should also help other people to have the confidence to admit their own subliminal biases. This does not imply that we can ever totally discard what may be submerged in our subconscious minds, but we can allow for these deep-seated feelings and let our understanding of them be one of the factors which comes into our making of judgements, about society as well as about literature.

There are many motives which may underlie the failure to treat other human beings as our equals. One of the less shameful of these is to see them as needing our support and protection, an attitude which has bedevilled from time immemorial the way women are treated by men. Lord Chesterfield wrote in a letter to his son, on 4 September 1748: 'Women are only children of a larger growth . . . a man of sense only trifles with them . . . as he does with a sprightly and forward child.' For many men, the consequence of this attitude has been that women are seen not only as needing protection, but also as not being fitted intellectually for the same kind of education as men.

A similar, sometimes benevolent, refusal to see people who are not able-bodied, or of white, preferably Anglo-Saxon, stock, as equally able to benefit from education, has also been one of the reasons for failing to give disabled or black people an equal place in society. Many white South Africans, for instance, have refused to recognize that the 'girl' who worked in the house and lived in the shack at the end of the garden was a mature woman with her own family responsibilities (cf. Naidoo, *Journey to Jo'burg*, 1985, p. 41; see Chapter 6); this was a symptom of the mind-set which kept apartheid going for so long, and prevented the majority population having equal access to education and jobs. The inability to recognize people different from ourselves as mature may be part of the reason for the horror that some people feel at the idea of the physically or mentally disabled having sex.

The sentiment that others are not yet ready for equality is particularly relevant when we are thinking about literature for children; there is a kind of kinship between the audience for the literature and the people who are depicted, particularly in the classics of the past. Yet some of the characters in the books are seen as being incapable of attaining the maturity for which their readers are destined. Often in the past, white children were expected to take a natural interest in black people, particularly 'piccaninnies', in a way not dissimilar to their interest in animals, and to cultivate a similar feeling of sympathy and kindness. In like fashion,

159

boys were expected to feel protective towards women and children; the Doctor in E. Nesbit's *The Railway Children* (1906) reflects the attitude of the times when he says to a young boy, 'girls are so much softer and weaker than we are' (ch. 13).

Many of the reasons for depriving people of their rights, however, arise out of far from benevolent motives; one of these which is strongly causative of inequality is fear. If these people *do* grow up, will they be Caliban-like monsters in our midst? Certainly some of the villains of earlier literature support the idea that Blyton, Captain Johns and even Dickens were subconsciously afraid of people from other 'races'. Children have often been thought to resemble savages and to need taming; savage races (and even the lower classes) have *not* been tamed and are therefore dangerous. At best, this results in the sense that the savage has a kind of mystique, comparable to that which some men feel women to possess. Those who are *other* are deemed to have qualities which the rest of us lack; while these social or racial or sexual inferiors are not more intelligent in a straightforward way, they are regarded as wily and crafty. They threaten the stability of the state, and if they get control, anarchy will ensue. Vestiges of such feelings exist even today, and may help to account for the way in which in Britain young black people are often encouraged to take up sport, which can be seen as a channelling of otherwise dangerous energies. The attitude that *they* possess qualities which ordinary people lack and which may therefore be threatening, surprisingly also occurs in literature in association with the disabled, notably the blind, who are sometimes depicted as being sinister.

The variety of responses to literature

Some of the books of which I have written earlier have been the subject of considerable controversy, between people who have seen them as anti-racist or anti-sexist documents, and those who claim that the portrayal of black or female characters reveals the underlying prejudices of the author.

Both sides may be right in their comments about racism and anti-racism in Fox's *The Slave Dancer*, Taylor's *The Cay* and Armstrong's *Sounder* (cf. Chapters 2 and 6) or feminism and anti-feminism in Lindgren's *Pippi Longstocking* (cf. Chapter 2); while the authors are trying to present a positive view, their subconscious assumptions about the qualities of black people and women may have been exposed.

It is however even more certain that readers' judgements about these and similar books will vary because of their own backgrounds, education and interests. Not only will a young able-bodied black woman and an elderly disabled white man read books differently, but all of us must admit that the experience of reading a book at different stages of our lives means that in a way it is not the same book. Heracleitos said you could never step into the same river twice; it would be equally true to say that you can never read the same book twice. As Wolfgang Iser (1974) says:

> The convergence of text and reader brings the literary work into existence, and this convergence can never be precisely pinpointed, but must always remain virtual, as it is not to be identified either with the reality of the text or with the individual disposition of the reader. It is the virtuality of the work that gives rise to its dynamic nature. (p. 275)

There are few if any topics about which the responses of all readers will be identical; while a broad consensus can probably be reached among most open-minded educated people that National Front propaganda or child pornography are bad and should not be seen in the classroom, even in these cases, opinions would be likely to differ as to the best way of dealing with them. Material less extreme than this will be viewed according to the way our different experiences of life affect our perceptions.

The audience addressed by the author may not always be the one it receives. If the author on the one hand was hoping to change the perceptions of white readers or on the other to build up the self-concept of young black readers, this will affect the way the a book is written; it may lead to antagonism among readers either unaware of the author's intentions or resistant against putting themselves into the position of the intended audience.

Appreciation of the effects of the variety of reader and author backgrounds, and the general impossibility of even authors themselves being aware of all their intentions or preconceptions, may lead to despair about whether there can ever be any objective standards, and the fear that we must therefore tolerate all kinds of material, in the school and in society. In fact, there is far more consensus about the quality of specific works of literature, than might be expected. This is because a literary education tends to form people into what Stanley Fish (1980) describes as 'an interpretive community' (p. 335), a group of people who share a particular understanding of a specific area of reality, in this instance literature.

If teachers and librarians and others professionally concerned with children's reading ensure that their own reading qualifies them to make judgements which receive some measure of agreement from others, then they have some claim to be arbiters of children's choices, at least in the sense of what should be provided within the classroom or the children's library or bookshop. While we would want adults to have enough judgement to resist the implicit and explicit messages conveyed by a book, we cannot expect children to be in the same position until they have been exposed to a wide range of literature; we want therefore to select books which will help them to reach a degree of critical reading which ultimately will empower them as adults to recognize when an author is seeking to influence them. Children may not initially be part of an interpretive community but they should be educated to become members.

The process of helping children towards making educated judgements demands a high degree of tolerance from adults, who may need to make a conscious effort not to be either too dismissive or too accepting of what young people say. Adults and children can all feel demolished when a book they love is ridiculed by someone else. Sensitivity to the feelings of others is essential.

The implication of my argument is that books need to be discussed in a non-judgemental context, so that people don't feel too put down even if they have been reared in a setting where values which we find unacceptable have been current. Often we may need to facilitate an awareness of the limitations of what might be described as the 'sacred texts' of their childhood. This is particularly difficult in the area of what is literally held sacred.

Christians need to realize that not everyone, for instance, has Christian names or regards the season of Christmas as being special; they will only be prepared to do this if people of other religions on their part acknowledge the same about their own sacred books and festivals. The obverse of this is the need to hold other people's religious ideas in reverence; we are not expected to believe them but should acknowledge with humility that the universe is beyond a simplistic explanation and that we may learn from others as we hope they may learn from us.

What people say they object to in a book may not always be the real cause of their unease – they may find it easier to talk about the trivial than to dig deeper for the real cause. I have quoted earlier Rae Alexander's dismissal of Boston's *The Chimneys of Green Knowe* (cf. Chapters 1 and 2), on grounds that the little black boy has stereotypically short curly hair, a complaint that I consider trivial, whereas I do think there are much more serious matters for concern in the book, such as Jacob's involvement with tribal magic and his use of the English language. These factors mean for me not that the book should be rejected but rather that it should certainly be discussed. It is always possible that the reasons given for rejection of a text may be superficial but may represent something deeper, which may have resulted from the passive ideology of the author, and which readers need to examine in relation to their own unquestioned assumptions.

Teachers and librarians

It is useful for all members of society to try to become aware of what they take for granted without question, of some of the ideas which they have buried in their subconscious from childhood; it is however particularly important for teachers and children's librarians to confront their own unchallenged assumptions, for they are in a formative position *vis-à-vis* the young. In practical terms this means in-service courses, training sessions and conferences which include a large element of workshop discussion. It is vital to allow this to take place in a non-threatening environment and a non-confrontational context, with no need for everyone to feel that they have to make their responses public, as sometimes these could be uncomfortable; there should be no wish to place people in a confessional situation. For people to be totally committed to the equality of everyone, they need to understand themselves, and to start from where they are. Organizers of such discussions should be pleased with what the participants have to offer, rather than making them feel ashamed to admit their feelings. Teachers also need to develop a consciousness of the effect of society in the areas of sexism and racism; as Naidoo (1992) says:

> A teacher who has not begun to examine how living in a society culturally seeped [sic] in racism for centuries has infiltrated their own substratum of beliefs, assumptions, perceptions and values, will not be in a position to help students engage in that difficult and often uncomfortable task. (p. 147)

This kind of awareness, both at a personal and a societal level, also needs to be part of initial training courses for both teachers and librarians. Most institutions are very conscious of how important it is to include equality elements into courses, but Iram Siraj-Blatchford (1993) fears that in the first instance, some black students may avoid the teaching profession because of perceived racism; in the same book, G. Crozier and I. Menter suggest that there may often be a dichotomy between what students in training experience in college and in the schools where they do their teaching practice. It is essential, in particular, that ethnic minority students should not feel disempowered by the kind of image of black people held by some members of a school community.

A particularly important misapprehension which initial and in-service courses should attempt to remove is the frequently encountered statement that 'Racism isn't a problem here because we don't have a black community', with the implication that such a school does not need to bother to supply an anti-racist perspective, and might even be wiser to exclude from the curriculum any books which focus on black people. This is a poor preparation for pupils who live in a country which is multi-ethnic and multi-cultural; they cannot be guaranteed to remain for all their lives in a white enclave. Naidoo's work (1992), which will be described in more detail below, was carried out in a school with almost exclusively white pupils. In any case, equality issues tend to go hand in hand; many books which focus particularly on one issue also display concern about other aspects of inequality. This is a natural result of consciousness-raising; starting by thinking 'Why should I, as a woman, or a person of a particular ethnic group, be deprived of rights which other people have?' is likely to lead to the inference that other people are deprived of rights which I have.

One of the bugbears of recent years is the fact that some people think that full equality for those of all races and both genders has already happened; they therefore regard individuals who are still worried about these issues as being 'politically correct' about trivialities. That full equality is not yet here, scrutiny of the proportions of women, black people or disabled people in the pictures of the Boards of Management of any of the privatized utility companies should soon reveal. Power in society is still largely in the hands of a white male élite, though fortunately there have been some improvements. What is needed is a change in the expectations of those who are too easily satisfied by subordinate positions, and this will be helped by books as well as by legislation. Putting yourself imaginatively into a position is one of the ways of affecting your ideas about your future. Even if the effect of books is a cumulative rather than a one-off thing, probably all of us can remember how at some points of our lives we have been influenced by them, in both attitudes and career choices. As far as language is concerned, what is termed by its enemies 'politically correct' and by its friends 'inclusive' language is good linguistic sense; language does influence thought, by providing categories in which we subdivide reality, and if the language which society and books use does not admit certain categories, it is difficult to recognize that they are there at all. David Crystal (1987), referring to what is known as the Sapir-Whorf hypothesis concerning linguistic relativity, says:

> Language may not determine the way we think, but it does influence the way we perceive and remember . . . people certainly find it easier to make a conceptual distinction if it neatly corresponds to words available in their language. (p. 15)

A useful practical principle which teachers and librarians might well apply is that of never using a book or having it in classroom or library unless being prepared to discuss it with children of the age who are likely to encounter it there. This of course does not allow for the contingency of children bringing to school books which the professional adult would prefer not to discuss with them, but such discussion may be able to be conducted on an individual basis. It is, however, worth noting that there is some danger in forcing our own views on the young before they are ready for them. The result can be that pupils will utter these ideas in a kind of ventriloquism, because they know they will be approved by the school. There is also a danger in being too earnest about subjects in which we believe strongly; communication is often best made with an injection of humour where this is possible.

Above all, teachers, librarians and all others involved with children should be acting out of a conviction about the importance of seeing everybody in society as having equal value. This is not something which can be achieved by legislation, nor indeed totally by education, though both can facilitate it. Literature can be a valuable instrument in this process, and adults may find it helpful, not only to be very familiar with a wide range of children's literature but also to read some of the books for adult readers which throw light on the development of contemporary situations and attitudes; a few suggestions are included in the references for this chapter.

Teachers and librarians also need to be well informed about how literature can enshrine ideology, and may find it helpful to look at Peter Hollindale's (1988) practical suggestions for 'locating the ideology of individual books'. One of the most useful and original of these is the idea of transposing components of a text. If this is done, he conjectures, an anti-sexist novel may be revealed as merely being anti-male, or a war story may 'attack the Germans for atrocities which are approved when the British inflict them' (p. 19). He also recommends scrutiny of the ending and of the characters, particularly to determine whether certain groups of people are omitted, or desirable values are only associated with 'niceness'.

In essence, all that has been said above could really be described as sound teaching; as Babette Brown (1988) claims, 'Anti-racist practice is good practice' and fosters children's all-round development. I would widen this to refer to all varieties of inclusive practices; to make all children, of both sexes and all ethnic groups, whatever their personal strengths and weaknesses, feel valued, is indeed good practice, for teachers, librarians, children's booksellers – and indeed, for parents.

The curriculum in English and Welsh Schools

In 1975, the ground-breaking Bullock Report, *A Language for Life*, included in its examination of the teaching of reading and related areas, a rather carefully titled chapter, 'Children from Families of Overseas Origin'. This gave explicit recognition to such aspects as the importance of culture, and the need to distinguish between children with a non-standard dialect and those whose first language was not English; it acknowledged (despite the unfortunate placing of the chapter in the section dealing with Reading and Language Difficulties) that having a second language was not necessarily a problem and concluded, 'the central recommendation of this chapter [is] a sensitivity and openness to language in all its forms' (p. 294).

Even before Bullock, the question of the most appropriate way to teach children whose first language is not English had been considered by the Equal Opportunities Commission, and subsequently a variety of documents, notably the Warnock Report (1978) and the Swann Report (1985) have addressed equality issues; the most important current influence on English and Welsh schools, in this and other areas, is the National Curriculum. The documents detailing the area of this concerned with English teaching were preceded by two versions of what is generally termed the Cox Report, *English for Ages 5 to 11* (1988) and *English for Ages 5 to 16* (1989); the thinking of these is generally reflected in the first English National Curriculum documents. It would not be appropriate here to go into much detail about the first version of the English National Curriculum or its preparatory documents; my intention is simply to draw attention to the way in which all of these enshrined many of the principles which I have already outlined in this and other chapters. They stress for instance that:

> Bilingual children should be considered an advantage in the classroom rather than a problem . . . [they] will make greater progress in English if they know that their knowledge of their mother tongue is valued . . . (1989,10.12)

While the report emphasizes the belief that 'all children should be enabled to attain a full command of the English language, both spoken and written' (10.5), cognisance is also taken of other dialects: 'The aim is to add Standard English to the repertoire, not to replace other dialects or languages.' (4.43). The Equal Opportunities Section (11) concentrates particularly on gender aspects, but that on Special Educational Needs (12) makes clear that the recommended policy is one of ensuring equal access to the curriculum to all children, whatever their disability, wherever possible. The chapter about literature places emphasis on 'social and cultural diversity' (7.4) and the desirability of drawing literature from different countries so that all pupils are made aware of 'the richness of experience' and 'the ideas and feelings of cultures different from their own', some practical suggestions being made as to sources (7.5).

Despite their many misgivings about the effect on their classroom work of the demands of the Cox Report and the National Curriculum which ensued, teachers of English, both primary and secondary, were in many respects happy with the spirit of these recommendations; much anxiety has, however, been expressed at the extent to which its much shorter 1995 replacement, *English in the National Curriculum* minimizes the impact of the original stress on literature from other sources than the great English tradition. Though a 'variety of cultures and traditions' (p. 13) are mentioned, the fact that the literature curriculum, particularly in secondary schools, places a great deal of emphasis on British authors from preceding centuries can easily tend to discourage the inclusion of authors from the rest of the world, with the result that pupils who are not of indigenous ancestry can easily lose sight of their own cultural heritage. 'The richness of dialects and other languages' (p. 2) is also mentioned, but there is a greater stress on the place of standard English than in the earlier documents, and there is considerable danger that a passing reference in the classroom to other literary traditions, foreign languages and non-standard dialects, will suffice to pay lip-service to the recommendations. Thus material which could do a great deal to enhance the self-concept of children from other languages and cultures may be omitted from the curriculum.

There is also no explicit attention in the English document to the other equality issues which did receive mention in 1989. It is apparent, however, that the National Curriculum as such places no obstacle to the kind of teaching which is implied by everything I have talked about so far, and indeed that those who embrace equality issues can be seen as fulfilling its explicit demands. What follows below is an attempt to provide more specific suggestions as to how these kind of areas can be treated in school.

Practical suggestions

Based on the material occurring throughout this book and some of the principles outlined above, there follow some recommendations related to the whole question of equality issues and literature. In mentioning titles I am in many cases not confining myself to books which are specifically concerned with equality issues; if one of the important ways of tackling such subjects is by means of literature, an understanding of how to *read* literature is essential, and this can be cultivated through encouraging a very wide range of reading.

Throughout this book, because of the nature of the subjects considered, I have inevitably been concentrating on the genre of realism; this certainly does not imply that I think fantasy should have no place in the classroom. Often issues can be more safely examined through a distorting mirror which lends them distance, as I have suggested in Chapter 8. Whatever genre is favoured, it will be unfortunate if teachers always have too didactic an emphasis, and ignore the need for children to enjoy fiction for its own sake!

Talk

It has often been suggested that there is not enough of a forum in schools for debate about sensitive subjects. Teachers are naturally cautious about introducing subjects which they know will run the danger of allowing certain sections of the class to indulge in comments which may be offensive to others. The practice of avoiding debate on such issues seems however unwise, for on the one hand it would be difficult to exclude all books which could give rise to it; books should not be available in the classroom or the school library if teachers or librarians are not prepared to talk about them. On the other hand, it is probably preferable to allow a forum for debate, so that if offensive remarks are made it will be within a situation where they can be challenged, rather than letting them occur only in the playground. A refutal needs to be given, for instance, of the 'facts' about the alleged 'inferiority' of some 'races'.

Literature should always be read in an atmosphere where it can be debated, rather than children simply being told, 'This is what the book is saying' or asked simply to copy down notes about other people's opinions concerning it. Nor should it simply be 'read around' the class, a sure way to kill nearly any book; if presented by someone of the reading competence of the teacher, difficult issues can be mediated by an adult voice and some of the tension which might arise from a child having for instance to read racist language will be reduced. This is not, however, to imply that books should not be read in small groups of, say, 4–6 children; this is often an excellent way of enabling children to have the experience of reading aloud in a less threatening context than the whole class, and also the opportunity of engaging in discussion on a small scale. If this practice is used, however, the teacher needs to be well aware of the kind of issues covered in every book read, and close at hand to discuss any controversial issues.

The teacher needs to be well prepared for talk about any questionable aspect of a book, and be ready to raise it if children look as if they're too embarrassed to do so.

Victor Watson (in Styles *et al.*, 1992) suggests that what is needed from the earliest age is 'the provision of a "space" in the school day and at home for sharing and talking about books.' (p. 7). Aidan Chambers, himself a children's author who is not afraid of handling controversial subjects (cf. Chapter 8), has also given some attention to the way in which debate about books can be handled in the classroom. The question to avoid asking children, he says, is 'Why?', which nearly always leads to trite or unhelpful answers. Rather, children should be given the encouragement which is contained in the title of his book about reading and talk in the classroom, *Tell Me* (1993). He emphasizes the respect with which children's utterances should be accepted:

> Because all too many children know that their responses are often dismissed as 'wrong', 'irrelevant', 'silly', 'not helpful', 'childish' (and worse) they learn to keep their thoughts to themselves. Dismissing what children 'really think' leads to their disaffection from school-based reading. (p. 45)

In *The Reading Environment* (1991) Chambers gives a good many valuable suggestions about practical measures to foster literature in the classroom, where he also considers aspects such as the choice of books, and practical details about classroom management in relation to books.

Fairytales

Among the earliest forms of literature to which children are likely to be introduced in the classroom are folk and fairy stories. Many of these involve aspects which have subsequently been questioned, such as the passivity of the heroines, the unpleasantness of step-mothers, as well as violence and horror. Such tales are not, however, sacrosanct as far as the version in which they are read, and even very young children are likely to discover that the story with which they have been familiar at home may not be the one told in the classroom, perhaps because the teacher is more resistant to the power of Disney than is the parent!

If then the stories have been altered over the years, they are available for children today to make their own changes, preferably however after they have become familiar with both the traditional versions and some of the conventions of fairytale, something which is unlikely in most cases to happen under the age of 8 (cf. Fremantle, in Pinsent, 1993, p. 58).

Once the formula has been grasped and some variant stories have been enjoyed, what better way of defying stereotypes of passive femininity, or villains who are ugly or deformed, than to tell, act out and write down, possibly with an adult as scribe, their own versions? Once children are familiar with the standard contemporary versions of stories, they will gain a good deal from playing with them, adapting them, perhaps with models such as Sczieska and Smith's *The Stinky Cheese Man* (1993) or Little, de Vries and Gilman's *Once Upon a Golden Apple* (1993). This practice will give them some understanding of the role of the author or even the community in creating material. Part of the process of accepting variants includes the use of folk-tales from other countries and some of the rich legacy of myth, elements of which are likely to be tantalizingly familiar and yet have unexpected twists.

Picture books

One of the many advantages of picture books is the fact that the illustrations can provide material which is not explicit in the text, or which may at times contradict it. Because of their generally simple text, they are accessible to all age groups, and provided older children are not given the impression that they are being presented with material which is beneath them, such books can be very useful in allowing the less able reader, or the child with as yet little knowledge of English, to explore ideas which are often too sophisticated for the ostensible audience of very young children to appreciate (see Godleman, in Pinsent, 1993, for suggestions of how to use these books with older pupils).

Children can in fact very easily become authors of this kind of material, and if it is a group venture, the strengths of different pupils can be utilized, such as design, drawing, colour, text, plot and computer expertise. It is possible to bring in characters from different ethnic backgrounds, to portray a variety of settings, clothes and food, in a way similar to that which Eileen Browne's *Handa's Surprise* (1994) does for the fruits and animals of Kenya.

Picture books can often pose questions about tolerance and about the position of females and the disabled, to children who might not be ready to understand them in a totally textual form. Among the many books which have been mentioned in other chapters as affording this kind of opportunity are David McKee's *Tusk Tusk* (1978), June Counsel's *But Martin* (1984), Michael Rosen and Bob Graham's *This is Our House* (1996) and Mary Hoffman and Caroline Binch's *Amazing Grace* (1991). (See Chapter 6 for further details.) None of these books is narrowly didactic, and all give opportunities to young people of all ages to discuss puzzles to which there is no single right solution. That such books are not below the dignity of older pupils to consider is amply displayed by Sharon Walsh (in Pinsent, 1993), talking about Anthony Browne, whose books also are rich in material for discussion.

Historical understanding

Even those who have never attempted to teach history in school will often be aware of the limitations of young children's understanding of time. Confusion between the Romans and the Normans indicates that mere matters of 1000 years may mean little to young children, who may be unsure whether their 'really old' parents and teachers are, say, 15 or 95! It is clear, therefore that it may not be easy to engender in young children a sense of historical relativity about fiction which reveals the prejudices of its period. This is probably the chief reason why discussion of books which may not have been intentionally racist when written but have become so in the light of subsequent understanding of human nature, such as *Little Black Sambo*, needs to be postponed to the secondary school. Nevertheless, as well as looking at books which can foster tolerance, such as those mentioned under the heading 'Picture Books' above, there are some possibilities which are not beyond children in Key Stage 2 (7–11 years). Looking at things we take for granted today, particularly the situation of children at home and at school in the past and within different societies, may often be illuminating, especially if film and television are used.

Pupils in the secondary school should be capable of more awareness of the historical situation when certain books were written, and the way in which the social background of authors like Kipling, Blyton and Bannerman will have led them to take for granted certain assumptions which are no longer acceptable. It is also helpful for children to learn about the conditions of the underclasses in earlier societies; there is so much of a danger that in looking at glossy images, they may not realize how thoroughly unpleasant it was to live in unhygienic and plague-ridden Elizabethan London. After all, the chances are that the majority of the ancestors of any one of us were probably among the poor, and any ideas of the supremacy of people in this country can vanish when comparisons are made between poverty even in Victorian England and poverty in Africa at the same time. This could help to banish the racist taunt about ancestors being in the jungle; any difference there is between an urban or a tropical jungle may well be in favour of life in Africa!

Looking at fashions in clothes can also be revealing; a speaker at a recent conference mentioned how astounded her pupils were when told at a museum of costume that Jane Austen wouldn't have worn knickers. The fact that what seems *the* absolutely essential item of respectable dress was not used by an author so associated with respectable society caused amazement, and a deepening awareness about differences in conventions. It can also be surprising for children to begin to realize that what we take as axiomatic in our society about entitlement to education was not so obvious 150 years ago; this can help to foster a sense of cultural relativism, and a means of questioning what there is in our current society which will no longer be acceptable 150 years hence.

Text and language

The area of education most specifically linked with the use of books is of course that of understanding how to read fiction. It has often become apparent that people who reject particular texts as racist or sexist do so without having a clear idea about the nature of fiction. Children need to be educated in how to read a novel, and this demands that their schooling is filled with numerous examples of story. As the work of Applebee (1977) indicates, children are indeed slow to the realization that not everything which is written down is necessarily true, and helpful in this process is the child's sense of play. Exploration of the question 'What would happen if . . . ?' in drama, their own writing or by reading some of the kind of fiction which poses it, such as Joan Aiken's *The Wolves of Willoughby Chase* (1962)(an England where the Hanoverians never banished the Stuarts and the Channel Tunnel was built in the nineteenth century) and Diana Wynne Jones' *Hexwood* (1993) (using the idea of parallel universes) can be very efficacious here.

Children need to acquire the awareness that the writer may deliberately lead the reader towards a particular point of view or assumption by the use of a first person narrator, or a focal character, who should not always be believed. Many of the books which do this are quite sophisticated and demand advanced reading skills (see reference section for some suggestions) but some picture books also employ this kind of approach, thus making it accessible for younger children. An interesting example is Jon Sczieszka and Lane Smith's *The True Story of the Three Little Pigs* (1989), as told by the wolf, which immediately raises questions as to the extent to which text should be believed, as, in a different way do John Burningham's books about Shirley, a little girl who has amazing adventures, presumably in her imagination, while her dull parents do everyday routine things. Reading novels and picture books can help provide for children an education of the emotions as the readers come to realize that they don't have to accept without question what the characters, or even the writer, seem to be wanting us to accept, nor do we have to like the characters. Children need gradually, according to their stage of maturity, to acquire an alertness to devices used to affect judgement of the reader, such as imagery and intertextuality (cf. Chapter 2). Again, books which at one level are for very young children may include a high degree of artifice on the part of the writer and illustrator, so that the child is being inducted into an understanding of what literature is about; a child who has experienced the kind of play with characters which Janet and Allan Ahlberg indulge in *The Jolly Postman* (1986) and its successors is on the way to appreciate the nature of fiction, as indeed is the child enjoying Sczieszka and Smith's *The Stinky Cheeseman and other Fairly Stupid Tales* (1993).

An effective way of creating awareness of what the author is doing, whether intentionally or not, may well be through looking at earlier and later versions of the same book. This can be very illuminating if for instance Blyton's *Noddy* books, in their earlier and their recent incarnations, Dahl's two versions of *Charlie and the Chocolate Factory*, or two versions of Lofting's *Doctor Dolittle* are examined (cf. Chapters 3 and 4 above). This sort of exercise can soon lead to discussion of whether any criticisms need to be made even of the revised versions.

Many interesting ideas are given in the Cox Report (1989) about techniques which can be used to facilitate an understanding of what literature is. An example of one of these is 'Hot-seating . . . individually, or collectively [a child or group of children] taking on role of a character to answer questions posed by the rest of group'. It is surprising how much insight children have into literature; often this remains undisplayed because conditions in the classroom don't always allow it to be expressed.

A sensitive issue which has been touched upon several times is that of the deliberate use of racist language spoken by unpleasant characters. There is ample material for discussion here, but I would emphasize that this is an area where the teacher's voice is an essential intermediary, rather than a child having to use in the authorized setting of the classroom terms which pupils know to be open to question. A not unrelated matter is the need for care about accurate pronunciation of foreign names of people and places in books; it is often all too easy for those who find them unfamiliar to adopt demeaning versions of them.

Attention to the rest of the world

Literary resources which relate to other countries range from collections of folk tales, through attractive and relatively objective portrayals of life in different places, to books which are clearly intended not only to inform but also to affect the feelings of readers. R. Schermbrucker's *Charlie's House* (1991) (see Chapter 6), for instance, emphasizes the poverty in an African shanty-town by the use of apparently unemotive description, accompanied by pictures; in its restraint, with guidance from the teacher, it can help children to formulate contrasts concerning life-styles.

Not all depictions of Africa or India should be of poverty or of rural scenes, or this may create an unrealistic image, which could be unrecognizable for children from cities in some of these countries. Children whose ancestors lived in other lands also need to know something about their own cultural traditions.

170

The history of slavery is another area which needs to be taken account of in the classroom, and books such as Rosemary Sutcliff's *The Lantern Bearers* (1959; Oxford: Oxford University Press) and Susan Price's *The Saga of Aslak* (1995; London: A. & C. Black), with central characters who are slaves of the Saxons and the Vikings respectively, make clear that this is a phenomenon which has happened in all societies and periods. This in no way exonerates what happened in the Southern States of America; rather it shows how all cultures have been both perpetrators and victims of this noxious practice.

Further information about relevant resources is given in the references to this chapter, but two organizations demand special attention. The first of these is Letterbox Library, which, among its other activities in working towards a non-sexist and non-racist school environment, is a valuable supplier of material from and about countries overseas. The second, the International Board on Books for Young People (IBBY) supplies a dimension which is often missing from children's literature in English, for so rich are our native resources that it is easy to forget the insights which may be derived from looking at the rest of the world.

Other aspects of classroom practice

One of the facts revealed by Ruth Lewis's study (1996)(see below) is that in many classrooms and schools, there are abundant books about ethnic minority groups in Britain and abroad which are not used adequately, and which might be of particular relevance to many of the children. It is very easy to feel that justice has been done to a book by buying it, and that when it rests on the shelves, it will do its own work in attracting readers. As Lewis discovered, many children were not only surprised but also delighted to discover that books had something to say about their own background and people of similar appearance to themselves. Finding time to talk to the children, individually or in small groups about these books, or reading to the class from them, is a simple measure, but one which it is easy to neglect.

Another large subject, to which it is impossible to do justice at this point, is that of dual language texts; these certainly have a part to play in consolidating the ethnic identity of children, giving them a sense of pride in their mother tongue and sometimes giving their relatives who are literate only in their mother tongue the chance to perform a mutually enriching role.

The obverse of the positive choice of books is the valuation and use of what the children may bring in, even if it raises questions; clearly it may not always be possible to do this collectively, but sometimes books from home may give useful evidence of issues which are important to the children. The children's own stories, especially those which they may write and illustrate about visits to other countries, or about subjects like age and disability, may also be an invaluable source for other children in the class; there has been much work in recent years about seeing children as authors (cf. Donald Graves, 1983), and children can co-operate in making books which are likely to be very attractive to the rest of the class (see Paul Johnson, 1990).

Human resources are often used too little; while many teachers are aware of the value of bringing poets and authors of children's books into the classroom, they may easily forget that the children's relations and other people from the local community, particularly the elderly, often have much to contribute in giving all children a picture of what life, whether in Britain or abroad, was like in the past.

171

The additional result of this is the fact that children are less likely to undervalue old people if they have seen them as sources of community history.

It may sometimes be worth encouraging children who speak a non-standard variety of English occasionally to make use of it, especially in Drama. There are often problems about writing dialect down, so that it may sometimes be preferable to leave it in an oral form; however much debate there may be about the desirability or not of standard English in speech, it is generally agreed that children need access to it in writing. Nevertheless, some debate about the extent to which dialect (including vocabulary and syntax, not only accent) can be written down is an excellent means of helping children towards an understanding of the nature of language, and relating to some of the Programmes of Study of the National Curriculum, such as 'to investigate how language varies according to context and purpose and between standard and dialect forms' (1995, p. 12, Key Stage 2, Speaking and Listening). Poetry in dialect can be vividly expressive.

Equality of opportunity also applies to access to non-fictional resources. On the one hand, teachers need to be aware that if their own personal preference is for narrative rather than factual material, it may not be shared by all their pupils; there is a need to value the enjoyment which many boys in particular have of factual material, and indeed, to encourage girls towards texts which they may at first reject because of its lack of obvious engagement with people and relationships. It is also important to facilitate girls' use of computer technology, especially CD-Roms, where they may need to become aware of resources which are potentially full of interest.

Much of what I have said so far inevitably sounds very serious, for these are important subjects, yet it would be a mistake to be too earnest. If literature is not enjoyed it is unlikely to make much impression upon the child reader. In this respect, the range of children's literature which has been described (cf. Lurie, 1991) as subversive can often be more effective than that which is too obvious in its didactic intent. Much of the popularity of Roald Dahl and Enid Blyton results from the feeling that they are on the side of the child against the adults, a feeling which may be somewhat delusive, as under the apparent chaos, a feeling for traditional values can often be detected.

More contemporary writers who similarly seem to be able to write on the wavelength of children include Paul Jennings, Morris Gleitzman, Paula Danziger, Judy Blume, Anne Fine, Jacqueline Wilson and Gene Kemp. By apparently turning the world upside down, such writers are often able to engage the interest of children in issues like the situation of the homeless, the environment, children with problems about their families, and disablement. The last thing that should be done, however, is to deprive children of a feeling of ownership of such potentially subversive material; whether it be the comics and magazines which they circulate within a circle of friends, or authors who are prepared to write about subjects such as the physical and relational problems of growing up, children will generally get more from a text if it is felt to be their own than if the teacher seems to be claiming it instead. A related aspect is that while boys often disclaim any interest in girls' books or magazines, they are frequently prepared to read them, either in secret or with the ostensible purpose of ridiculing them, but really to discover about aspects of physical development and relationship, about which the girls' books may be more informative than boys' fiction is. The role of the teacher here seems to be one of remaining very low key!

Some school-based projects

It is of interest to look at some projects carried out in schools, with the intention of helping pupils towards a greater openness in their attitudes in the areas of gender and 'race'. Two of these, based in Primary schools, were carried out in connection with the Roehampton Institute London MA in Children's Literature and are unpublished; the third, Beverley Naidoo's secondary school research project, is described in detail in *Through Whose Eyes* (1992).

Laleh Kazemi's Graduate Diploma project (1996) was entitled *Children's Heroes and Heroines: One Class's Response to Two Dominant Heroines*. The class in question were 5-year-olds in an inner-city school, who were already enjoying a range of picture books and showed a predilection for stories 'where the hero is male, active and able to save the day while the female is beautiful, passive and patiently waiting for the hero to solve the problems' (p. 4). The children were given the opportunity to draw pictures representing their favourite personalities from stories, and there is little surprise, even at such an early stage, in how stereotyped their responses were; in these quotations, their spelling has been normalized.

With few exceptions, the girls opted for female heroines: Barbie 'because it is girlie'; Cinderella 'because she wears nice things' or 'because she has pink on'; and Pocahontas 'because she has animals and she is beautiful'. Most of the boys were equally committed to male heroes: Power Rangers 'because they are heroes'; Sonic the hedgehog 'because they fight'; Spiderman 'because he ties people up'. While some children's reasons for choice were less gender specific, such as possessing the video of a character, the explanations of these very young children for their preferences cannot really be viewed with equanimity!

Kazemi presented the children with two picture books with non-traditional heroines. The first of these, *Once there were Giants* (1989) by Martin Waddell and Penny Dale, follows the change in the narrator between seeing all the grown-ups around as giants, to her realization that she is becoming a 'giant' herself as she grows up. Since the heroine competes with boys, it is at first difficult to tell her sex, which only becomes clear half way through the book, a fact which caused some anxiety to the children, who felt the need for more definitive gender markings. An aspect which seemed particularly to shock the pupils was a scene where the narrator punches her brother and in return receives a black eye. The general feeling was that the girl should not punch, even if her brother did, and partly because of this, the book never became truly popular with the class; the response of one girl is typical: 'She fights like a boy. I don't fight. I don't like her. Because she's horrible.'

The heroine of the second book, Babette Cole's *Tarzanna* (1991) (cf. also Chapter 5 above), lives in the jungle where one day she discovers a new animal, Gerald; when they visit Gerald's country, they liberate the zoo animals and return them to the jungle. Despite the clear analogy between this character and Tarzan, whose exploits the boys had imitated in the playground, the children seemed quite certain about the differences: Tarzan does not have lipstick, nail varnish or long hair, and 'he rescues Jane'. Tarzanna's corresponding rescue of Gerald seemed to

173

count for less. Neither Tarzanna nor the heroine of the Waddell book ever became figures of playground games.

The extent of the stereotyping already internalised by the young children, which remained resistant to attempts to suggest that some kinds of behaviour need not always be gender-linked, is very considerable. Commercial forces in particular, as evidenced by the way in which the children's personal choices reflect the influence of television, reinforced by peer pressure, seem to be more significant than the effect of school. Nevertheless, the fact that the project was enjoyed and led to a good deal of debate could still be a small step towards making these children aware that other positions about gender were possible.

Ruth Lewis's MA Dissertation (1996) investigated two main areas: the extent to which teachers make adequate use with ethnic minority pupils of some of the excellent resources which are available, and the response of such pupils to stories about characters from a range of backgrounds. A questionnaire was distributed to a number of teachers, and replies were received from 17 of them, representing a total of 536 pupils in seven different primary schools; of these, at least 127, nearly a quarter, spoke English as an additional language. Teachers were asked to keep a record of the stories read to their classes over a period of 4 weeks; the results indicated that the amount of reading aloud to the class declined as the children got older, from an average of 15 books read during the 4–week period to the Key Stage 1 children (5–7 years) to an average of only four to the Key Stage 2 pupils (7–11 years).

Of a total of 145 stories read to the children, Lewis could only be sure that ten were 'either reflecting cultural backgrounds other than Britain or showing Britain as a multiculturally diverse society' (p. 21). There seemed little correlation between the number of children in the class with English as an additional language and the teachers' choice of books about other cultures.

Lewis went on to interview eight children, four boys and four girls, in their final year (10 or 11 years old) at a primary school where about a quarter of the children are from an ethnic minority background, many being bilingual. Details of the eight children's linguistic and cultural backgrounds are to be found in Table 4, where the choice made by each child of a story to read or have read to them is also indicated. The selection offered included 'legends from Asia, European Fairy Tales, short stories by European, Jamaican and Asian authors and picture books about contemporary children from different cultural backgrounds' (p. 27).

Interviews were conducted using Aidan Chamber's (1993) 'Tell Me' framework (see section on 'Talk' above). The following comment is typical of those made by many of the children in encountering stories which featured people from similar ethnic backgrounds to themselves: 'I didn't know there were stories like this. I would like more stories like this.' (p. 40). One boy was able to relate his choice to his own visit to Pakistan, feeling that the pictures did not do justice to the modern city 'just like New York' he had visited; he was also very surprised to learn about the Indus civilization – nothing that he had encountered at school had made him aware that early civilizations involved anyone other than the Romans or Greeks. Several of the children displayed pride in knowing how to speak or read languages unfamiliar to the teacher conducting the interviews, and they also felt happiness in seeing people like themselves in the books. Generally speaking, the interviews also gave the children the opportunity to talk about their own experiences, and in

Table 4 Links between pupils' cultural backgrounds and choice of books.

Name and gender	Languages	Cultural background	Books chosen	Cultural background of chosen book	Cultural link
A. D. (f)	Gujarati/ English	India/Africa/ England	*Grandpa Chatterji*	England/India	Yes
H. D. (f)	Gujarati/ English	India/Africa/ England	*Dial-A-Story* short story 'Pebble on the Beach'	England/India	No
S. S (f)	Urdu/ English/ Arabic	Pakistan	*Beauty and the Beast*	European	No
E. M. B. (f)	French/ English	Africa (Ivory Coast)	*Grace and Family*	England/Africa	Yes
S. K. (m)	Urdu/ English/ Arabic	Pakistan	*Clues in the Desert*	Pakistan	Yes
S. B. (m)	Panjabi/ English	India	*Amal and the Letter from the King*	India	Yes
T. G. (m)	Panjabi/ English	India	*Mouth Open, Story Jump Out* short story: 'Bravé Dangé'	West Indies	No
M. H. (m)	Somali/ Swahili/ English	Africa (Somalia and Kenya)	*Tortoise's Dream*	Africa	Yes

Reproduced with permission from Ruth Lewis's MA dissertation, *The Access of Children from Ethnic Minorities to Children's Literature* (1996).

some instances to relate the books to their own problems, for instance with a step-parent.

From Lewis's study, it is difficult to resist drawing the conclusion that on their part, many teachers are either reluctant to use, or, more probably, unaware of, the many attractive books now available representing children from other cultures. On their side, however, there are many children who would profit from such books, in some cases by learning about their own cultural heritage and, for indigenous British children, by widening their horizons to include the rest of the world.

Beverley Naidoo's research project forms the subject of her book, *Through Whose Eyes* (1992); it is also usefully summarized by her in *A Multi-cultural Guide to Children's Books* (Stones, 1994), where Naidoo writes of the impetus behind her own fiction, which she sees as 'an attempt to explore perspectives and voices which my apartheid childhood prevented me from seeing and hearing'. Her project was an attempt to investigate the potential of a work of fiction 'to change someone's way of seeing'. A class of 30 13-year-olds in a predominately white area of England were presented with a range of books which strongly indicted racism, and their responses, both individual and group, were recorded and analysed. One of Naidoo's conclusions is particularly interesting:

Throughout the course, there was a greater tendency amongst the girls towards associating themselves with non-racist views and to valuing their empathetic feelings. This was not exclusive to the girls, but it is clearly important to ensure that female voices are heard in the wider classroom and impossible to tackle racism and ethnocentrism effectively in isolation. Put bluntly, if a predominantly white classroom and school give priority to white male voices and experience, what is the likelihood that racism can be properly addressed? (1994, p. 11)

Naidoo also emphasizes what she calls 'contradictory consciousness', where students who declared themselves as solidly in favour of equality nevertheless revealed assumptions which contradicted their theoretical values. This is the phenomenon which Hollindale (1988, p. 12) highlights in talking about 'passive ideology'; it is something which everyone can experience and one of the chief reasons why it is important for all of us to try to discover our underlying assumptions, so that we can take them into account.

I have chosen to look at these three examples relating to widely differing topics and age groups because in different ways they demonstrate the difficulties and the fact that for even a small degree of progress to be made, a high degree of patience and tolerance is needed by all concerned. Nevertheless, all over Britain and North America, attempts are being made to make children more aware of everybody's rights and qualities, and to use some of the wealth of fictional material which is now available.

Conclusion

It is encouraging to see that there has been a considerable increase in recent years in the provision of high-quality material related to a range of equality issues. A notable development is the way in which people who started out with a particular perspective have widened it during the last 10–15 years. Letterbox Library, founded in 1983 with a brief related to providing a good inexpensive source of non-racist and non-sexist books, has taken on board more recently other subjects, such as the environment; their Winter 1996 issue is devoted to disability. Verna Wilkins, who set up Tamarind Press because she found a lack of black characters in fiction for her own children to identify with, has always had a strong consciousness of gender issues. Recently she too has written books featuring disabled characters, as also has Beverley Naidoo, whose work dealing with racial justice issues has demanded attention in this and previous chapters.

We may not yet have arrived at true equality for males and females, for people of all languages, cultures and ethnic origins, and for those with varying degrees of physical or mental disability, but it is now far more usual for dominant characters representing all these areas to be encountered in print than it was 25 years ago. There is now no lack of fictional role models, and certainly no shortage of interesting stories featuring them. There is no longer any need to be apologetic about literature which does not focus on white males; in fact some teachers have become worried about there being insufficient fiction today featuring boys. If that is the case, then perhaps they need to be directed to some of the stories with female main characters, whose adventures are just as riveting!

176

Even if literature is not the only or indeed the most important agent for change of attitudes in society (a contention which is open to debate), no one could deny that it is an important instrument in the process. It may be, as Holland (1968;1989) says, that its most important role is to increase flexibility of mind (p. 340), but that in itself is an objective well worth the aim. Naidoo (1992) recounts the story of a young man who asked her, 'Has a book ever changed your whole life?' as a prelude to describing a book which had completely altered his outlook (p. 9). Many of the texts which I have mentioned in this book have the potential to do the same for child readers. Adults can never tell how any book may affect a particular child; the only thing they can do is to know the books and make them available, and to know the children well enough to direct them towards the most appropriate book at the right stage, if and only if such aid seems to be needed. By their openness and readiness to discuss issues raised, they can help children work through their own puzzles about some of these sensitive issues, and thus play a small but significant part in the process of making our society more equal.

References

Note that an extensive bibliography is also given at the end of this book.

Organisations

Books for Keeps, 6 Brightfield Road, London SE12 8QF; Tel. 0181 852 4953

Book Trust, Book House, 45 East Hill, London SW18 2QZ; Tel.0171 870 9055

Centre for Language in Primary Education, Webber Street, London SE1 6QW; Tel.0171 401 3382/3

Council for Racial Equality, Elliot House, 10/12 Allington Street, London SW1E 5EH

Development Education Centre (Birmingham), Gillett Centre, 998 Bristol Road, Selly Oak, Birmingham B29 6LE

Federation of Children's Book Groups, 6 Bryce Place, Currie, Midlothian, Scotland, EH14 5LR; the journal of the organisation is *Carousel*, 7 Carrs Lane,Birmingham, B4 7TG; Tel. 0121 643 6411

Frances Lincoln Ltd., Apollo Works, 5 Charlton Kings Road, London NW5 2SB

International Board on Books for Young People(IBBY), c/o Children's Literature Research Centre, Roehampton Institute London, Downshire House, Roehampton Lane, London SW15 4HT; Tel.0181 392 3346

Letterbox Library, Unit 2D, Leroy House, 436 Essex Road, London N1 3QP; Tel.0171 226 1633; Fax 0171 226 1768

Reading and Language Information Centre, University of Reading, Bulmershe Court, Earley, Reading, RG6 1HY; Tel. 01734 318650

Tamarind Press, P. O. Box 296, Camberley, Surrey, GU15 1QW; Tel. 01276 683979

Working Group against Racism in Children's Resources, 460 Wandsworth Road, London SW18 3LX; Tel. 0171 627 4594

Sources of material: lists and other publications

Commission for Racial Equality (1996) *From Cradle to School: A Practical Guide to Racial Equality in Early Childhood Education and Care.*

Hollindale, P. (1988)*Ideology and the Children's Book*. Stroud: Thimble.

Hunt, P. (ed.)(1992) *Literature for Children: Contemporary Criticism*. London: Routledge.

Mathias, B. (n.d.) *Everyone is Different: A Special Needs Booklet*. Harmondsworth: Penguin.

Mathias, B. (1993) *Barncoats Special Needs Directory*. Falmouth: Bishop & Barncoats.

Stones, R. (ed.)(1994) *A Multicultural Guide to Children's Books 0–12*. London: Books for Keeps; Reading: Reading and Language Information Centre.

Sylvester, R. (1991) *Start with a Story: Supporting Young Children's Exploration of Issues*. Birmingham: Development Education Centre.

Waterstones *Guide to Children's Books*. London: Waterstones.

Whyte, J. (1983) *Beyond the Wendy House: Sex Role Stereotyping in Primary Schools*. York: Longman [Although this was published some time ago, it still has useful points to make.]

Working Group against Racism (1996) *Guidelines and Lots More Titles: Picture Books*. London: WGARCR.

Some (mostly fiction) books for adults

Achebe, C. (1958) *Things Fall Apart*. London: Heinemann.

Angelou, M. (1969;1984) *I Know Why the Caged Bird Sings*. London: Virago.

Atwood, M. (1986) *The Handmaid's Tale*. London: Cape.

Brady, J. (1993) *Theory of War*. London: Deutsch.

Carter, A. (1979) *The Bloody Chamber*. London: Gollancz.

Carter, A. (ed.) *The Virago Book of Fairy-tales*, London: Virago.

Coetze, J. M. (1983) *Life and Times of Michael K*. London: Secker & Warburg.

Elkin, J. and Duncan, C. (1992) *Free My Mind: An Anthology of Black and Asian Poetry*. Harmondsworth: Penguin.

Gilman, C. P. (1995) *The Yellow Wallpaper*. Harmondsworth: Penguin.

Gregory, J. (1995) *Goodbye Bafana*. London: Hodder.

Hockenberry, J. (1995) *Declarations of Independence: War Zones and Wheelchairs*. London: Viking.

Johnson, C. (1991) *Middle Passage*. London: Pan.

Kafka, F. *Metamorphosis*. (First published 1913).

Morrison, T. (1987) *Beloved*. London: Chatto.

Ngugi, J. (1967) *A Grain of Wheat*. London: Heinemann.

Twain, M. *Huckleberry Finn*. (First published 1884).

Walker, A. (1983) *The Color Purple*. London: The Women's Press.

Walker, A. (1992) *Possessing the Secret of Joy*. London: Cape.

Children's books which have an unreliable narrator or focal character

(Note that these books and those in the following list do not necessarily have any specific relevance to the kind of equality issues which have been discussed. They are included here rather from the point of view of helping children towards an awareness of the author's techniques in creating scepticism about what a key character believes.)

Bawden, N. (1973) *Carrie's War*. London: Gollancz.

Cormier, R. (1977) *I am the Cheese*. London: Gollancz.

Doherty, B. (1991) *Dear Nobody*. London: Hamish Hamilton.

Fox, P. (1973;1979) *The Slave Dancer*. Basingstoke: Macmillan.

Guy, R. (1974) *The Friends*. London: Gollancz.

Kemp, G. (1977)*The Turbulent Term of Tyke Tyler*. London: Faber.

McNaughton, C. (1993) *Have you Seen who's Just Moved in Next Door to Us?**. London: Walker.

Mayne, W. (1985) *Drift*. London: Cape.

Milne, A. A., *Winnie the Pooh*. (First published 1926)

Stevenson, R. L., *Treasure Island*. (First published 1883)

Taylor, T. (1970) *The Cay*. London: Bodley Head.

Picture books which employ sophisticated literary devices

Ahlberg, A. and Ahlberg, J. (1978) *Each Peach Pear Plum**. London: Kestrel.

Ahlberg, J. and Ahlberg, A. (1986) *The Jolly Postman**. London: Heinemann.

Browne, A. (1989) *The Tunnel**. London: Julia MacRae.

Browne, E. (1994) *Handa's Surprise*. London: Walker.

Burningham, J. (1977) *Come Away from the Water, Shirley**. London: Cape.

Little, J. *et al.* (1991) *Once Upon a Golden Apple**. Harmondsworth: Penguin.

Provensen, A. and Provensen, M. (1988) *Shaker Lane**. London: Julia MacRae.

Sczieszka, J.and Smith, L. (1989) *The True Story of the Three Little Pigs**. Harmondsworth: Penguin.

Sczieszka, J.and Smith, L. (1993) *The Stinky Cheese Man and Other Fairly Stupid Tales**. Harmondsworth: Penguin.

Trivizas, E. (1993) *Three Little Wolves and the Big Bad Pig**. London: Heinemann.

Waddell, M. and Dale, P. (1989) *Once There were Giants*. London: Walker.

Willis, J. and Ross, T. (1992) *Dr Xargle's Book of Earthlets**. London: Andersen.

References

Note that details of children's books referred to, and of resource lists and guidelines, are also to be found at the end of the appropriate chapters.

Applebee, A. N. (1978) *The Child's Concept of Story*. Chicago: University Press.

Appleyard, J. A. (1990) *Becoming a Reader: The Experience of Fiction from Childhood to Adulthood*. Cambridge: Cambridge University Press.

Barker, M. (1989) *Comics: Ideology, Power and the Critics*. Manchester: University Press.

Barrs, M. and Pidgeon, S. (eds) (1993) *Reading the Difference: Gender and Reading in the Primary School*. London: Centre for Language in Primary Education.

Bettelheim, B. (1976) *The Uses of Enchantment*. London: Thames and Hudson.

Brown, B. (1988) 'Anti-racist practice is good practice', *Nursery World*. 22 September.

Bruner, J. (1986) *Actual Minds, Possible Worlds*. Cambridge, Ma.: Harvard University Press.

Bullock, A. (1975) *A Language for Life*. London:.

Carpenter, H. and Prichard, M. (1984) *The Oxford Companion to Children's Literature*. Oxford: Oxford University Press.

Chambers, A. (1991) *The Reading Environment: How Adults Help Children Enjoy Books*. Stroud: Thimble.

Chambers, A. (1993) *Tell Me: Children Reading and Talk*. Stroud: Thimble.

Cherland, M. R. (1994) *Private Practices: Girls Reading Fiction and Constructing Identity*. London: Taylor & Francis.

Christian-Smith, L. K. (ed.)(1993) *Texts of Desire: Essays on Fiction, Femininity and Schooling*. London: Falmer.

Claire, H. *et al.* (eds.)(1993) *Equality Matters*. Clevedon: Language Matters.

Collins, F. H. (ed.) (1997) *Reading Voices*. Exeter: Northcott House.

Cox, C. B. (1988) *English for Ages 5 to 11*. London: Department of Education and Science.

Cox, C. B. (1989) *English for Ages 5 to 16*. London: Department of Education and Science.

Crystal, D. (1987) *The Cambridge Encyclopedia of Language*. Cambridge: Cambridge University Press.

Department for Education (1995) *English in the National Curriculum*. London:.

Dixon, B. (1978a) *Catching Them Young 1: Sex, Race and Class in Children's Fiction*. London: Pluto.

Dixon, B. (1978b) *Catching Them Young 2: Political Ideas in Children's Fiction*. London: Pluto.

Dixon, B. (1982) *Now Read On: Recommended Fiction for Young People*. London: Pluto.

Eagleton, T. (1983) *Literary Theory: An Introduction*. Oxford: Blackwell.

Evans, E. (ed.)(1992) *Reading Against Racism*. Milton Keynes: Open University.

Fish, S. (1980) *Is There a Text in this Class?: The Authority of Interpretive Communities*. Cambridge, Ma.: Harvard University Press.

Fox, G. *et al.* (eds)(1976) *Writers, Critics, and Children*. London: Heinemann.

Garner, J. F. (1994) *Politically Correct Bedtime Stories*. London: Souvenir Press.

Gifford, D. (1988) *Happy Days. 100 Years of Comics*. London: Bloomsbury.

Gilligan, C. (1982) *In a Different Voice: Psychological Theory and Women's Development*. Cambridge, Ma.: Harvard University Press.

Graham, J. (1990) *Pictures on the Page*. Sheffield: NATE.

Graves, D. (1983) *Writing: Teachers and Children at Work*. London: Heinemann.

Griffith, P. (1987) *Literary Theory and English Teaching*. Milton Keynes: Open University.

Hancock, S. (ed.) (1997) *Guide to Children's Reference Books*. Aldershot: Scolar.

Heath, S. B. (1983) *Ways with Words*. Cambridge: Cambridge University Press.

Hill, J. (ed.)(1971) *Books for Children: The Homelands of Immigrants in Britain*. London: Institute of Race Relations.

Hobsbawm. P. (1972). *A Reader's Guide to Charles Dickens*. London: Thames & Hudson.

Holland, N. (1989; 1st edn 1968) *The Dynamics of Literary Response*. New York: Columbia University Press.

Hollindale, P. (1974) *Choosing Books for Children*. London: Paul Elek.

Hollindale, P. (1988) *Ideology and the Children's Book*. Stroud: Thimble.

Hunt, P. (ed.)(1992) *Literature for Children: Contemporary Criticism*. London: Routledge.

Iser, W. (1974) *The Implied Reader: Patterns of Communication in Prose Fiction*. Baltimore: Johns Hopkins University Press.

Johnson, P. (1990) *A Book of One's Own: Developing Literacy Through Making Books*. London: Hodder & Stoughton.

Kazemi, L. (1996) *Children's Heroes and Heroines*. Roehampton Institute London: Unpublished Graduate Diploma Project.

Klein, G. (1985) *Reading into Racism: Bias in Children's Literature and Learning Materials*. London: Routledge.

Lewis, R. (1996) *The Access and Response of Children from Ethnic Minorities to Children's Literature*. Roehampton Institute London: Unpublished MA Dissertation.

Lodge, D. (1981) *The Modes of Modern Writing: Metaphor, Metonymy, and the Typology of Modern Literature*. London: Arnold.

Lodge, D. (1981) *Working with Structuralism*. London: Routledge.

Lodge, D. (1990) *After Bakhtin: Essays on Fiction and Criticism*. London: Routledge.

Lurie, A. (1991) *Not in Front of the Grown-Ups*. London: Sphere Books.

Mathias, B. (1993) *Barncoats Special Needs Directory: Books For and About Children with Special Needs*. Falmouth: Bishop & Barncoats.

Meek, M. *et al.* (eds)(1977) *The Cool Web: The Pattern of Children's Reading*. London: Bodley Head.

Meek, M. (1982)'The Role of the Story', in *Story in the Child's Changing World*. Proceedings of the 18th Congress of the International Board on Books for Young People, Cambridge, 1982

Meek, M. (1988) *How Texts Teach What Readers Learn*. Stroud: Thimble.

Mellor, B. (1984) *Changing Stories*, London: ILEA English Centre.

Milner, D. (1983) *Children and Race: Ten Years On*. London: Ward Lock.

Morris, P. (ed.)(1994) *The Bakhtin Reader*. London: Arnold.

Naidoo, B. (1992) *Through Whose Eyes? Exploring Racism: Reader, Text and Context*. Stoke-on-Trent: Trentham.

Nodelman, P. (1988) *Words about Pictures: The Narrative Art of Children's Books*. Athens: University of Georgia Press.

Pardeck, J. T. and Pardeck, J. A. (1987) 'Bibliotherapy for Children in Foster Care and Adoption', *Child Welfare*, **LXVI(3)**, 269–78.

Opie, I. and Opie, P. (1959) *The Lore and Language of Schoolchildren*. Oxford: Oxford University Press.

Pardeck, J. A. and Pardeck, J. T. (1984) *Young People with Problems: A Guide to Bibliotherapy*. London: Greenwood Press.

181

Pinsent, P. (1990) 'Anti-Racism and Children's Literature', *The School Librarian*. **38(2)**, 45–50.

Pinsent, P. (ed.)(1992) *Language, Culture and Young Children: Developing English in the Multi-Ethnic Nursery and Infant School*. London: David Fulton.

Pinsent, P. (ed.)(1993) *The Power of the Page: Children's Books and Their Readers*. London: David Fulton.

Pinsent, P. (1994) '"We speak English in this school": the experience of immigrant children as depicted in some recent books'. In Broadbent *et al.* (eds) *Researching Children's Literature: A Coming of Age*. Southampton: LSU Publications, pp. 66–74.

Pinsent, P. (1996)'Race and feminism in some recent children's books', *Feminist Theology*, **13**, 96–107.

Pinsent, P. (1997)'Race and Ideology in Textbooks', *Paradigm: The Journal of the Textbook Colloquium* (in press).

Pinsent, P. (1997) 'Reference books for children: A brief historical survey', in Hancock, S. (ed.) *Guide to Children's Reference Books*. Aldershot: Scolar.

Quicke, J. (1985) *Disability in Modern Children's Fiction*. London: Croom Helm.

Reynolds, K. (1990) *Girls Only: Gender and Popular Children's Fiction in Britain, 1880–1910*. Hemel Hempstead: Harvester.

Reynolds, K. (1994a) *Children's Literature in the 1890s and the 1990s*. Plymouth: Northcote House.

Reynolds, K. (ed.) (1994b) *Contemporary Juvenile Reading Habits: A Study of Young People's Reading at the End of the Century*. London: Roehampton Institute, Children's Literature Research Centre.

Reynolds, K. (ed.) (1996) *Young People's Reading at the End of the Century*. London: Roehampton Institute, Children's Literature Research Centre.

Roehampton Survey (1996) – see Reynolds, 1996.

Sacks, O. (1989) *Seeing Voices*. London: Pan.

Said, E. (ed.)(1987) Introduction to R. Kipling, *Kim*. Harmondsworth: Penguin.

Said, E. (1993) *Culture and Imperialism*. London: Chatto.

Sarland, C. (1991) *Young People Reading: Culture and Response*. Milton Keynes: Open University.

Sheridan, E. M. (ed.)(1982) *Sex Stereotypes and Reading: Research and Strategies*. Deleware: International Reading Association.

Siraj-Blatchford, I. (1993)'Race', Gender and the Education of Teachers*. Milton Keynes: Open University.

Snowling, M. (1987) *Dyslexia: A Cognitive Developmental Perspective*. Oxford: Blackwell.

Stephens, J. (1992) *Language and Ideology in Children's Fiction*. London: Longman.

Stibbs, A. (1991) *Reading Narrative as Literature: Signs of Life*. Milton Keynes: Open University Press.

Stinton, J. (ed.)(1979) *Racism and Sexism in Children's Books*. London: Writers and Readers Publishing Cooperative.

Styles, M. *et al.* (eds.)(1992) *After Alice: Exploring Children's Literature*. London: Cassell.

Thistlethwaite, S. (1990) *Sex, Race, and God: Christian Feminism in Black and White*. London: Chapman.

Walkerdine, V. (1984) 'Some Day My Prince Will Come'. In McRobbie, A. and Nava, M. (eds) *Gender and Generation*. London: Macmillan.

Warner, M. (1994) *From the Beast to the Blonde*. London: Chatto.

Wells. G. (1987) *The Meaning Makers*. London: Hodder & Stoughton.

Zipes, J. (1986) *Don't Bet on the Prince*. Aldershot: Gower.

Zipes, J. (1993; 1st edn 1983) *The Trials and Tribulations of Little Red Riding Hood*. New York & London: Routledge.

Index of Authors

Index of Subjects